1980

The
Rulers of
Belgian Africa
1884–1914

Prepared under the auspices of the Hoover Institution.

The Rulers of Belgian Africa 1884–1914

L. H. Gann and Peter Duignan

Princeton University Press, Princeton, New Jersey

Publication of this book has been aided by a grant from the
Paul Mellon Fund of Princeton University Press
This book has been composed in Linotype Times Roman

CONTENTS

Figures

Tables

PREFACE

THE present work forms part of a multivolume series designed to elucidate the social background, preconceptions, and work of the white military officers and bureaucrats who conquered and administered the European colonies in Africa during the age of the "New Imperialism." It runs in harness with *The Rulers of German Africa, 1884-1914*, and *The Rulers of British Africa, 1870-1914* (both published by Stanford University Press). The literature on imperialism fills many library shelves, but there is as yet no comparative work that covers the sociology of the empire builders, nor one that deals with the nuts and bolts of the imperial edifice. Our work tries to fill a gap in the literature on Belgian Africa. It is not a full-scale history of the Belgian Congo, much less an exhaustive account of white-black relations in the vast territories under the Belgian tricolor. Rather, it is an essay in Euro-African history, focusing on the rulers, although we do not exclude the role played by the colonial subjects in the drama of empire.

Our general approach is somewhat unfashionable. We believe, as Marx, Engels, Livingstone, and Kipling all believed before us, that European colonization—for all its evils—played a progressive as well as a negative role in the backward regions of the Victorian world. European colonization had some of its roots in the desire for profits and glory, but it was also part of an overspill of the European domestic reform movement. The best of the colonizers wanted to "improve" the heathen in the African bush as well as the poor in the slums of the métropole. European colonization, in our view, was linked to the wider process of cultural transfusion that spread Western techniques and Western values to the remotest corners of the globe. The white invaders in the Congo differed from all previous conquerors—Swahili, Chokwe, Tutsi—in that whites had at their disposal philosophies of governance, scientific techniques, and modes of production that were qualitatively rather than quantitatively different from those available to their predecessors. The whites tried to shape a new Africa in their own image. Up to a point, they succeeded.

Our study of the Belgian colonial pioneers is briefer than the companion volumes on the German rulers of Africa, and briefer still than our study of the British rulers of Africa during the same period. Belgian administrators published fewer reminiscences than their British and German confrères. The Belgian archival material bearing on colonial personnel that has been made accessible to historians is scantier than the equivalent holdings in Great Britain and Germany, and the secondary literature on Belgian colonialism is less extensive than the work done on British and German empire building. Although the quality of Belgian scholarship remains high, lamentably few Belgian academics now take any interest in yesterday's empire. The Belgian possessions in Africa were not only smaller than Great Britain's and Germany's, they were also more marginal to metropolitan society than the British, or even the German, colonies. In Great Britain there was a strong colonial tradition, a far-flung "old boys' network" of men who wanted their sons to serve the empire overseas. German colonialism never acquired this popular appeal; nevertheless, the Kolonialgesellschaft numbered its supporters in tens of thousands. No colonial lobby of equivalent numerical strength existed in Belgium.

Though smaller than the Kolonialreich, the Belgian Congo covered a huge area nonetheless. It comprised many people: pygmy hunters in the forests, Swahili-speaking freebooters from the East Coast, Lunda agriculturists, Chokwe hunters, and many others. The area was more than eighty times the size of Belgium and included a great variety of climatic and geographic zones ranging from tropical rain forests to arid steppes. Its economic importance to the Belgian motherland was originally negligible.

PREFACE

The Congo Free State was the personal creation of King Leopold II, who initiated an empire under the guise of international humanitarianism. Leopoldine colonialism came to be accounted as one of the worst in modern African history. After Leopold's private empire was taken over by the Belgian state in 1908, a variety of reforms were introduced. The new colony was administered through a tightly knit partnership of government, missions, and interlocking companies. In terms of Belgium's total commerce, the importance of the Congo remained small; in African terms, however, Belgian trade and investment involved considerable sums.

The Belgians introduced far-reaching changes into the colony. They provided the basic infrastructure of modern transport. Having first practiced a ruthless form of *Raubwirtschaft* (destructive exploitation), they subsequently encouraged new forms of economic enterprise and made a start—however slight—in providing modern social services. Above all, they built a Western-type army and a Western-type administration. They unified a huge African region under one flag. Modern Zaïre owes its creation to Belgian imperial enterprise.

In outlining the story of Belgian Africa, we have concentrated attention on the civil servants and soldiers who built this empire. We have sought to produce a brief interpretative study based upon case histories and selective samples rather than an exhaustive description. Since we have covered numerous parallel topics, we have had to accept some repetition.

Our work has been lightened by generous aid received from many institutions and individual scholars. Thanks are due to the respective heads of the Archives du Palais Royal, Archives africaines, Archives générales du Royaume, Musée de Tervuren, and the Bibliothèque africaine, all in Brussels. We also thank Professors Bruce Fetter, Jean-Philippe Peemans, William Norton, Jean Stengers, Jan Vansina, and Crawford Young, who have given us advice or who have read the manuscript in part or as a whole. In addition, Professor Vansina has generously made available to us an essay, as yet unpublished, of his own. Mme. L. Ranieri gave advice.

This work was made possible through the assistance of a research grant from the National Endowment for the Humanities, but the findings and conclusions here do not necessarily represent the views of the Endowment. We are equally indebted to the Earhart Foundation for their generosity in supporting the Hoover Institution's "Builders of Empire" project, of which this volume forms a part.

Abbreviations

The
Rulers of
Belgian Africa
1884–1914

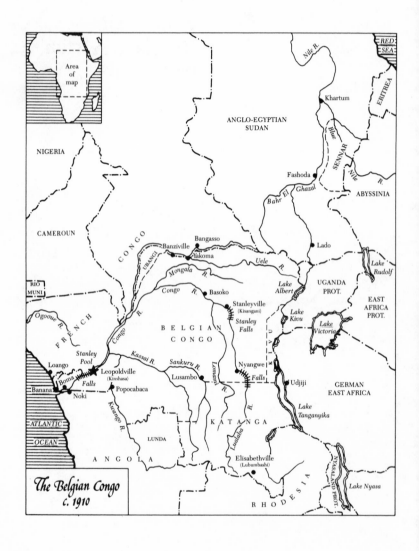

The Belgian Congo
c. 1910

ONE

BELGIUM: THE METROPOLE

WHEN Leopold II acceded to the throne of Belgium in 1865 as the second king since Belgian independence in 1831, he became sovereign of what still seemed a somewhat precarious state. His little kingdom barely exceeded five million inhabitants. It was flanked by two powerful neighbors, Prussia and France. Its continued neutrality, though guaranteed by treaties, appeared far from secure. To make matters worse, Belgium was divided by language and class: the ethnic cleavage ran between French-speaking Walloons and Gallicized Flemings on the one hand and Flemish people on the other.

The Flemish-speaking parts of the country—East and West Flanders, part of Brabant, Antwerp, and Limbourg—depended mainly on agriculture. The natural fertility of the Flemish provinces, other than Limbourg, often left much to be desired; unremitting toil and great agricultural skill were required to provide Belgium with its crops of barley, oats, beetroot, and potatoes. By and large, the Flemish portions suffered the greatest poverty; conditions in the countryside at times resembled those of Ireland, and the Flemings made up a large proportion of the country's unskilled workers. The southern provinces (often referred to as Wallonia)— Namur, Liège, Hainaut, and Luxembourg—were French-speaking. Discoveries of extensive coal deposits during the nineteenth century gave Wallonia a commanding lead in the country's industrialization. The Walloons comprised within their ranks a large portion of Belgium's middle and upper middle classes, and they supplied most of the senior civil servants and army officers, and a large segment of the skilled workers and miners.

Modern Belgium was shaped by the French Revolution. Two decades of French occupation (lasting until 1814) profoundly modified the old local and seignorial loyalties that had characterized the ancient regime in the Austrian Netherlands and the bishopric of Liège. The new rulers spoke French, looked to Paris, and believed in the supremacy of the secular state. Their culture overlaid the older Catholic, Flemish, and localist traditions without destroying them. Between 1815 and 1830 Belgium formed part of the Kingdom of the Netherlands. In 1830 it broke away from this union, and its French-speaking bourgeoisie set up an independent kingdom shaped in their own image. French was the language of the court, of polite conversation, of big business, scholarship, and government. Most French speakers were ignorant of Flemish. They usually had little notion of the brilliant literary revival that enriched Flemish during the 1800s, and they despised the language as a *patois* fit only for carters and housemaids. The French-speaking component was strengthened by ambitious Flemings anxious to make their way into the higher ranks of the army and administration by adopting the French tongue, thereby confirming French in its predominance.

Belgium's linguistic division had religious as well as social overtones. The Flemings were mostly Catholics; the Walloons, especially those in the larger towns, counted many anticlericals among their number. The vast majority of Flemings looked for guidance to the Church, the most powerful institution in the Flemish countryside, a great cultural as well as a religious organization, and an important avenue for mobility and status for peasant sons from Flanders. Most French-speaking Walloons, on the other hand, would not learn Flemish, and Church influence among the French-speaking bourgeoisie was paralleled by a massive Masonic network in Wallonia.

The ethnic division between Flemings and Walloons was, admittedly, not nearly as severe in the late nineteenth century as it was to become in the middle of the twentieth. The

4

main cleavage ran between Catholics and Liberals. Belgium, nevertheless, remained a divided country.

SOCIAL STRUCTURE AND ECONOMY

The highest place in Belgian society was occupied by the nobility and the haute bourgeoisie. The nobility consisted primarily of French speakers who used Flemish only to converse with their servants and tenants. The more recently created Belgian noblemen, unlike their confrères in France and Germany, were not distinguished from the rest of the population by the *particule*, by a *von* or *de*; they did not necessarily hold titles, but took their position from descent and social acceptance by their peers. As in Britain, the aristocracy of Belgium was open to new blood by marriage, by promotion to high civil or military office, and by financial success. Freethinking merchants and atheist professors had no wish to mingle with the aristocracy, but many a rich banker or manufacturer—especially if he were a Catholic—sought acceptance by the aristocracy, elevation to the baronage, and eventual listing in *High Life in Belgium*, the indispensable register of social success.

Although in economic as in political terms the Belgian aristocracy was not comparable to the British, the Belgian nobility was far from negligible. The aristocracy had a stake in the land. In Flanders especially, men of distinguished birth owned considerable estates, which they usually leased to tenant farmers. During the nineteenth century they began to invest the proceeds from their agricultural enterprises in industry, and names of noble lineage increasingly appeared on the boards of banks and great companies. Aristocrats held many commissions in the cavalry and the dragoon regiments of the army; the nobility were also well represented in the magistracy. They did not dominate the armed forces or the administration as a whole, however, and the bulk of Belgian land was held by small proprietors, not by noblemen. The social power of the nobility thus was incomparably

5

weaker in Belgium than it was, say, in Mecklenburg or West Prussia.

By far the most powerful social group in nineteenth-century Belgium was the middle class, especially the French-speaking segment that had led the revolution against Holland in 1830 and had played the main part in creating modern Belgium. The rise of the bourgeoisie was impeded neither by historical tradition nor by an all-powerful aristocracy. Moreover, these men used Belgium's advantages of an excellent communications system, a productive agriculture, and great coal reserves. Industrial skills were widespread, labor was cheap, and technical education was excellent. In 1861 free trade triumphed as a principle of political economy, and Belgian wealth advanced dramatically.

The class of businessmen who built the new economy consisted largely of "new men," hard-fisted entrepreneurs accustomed to dealing harshly with established workmen and more harshly still with migrant laborers; unlike their British confrères, they were ready to use the military against strikers. It was they who built the new Belgium, the Belgium of steel mills and coal mines, a country hard and bracing—utterly different from the old Pays Bas, with its economy based on textiles and consumer goods, its transport system centered on canals, and its cities beautiful but staid like Ghent. The new industrial pioneers rarely derived from the ranks of the landed aristocracy or the traditional urban patriciate; they were apt to come from humble homes where men made few demands on life. The new captains of industry held a reputation for frugality and single-minded dedication to their enterprises; they allowed themselves few luxuries other than an occasional party given in honor of their relatives or an occasional trip to Ostende or Paris.

The typical manufacturer was a self-made man, American style, who had come up from humble circumstances. He might make his way to success by going directly into business or by working through institutions of higher learning. Belgium had an excellent system of industrial training, and

6

at the universities of Louvain and Brussels able students were granted free instruction. The "new man" might begin the climb to the top in the army, also a ladder for upward mobility. There were, of course, exceptions. The great capitalists included men like Maurice Despret, whose father was a director of the Société générale. Young Maurice was well connected, but the commercial ethos of his class did not permit him to join his father's establishment; he had to look for a job in another bank before working his way up to the presidency of the Banque de Bruxelles.

More typical are the life stories of such industrial pioneers as Baron Evence Coppée (1851-1925), a mining engineer who became a coal magnate; Jean Jadot (1862-1932), a railway engineer and later one of Belgium's great financiers; Baron Edouard Empain (1852-1929), the son of a village schoolmaster, a draftsman in his early career, and subsequently a major railway entrepreneur and adviser to Leopold II; Adrien Hallet (1867-1925), an agronomist, later a plantation lord; and Ernest Solvay (1838-1922), a bookkeeper who founded a great fortune on the manufacture of soda. For these people life was hard—so hard that some of them began their careers by joining the army before going into business. Magnates with a military background included Emile Francqui (1863-1935), the son of a poverty-stricken attorney, and Albert Thys (1849-1915), a great railway builder who began his career at the age of seventeen by enlisting in the armed forces.

In 1912 Belgium was the world's most highly populated country, with 252 people per square kilometer, compared with 144 in Great Britain, 120 in Germany, and 73 in France. Thus Belgian agriculture, sustained by growing internal markets and by the excellent system of internal communication, was one of the most productive in Europe. Belgian farmers, who made up only 23 percent of the population and were mostly medium- and small-scale producers, enabled their countrymen to eat reasonably well by dint of the tillers' hard work and a highly intensive system of cultivation. They were

7

famed for the production of potatoes, beetroot, and vegetables, for the excellence of their dairy products and beef, and for their extensive use of fertilizers and agricultural machinery. (In 1914 their crops covered 17,363,174 hectares; 521,495 hectares were forest land, and only 190,444 were uncultivated or fallow. The rest of Belgium consisted of built-up areas, marshland, mining reserves, and so forth.)

The condition of the rural population varied enormously. The French-speaking farmers in regions such as Luxembourg province were usually better educated than their Flemish-speaking counterparts; many Walloons went into the administration, in which French speakers held a dominant stake. The Flemish peasantry included a great number of small landholders or men with no landholdings at all, who subsisted on potatoes and other cheap food. They formed a pool of ill-remunerated labor in both the cities and the countryside. Flemish laborers, organized in gangs under their own gang bosses, traveled as far afield as France and western Germany to harvest crops and to perform other forms of heavy manual labor. Politically conservative, they were strongly influenced by the Church, while their educated sons commonly opted for the French-speaking milieu of Brussels or took up the cause of socialism.

The Belgian working class also lived under widely varied conditions, and generalizations are hard to make. The three decades preceding World War I saw a considerable rise in wages. Between 1880 and 1913, for example, the wages of miners rose from 920 to 1,580 francs, and the average income per person increased from 510 to 850 francs between 1895 and 1913. The cost of living was low; yet, overall, the Belgian working class was one of the most impoverished in Western Europe. In 1903 an unskilled worker in the Ardennes, an ill-favored region, earned no more than a franc a day, compared with the five francs earned by a miner. The laboring poor in Belgium were also among the least educated in Western Europe; in 1882, 42.25 percent of the population was unable to read and write, and by 1910 the illiteracy rate

8

still stood at 37.63 percent. Luxembourg had the best system of education, followed by Namur, Liège, and Brabant, with the Flemish provinces far behind. Free and obligatory primary education was not introduced until 1914—more than forty years after the British Elementary Education Act of 1870. The Belgian working class also lagged in a political sense: whereas most male workers in Great Britain were enfranchised between 1867 and 1884, it was 1919 before Belgium adopted universal male suffrage on the principle "one man—one vote." (Universal suffrage had been established in 1893, but it was tempered by a system of plural voting that gave more than one vote to electors fulfilling certain conditions regarding income, education, and family. Reform of the system was extended in 1899 by the grant of proportional representation. In 1919 manhood suffrage was accepted "pure and simple," the voting age was lowered to twenty-one, and certain categories of women were given the vote.)

Belgian economic achievement, however, was extraordinary. By the end of the nineteenth century the kingdom had become one of the most advanced countries in the world. Belgium built the first railway network on the European continent. Railway construction in turn stimulated such industries as coal mining, iron working, and engineering. Belgian prosperity rested on steam power; between 1846 and 1900 the consumption of steam power rose from 40,000 to 430,000 horsepower. An elaborate banking system and one of the world's most efficient transport networks firmly bolstered the nation's economy, and until the end of World War I Belgian industry benefited from low labor costs. Belgian wages rose slightly during the 1860s, but declined during the severe depression that struck at European prosperity between 1873 and 1896; wages returned to the level of the 1860s only in 1898, beginning a period of general economic recovery that continued until World War I.

Belgian foreign trade, which had nearly trebled between 1860 and 1880, stagnated during the depression (see Table

9

1). Once the economy recovered, however, Belgium emerged as a major commercial and industrial power. By the end of the century it had developed great metallurgical industries, and was an important producer of iron, steel, textiles, chemicals, and machinery, especially steam engines, cable cars, railroad material, and the like. The Belgian transport system was more closely meshed than any other in the world. The population of the little kingdom had risen from 5 million in 1865 to 7.5 million by 1909. National wealth had grown at a still faster rate during the same period—from an estimated 11 billion gold francs to 51 billion. Belgium had become one of the most highly urbanized countries in Europe, was one of the world's great trading nations, and was export-

TABLE 1

Value of Belgian Trade
(In Millions of Belgian Francs)

Year	Imports	Exports	Transit
1860	516	469	408
1880	1,680	1,216	1,008
1895	1,680	1,385	1,219

SOURCE: *Brockhaus Konversations-Lexikon*, vol. 2 (Leipzig, 1895), 670.
NOTE: Thirty francs at the time equaled £1.0.0.

ing some one-third of its total production—a higher proportion even than that of Great Britain.[1] Most of this commerce centered on Western Europe. In 1895, for instance, Belgian exports to the main Western European countries amounted to more than 1,100 million francs out of total exports valued at just under 1,400 million. Belgian industrialists had also begun to make their mark on many other parts of the world —Russia, the United States, and the Argentine—as builders of railways, cable cars, and ironworks.

These industries owed an enormous debt to family firms begun by small entrepreneurs. During the latter part of the century, however, family firms in Belgium (as elsewhere)

10

increasingly gave way to powerful corporations. One of the pioneers in this process was Baron Empain, Leopold's principal business adviser. He played an important part in developing the general investment company, that is, a single trust endowed with holdings in many different companies, each of which, in turn, might use the parent trust as a savings bank and as a source of expert advice. Empain also specialized in the concession business and in the provision of public services. He controlled an international cable-car and railway empire, his most famous achievement being the Paris Métro. His railways operated as far afield as Russia, Spain, and China; his tramcars rattled up and down the streets of cities as near as Boulogne and as distant as Cairo and Astrakhan. An enterprise typical of such great financial powers was Sofina (Société financière de transports et d'entreprises industrielles), founded in 1898, one of the world's largest companies in the field of financing and managing hydroelectrical and transport undertakings. Sofina, in turn, controlled numerous subsidiaries abroad, such as Gesfürtel (Gesellschaft für elektrische Unternehmungen) in Germany.

The process of financial concentration also took place in the banking world. Before World War I the most powerful financial combine was the Société générale, founded in 1822, which initially derived most of its profits from the development of landed properties; later it turned to commercial and investment banking. It soon established close connections with major industrial enterprises, particularly with coal mining. The Société became the first organization to practice what became known as "mixed banking," a system subsequently followed by German and most other large continental banks. Additional powerful ventures included the Banque de Bruxelles and the Crédit Anversois, organizations that gradually displaced the smaller local banks from their accustomed place within the Belgian economy.[2]

Before 1900 the bankers of Belgium had become experienced in investing Belgian funds abroad. Early in the nineteenth century these capitalists had played a valuable part

11

in financing the coal-mining and metallurgical industries of western Germany and northern France; from 1865 on, Belgian lenders put substantial funds into railway building, and after 1875 into the foreign construction of electric tramways. Belgian capital exports declined after 1884, but with the revival of prosperity during the 1890s the bankers once more began to lend money to foreigners on a large scale. Belgian money and Belgian skill helped to develop iron and steel industries as well as railways and tramways in Russia and in countries as distant as the Argentine (see Table 2).

TABLE 2

Belgian Capital Invested Abroad, 1895

Field of Interest	Capital Invested (in millions of Belgian francs)	Percentage of Total Investments
Agriculture and agricultural processing industries	13	3
Extractive industries	102	25
Metal industries and engineering	46	12
Transportation	190	46
Miscellaneous industries	18	4
Public utilities	40	10
Commerce	2	—
TOTAL	411	100

SOURCE: Ginette Kurgan-van Hentenryk, *Léopold II et les groupes financiers belges en Chine: La Politique royale et ses prolongements, 1895-1914* (Brussels, 1972).

In theory a free-trading country, Belgium was firmly committed to a doctrine of private enterprise. In practice, however, the economy was controlled in a variety of ways. Kinship played an even greater part in the operation of Belgian than of Swedish or German capitalism. Belgium's great enterprises were linked to great interlocking family networks. In addition, the state began to intervene in the private economy relatively early. In 1886 the state had begun a hundred-million-franc public-works project aimed primarily at extending the country's logistic infrastructure: port facilities were built at Zeebrugge, railway lines were extended and modernized, and canals were improved. When great new coal deposits were discovered in the Kempen basin of northeastern Belgium, the state set up a reserved zone in which grantees could secure concessions only by means of special legislation. The principle of state intervention was accepted in the metropolitan economy long before the Belgian state began to intervene in colonial enterprise.

POLITICS AND ADMINISTRATION

Belgium was bitterly divided politically. Farmers clashed with townsmen, employers contended with workers. Advocates of protection disagreed with spokesmen of laissez faire, who in 1865 succeeded in turning Belgium into one of the classic free-trade countries of Europe. Economic cleavages were exacerbated by religious and ethnic differences. Until the emergence of the Socialist party at the end of the 1800s, Belgian politics were overshadowed by struggles between Catholics and Liberals. Their ideological rifts went deep; even small towns were split into factions. Good Liberals read anticlerical papers and bought their meat only from Liberal butchers, their bread from Liberal bakers, and their shoes from Liberal cobblers. Good Catholics preferred Catholic journals and patronized Catholic butchers, Catholic bakers, and Catholic cobblers. Liberal processions marched through the streets displaying blue flags; Catholic processions proudly carried yellow banners. Militant Liberals violently set upon religious processions; faithful Catholics disrupted civil funerals. Even minor political quarrels over the control of a school or the use of a cemetery might have nationwide political repercussions.

Before the franchise reforms of 1893, the mass of the population was excluded from the vote by elaborate property qualifications. Only about 120,000 Belgians, the so-called censitaires, were allowed to vote. This system enabled the

13

well-to-do Liberal middle classes in the towns and the larger Catholic landholders in the countryside to dominate Belgian politics. Sustained popular unrest finally forced the propertied classes to make concessions. In 1893 the franchise was replaced by a somewhat wider suffrage, modified by plural votes for men of wealth, learning, and social standing. (Subsequent electoral reforms were equally slow: universal male suffrage came in 1919, and universal voting rights for women in 1948.) The 1893 electoral regime, however, did away with the political monopoly hitherto held by the middle and upper classes. The Catholic masses came to dominate parliamentary politics, and the old Liberal party—the stronghold of the French-speaking upper middle class and of professional men in the cities—was reduced to secondary importance. Under Catholic auspices, Belgium embarked on a course of far-reaching social reform. Improvements in education led to a gradual decline of the country's inordinately high rate of illiteracy. Many new laws were passed to improve industrial working conditions. In addition, the government began to take steps to reduce the grievances of the Flemish speakers who comprised slightly more than half the population, and in 1898 the Belgian legislature passed an act establishing equality between the French and Flemish languages in the courts.

The Socialists remained a minority party, but their influence was far from negligible. Flemish peasants and their educated sons were often *Flamingants*, adherents of the Flemish ethnic cause, while Socialists derived largely from the ranks of urban workers; hence Antwerp and Ghent had active Socialist parties with a strong Flemish following, while Namur and Luxembourg remained Catholic bastions. The Socialist party stood for a moderate program of social reform, and its base consisted of the labor unions (*syndicats*), cooperatives, mutual insurance societies, and political study groups organized into semiautonomous federations.

This party—and, to a lesser extent, its rivals—was more than a parliamentary organization. The cooperatives pro-

14

vided cafés, meeting rooms, dance halls, libraries, and gymnasiums; they furnished old-age pensions and assistance to the needy; they maintained clinics and carried out educational work. As Thomas H. Reed, an American political scientist, wrote after World War I: a Belgian Socialist might, if he chose, live an almost exclusively Socialist life. As a child he learned to sing and dance with the *enfants du peuple*. As a youngster he would go on long hikes with the *jeunes gardes*. If he were inclined to athletics, he would find a place on a Socialist soccer team that played on a Socialist field. If he tended toward more intellectual pursuits, he would join a Socialist dramatic club or a Socialist chess club. Once he began to work, he acquired membership in a Socialist union, read Socialist newspapers, spent his evenings in a Socialist café or cinema, and found relief in a Socialist clinic where a Socialist doctor prescribed drugs compounded in a Socialist pharmacy. When he died, he might sink into oblivion in the blissful consciousness that his children would be even more Socialist than he had been.

Catholic organizations promoted nothing like this degree of homogeneity. Nevertheless, the Church provided a strikingly effective source of unity for a party that was made up of divergent social and economic interests, workers, peasants, and middle-class people, Flemings and Walloons. Catholics likewise organized their own trade unions and mutual aid societies that operated alongside the anticlerical organizations of the Socialists.

Despite internecine divisions, Belgium was widely admired in Europe as the very model of a soundly run constitutional state. The little kingdom was one of the few advanced European nations to escape the direct impact of the 1848 revolutions. Its ruling dynasty was connected to many royal houses, especially to the British monarchy, and it also enjoyed a European reputation for judicious moderation and a diplomatic influence quite out of proportion to its modest origins in a petty German dynasty.

According to the constitution, the Belgian legislature was

15

supreme. Nevertheless, Leopold II held an unusually power-ful position. His father, Leopold I, the first king of independ-ent Belgium, had played an important part in setting the kingdom on its feet. The confused state of the parties, along with the internal and external troubles of his new monarchy, had allowed him to build an influential position for the crown within the framework of a parliamentary state. It had been at Leopold I's suggestion, for example, that the Belgian state had built the first railway lines on the continent. Leopold II, a man of restless energy with a flair for business and an urge for speculation, had maintained the significant role of the monarch in the nation's affairs. Financiers, merchants, and manufacturers received invitations to court functions during his reign. Baronies were bestowed upon business magnates. The so-called metallo-aristocracy became well regarded by the highest families in the land, with the sovereign leading the list of admirers.

Leopold also occupied a powerful position within the country's administrative framework. According to the con-stitution, legislative power was exercised collectively by the king and the two houses. The monarch convoked, prorogued, and dissolved the Chamber; he stood at the head of the ex-ecutive power; and he appointed his ministers, who served the sovereign as long as they enjoyed the confidence of the legislature. A cabinet minister presided over each of the major government departments. (Each minister later came to be assisted by his own "cabinet," a small group of men whom he brought into office, who wielded a great deal of effective power, and who generally followed him into retire-ment.) Every department was organized into a number of *directions générales* or *inspections générales*. Below the sec-retaries-general and inspectors-general there was an imposing array of first councilors, directors, adjunct directors, and others, who among them made up the top layer of the service.

This bureaucracy—bourgeois in origin, urban in orienta-tion, and mainly French-speaking in its higher levels—was subject to numerous limitations. Administrative centraliza-

16

tion, combined with overly complex administrative routine, often produced delay. Ponderous methods of conducting official business were accentuated in many cases by the absence of modern office equipment and the scattered location of government offices. Throughout the service, critics complained, there was an undue addiction to precedent and *paperasserie* (red tape). The founders of the Belgian monarchy had attempted to set up a service free from patronage and dedicated to political neutrality. They had succeeded in avoiding a spoils system; yet promotion was not infrequently affected—or at least thought to be affected—by party considerations.[3] The number of functionaries was not very large in the nineteenth century, nor was the multiplication of offices as great as in neighboring France. The highest officials in the land, including the most senior academics, did well for themselves, while junior officials made a bare living.[4]

The judicial system was relatively simple. The Belgian system of justice rested on the French Code Napoléon, as modified by the older laws of the provinces. In order to operate, the system required a large number of judges, and this multiplicity of judicial offices may have tended to keep down the average level of salaries. Many of the most able jurists were said to prefer making a living in private legal practice or in industry.[5] Nevertheless, the system had many virtues. Corruption was rare, and the service was rigidly supervised through a complex network of inspections. The higher civil servants were well educated, and while the great majority of those at the top level were trained in the legal profession, the ranks of high-echelon administrators contained a number of men with backgrounds in other disciplines, including engineering. Justice was administered honestly by a well-qualified, well-trained magistracy:

> The quality of Belgian civil servants is on the whole very good. They are a class scrupulously honest. The higher officials are often men of splendid training and high

17

talent. . . . [A] critic of administrative methods . . . pays tribute to them as "men who, for a meager salary, give to the state . . . all their time, all their labor, all their thought."[6]

Though a unitary state, Belgium had a vigorous form of local government. The Belgian provinces (corresponding to French *départements*) and the *communes* were in no sense mere agents of the central authorities; they were distinct from the local services of the national administration—and much more important. Each province and each *commune* was a legal entity with defined legislative and executive powers. Each was sustained by a strong sense of local patriotism and local initiative, making Belgium, with its two linguistic cultures, an odd blend of a federal and a centralized state, distinguished by a dynamic economy and an active and creative cultural life.[7]

The Army

International treaties obliged Belgium to follow a course of neutrality. But whereas Switzerland, Europe's other neutral state, was willing to defend its inviolability by means of a militia recruited by universal military training, most Belgians would not serve in the armed forces. (A modified form of the draft was introduced in 1909; full-scale conscription came only in 1913.) Belgium relied on an army that to all intents and purposes was a professional force. Its record before World War I is not particularly glorious. The Belgian army had originated during the war of independence against the Dutch. Its officer corps had begun as a heterogeneous body that included many Belgian volunteers who had never seen service, many foreign-born officers, and a large number of former sergeants who had switched from the Dutch to the Belgian service. Hastily raised and ill-prepared, the new army did not do well against the Dutch; Belgian independence was finally secured by British, and especially French, intervention.

After the war of independence, the army was reconstituted with the help of foreign officers, including many French and Polish expatriates. Small as it was, it acquired an excellent professional reputation. Its educational institutions were efficient. They included the Ecole militaire, which was set up in 1834 to train junior officers, the Ecole de guerre, established in 1869 to provide advanced instruction to staff officers, and the Institut cartographique, a nursery for colonial explorers and conquerors. The supply service was highly competent, and the Albini rifle, introduced in 1867 and subsequently replaced by the Mauser, was a serviceable weapon. In the Franco-Prussian war of 1870-1871 both combatants respected Belgian neutrality and few doubted that the Belgian army, inexperienced as it was, would give a good account of itself.

The composition of the army's officer corps reflected the social compromise upon which Belgium had been founded. The army insisted on high educational entrance qualifications, including a thorough grounding in the sciences and mathematics. These skills were best taught at the state-supported secondary schools, with their anticlerical bias, rather than in Catholic institutions, where teachers stressed Latin and other humanistic studies. A substantial proportion of the officer corps therefore derived from the ranks of the French-speaking bourgeoisie and were thus urban in background and Liberal in orientation. By and large, they were a hard-working lot infused with the spirit of self-denial that characterized their fellow citizens in civilian clothes. A British observer explained in the 1850s: "The officers of the Belgian Army are of a different class to ours, because they continue at all times to study among themselves, as their promotion depends on it; and when our young gentlemen here are talking of breaking looking-glasses and furniture, the Belgian officers are talking over military matters and studying them."[8]

The role of the nobility in the army was far from insignificant, but the proportion of aristocratic officers steadily declined. In the mid-1800s noblemen had served in various branches of the military, including the artillery and the cavalry. By 1910 they were represented mainly in the mounted regiments (from a functional standpoint, the most useless unit in the event of a European war); 35 percent of the cavalry captains then were noblemen, but captaincies in the other armed forces were held by commoners. The Belgian officer corps did not in any sense constitute a rigid social class. Qualified rankers were willingly admitted, and able and ambitious noncommissioned officers could rise to the top provided they were able to surmount the educational hurdles in their way. Sergeants with experience and education received commissions as *sous-lieutenants* as a matter of course, in a manner inconceivable in the British or Prussian armies.

The army did not have to compete with a fleet for funds or prestige, for Belgium's tiny navy had been abolished in 1869 as an economy measure. The military also enjoyed royal patronage. Leopold II never ceased to defend the interests of an army that he regarded as a safeguard of Belgian neutrality and social order. There were no mutinies, discipline was strict, and the private soldier regarded a *sergent-moniteur* as a demigod.

Nevertheless, the army suffered from serious weaknesses. It was numerically small. In 1904 the regular army consisted of: nineteen infantry regiments, each composed of three or four active battalions and an equal number in reserve; eight cavalry regiments; and 104 batteries of artillery. Its effective strength amounted to just under forty-four thousand men. The *gendarmerie*, a mounted force of just over three thousand men, was a *corps d'élite* that might be classed as a first-class heavy cavalry. The *garde civique* and its allied units numbered about forty-two thousand men, but, in the magisterial language of the *Encyclopedia Britannica*, "the mass of the *garde civique* does not pretend to possess military value. It is a defence against sedition and socialism."[9]

Especially in its lower ranks, the army was poorly paid. Junior officers complained that they could not live on their pay. Promotion was slow; few professional officers were able to advance beyond the rank of *capitaine-commandant*. The officer corps also suffered from social isolation. In 1887 Belgium for the first time instituted reserve officer commissions, but there was nothing comparable to the great corps of reserve lieutenants and reserve NCOs that constituted the strength of the German army. Drill was unintelligent and rigid. The army's outlook was defensive. Even by 1914 it was ill provided with cadres, and its plans for waging war were inadequate.

Until the introduction of conscription in 1913, the Belgian army was overwhelmingly an army of the poor. Most of the bourgeoisie refused to serve in the ranks and preferred to pay for *remplaçants*. Belgium spent relatively little on its armed forces: in 1880 the military accounted for only 18 percent of the Belgian national expenditure, compared with 30.3 percent in France and 30.8 percent in Holland. Yet the Belgian public regarded even this limited percentage as a waste of the taxpayer's money. The *jeunesse dorée* and most merchants were inclined to look down on soldiers. The army was widely unpopular and was criticized in a way that would have been inconceivable in France and Germany. Many Catholics denounced it as a school of atheism, idleness, and harlotry, where peasant lads were weaned away from their ancestral faith and schooled in vice. Most of the long-serving soldiers were indeed Flemish-speaking countrymen, poorly paid and poorly educated, led by French-speaking officers, and commanded in the French language. Socialists censured the army as an instrument of class oppression and as a means for breaking strikes. After the army's unfortunate experience in repressing revolutionary miners' strikes in 1886, General van der Smissen, a leading Belgian soldier, expressed his fears to the king that the defense of the social order should not be left to an army composed solely of proletarians.

Above all, the army was bored. Many units were stationed in small villages, a particular hardship for urban-born officers. Drill was dull, tactical training unimaginative, and social life stifling. Before 1900 only half the captains and one-quarter of the lieutenants had received authorization to marry. These conditions improved somewhat during the era preceding World War I, when the danger of German invasion grew more obvious. Sport became more popular. Officers could marry more easily. Armaments improved, and the army obtained Krupp 7.5-cm. rapid-firing guns. Military strength increased, and when war broke out in 1914, Belgium was able to mobilize one cavalry division and six infantry divisions.

Despite the gradual improvements, the army considered itself the Cinderella within the nation. The more enterprising officers experienced a strong sense of professional frustration, and many of them preferred to serve foreign nations. During the nineteenth century Belgium sent abroad a substantial number of military as well as civilian labor migrants. Belgians fought for the French in Algeria, and for Emperor Maximilian in Mexico. When Belgium decided to participate in an international expedition against the Boxer Rebellion in China (1900-1901), the number of volunteers, both commissioned and noncommissioned, far exceeded the places available in the Belgian contingent. Well-educated, but exasperated by its condition, the Belgian officer corps was a ready-made reservoir of volunteers.

For an example of an exasperated young officer we may take the case of Charles Lemaire—by no means a flag-waving young man in love with a new pair of epaulettes. A man of outstanding ability, a keen soldier, and a well-known colonial publicist, Lemaire later became the first director of the Ecole coloniale supérieure established after World War I. He was typical in many ways of the young officers who first

22

sought their professional fortunes overseas. Lemaire was born in 1863 in Cuesmes-lez-Mons, the son of a small-town *percepteur des contributions*. His father died when he was young, and he was strictly brought up by his grandfather, whose guiding principles later became those of the Ecole coloniale: "Don't lie, don't steal, don't gamble, don't borrow."

Lemaire first went to the *école primaire* at Cuesme, and then to the *athénée* at Mons. He did well in natural sciences and mathematics, both subjects stressed at the Ecole militaire, which he entered in 1881 and where he enjoyed some of the best years of his life. The institution was beautifully situated in the Abbaye de la Cambre, whose charm and pleasant rural surroundings made up for its lack of comfort (not until 1908 was the school transferred to the cold, classical-style quarters of the Cinquantennaire). The Ecole militaire was to Lemaire a substitute family that provided him, a young agnostic, with the moral precepts and sense of personal security that he had lacked in the secular state schools where morality was not taught in the classrooms. In 1886 he was commissioned and joined the 2nd regiment of artillery, but he was soon disillusioned with army life at home. Garrison duties were dull, and he was upset by the low esteem in which the army was held.

When his grandparents died there were no more family ties to hold Lemaire in Belgium, and he determined to serve in the Congo. Two of his classmates at the *école primaire*, Félicien Cattier and Jules Cornet, were also destined to achieve fame in the Congo—the former as a critic of government and the latter as a geologist. The Congolese enterprise seemed to Lemaire a great humanitarian and "utilitarian" venture. In an article addressed to his fellow officers he wrote that Leopold's adventure might provide a secular mission field for an officer corps that was unsure of its place in society. A "civilizing mission" in Africa might help to reconcile class divisions at home and provide an alternative to "collectivism":

23

In our little Belgium the army has sunk into a depressing state of moral torpor. Only its officer corps has kept up with its neighbors, the men who stand on guard over the fortresses of Germany and the *camps retranchés* in France. But our officer corps is not well known. Are we not commonly referred to as old women, sabre-rattlers, coffeehouse heroes, and leathernecks? The modern officer in fact is a worker and often a scientist. . . . Hundreds of young officers have shown their *élan* in the Congo. There they have experienced a world of its own, with its own customs, its own ideas and its own prejudices, a world not yet touched by the canker of money. One day, perhaps, this little world will become a tabernacle of honor, the last refuge of virtue.[10]

Before Lemaire set out for Africa, he made a point of visiting Westminster Abbey in London to pay homage to the memories of Newton, the giant of science, and Livingstone, the king of explorers. He departed for the Congo determined to serve the cause of progress and humanity. As the years went by, he was to be bitterly disappointed.

Royal Colonialism: The Beginnings

When Leopold II began to build his African empire, the Belgian stake in Africa was negligible. Belgium conducted the bulk of its trade with Western and Central Europe and, to a lesser extent, with Russia, the United States, and Argentina (see Table 3). The greater portion of Belgium's foreign investments had likewise been placed in Europe, while most of the remainder had been lent to Latin American creditors (see Table 4).

Africa played little part in the calculations of Belgian businessmen. There was no Belgian *entrepôt* trade on the shores of the Congo and no Belgian merchant marine looking for African cargoes. African ventures thus held no appeal for solid businessmen of the traditional kind. Men like Jules Malou, the leader of the Right in the Senate, a director of the

TABLE 3

Value of Belgium's Foreign Trade, 1895
(In Millions of Belgian Francs)

Country	Total Imports	Total Exports
France	300	284
Germany	199	311
Great Britain	193	267
Netherlands	175	165
United States	133	47
Russia	117	22
Rumania	100	9
Argentina	93	14
British India	53	20
Sweden and Norway	46	16
Italy	20	25
Spain	20	22
Switzerland	4	34
Congo	ca. 5	—

SOURCE: *Brockhaus Konversations-Lexikon*, 2:670.

TABLE 4

Belgian Foreign Investments, 1895

Investment area	Capital Invested (in millions of Belgian francs)	Percentage of Total Investments
Europe		
Russia	116	18
Italy	48	7
France	25	4
Germany	18	2
Other	176	26
SUBTOTAL	383	57
Outside Europe		
Latin America	173	26
Africa	71	10
Other	46	7
SUBTOTAL	290	43
TOTAL INVESTMENTS	673	100

SOURCE: Kurgan-van Hentenryk, *Léopold II et les groupes financiers belges*, p. 45.

Société générale, and one of the leading figures in the financial world of Belgium, remained aloof—as did Belgian public opinion as a whole. Most Belgians had no thought of emigrating; those who did preferred to go to nearby France rather than to distant Africa. They were indifferent to colonization overseas, not for anti-imperialist reasons, but because of an intense preoccupation with local issues that sometimes assumed almost apocalyptic dimensions in the eyes of late-nineteenth-century Liègeois or Bruxellois. Anticlerical Liberals feared the supposed machinations of the Catholic Church; Catholics dreaded Masonic conspiracies and secular education; Socialists loathed their real and supposed oppressors and looked to the onset of a new order. With so much at stake, the diversion of energy into some quixotic venture in Africa seemed not only risky but also absurd. To its many opponents, especially to the Socialists, Leopold's African venture was at once royalist, capitalist, militarist, and clerical. Royal colonialism exploited both Congolese tribesmen and Belgian taxpayers for the sole benefit of a clique; hence no patriot should have anything to do with colonization in any shape or form.

The foundation of the Congo Free State, therefore, owed nothing to public opinion and little, initially, to the Belgian bourgeoisie. The state was created primarily by the king. Leopold II, a royal businessman, was skilled in financial manipulation, ruthless in dealing with his equals, devoid of gratitude to his subordinates, and ready to stoop to large-scale deception. Belgium's internal capital markets were never sufficient for Leopold's needs, but his international connections as a sovereign monarch afforded him access to the stock markets of Paris, Vienna, and Berlin. Like Cecil Rhodes, he was a master of financial suasion. He was equally accomplished in the art of propaganda, adroitly blending humanitarian motifs—especially the antislavery cause—with appeals to patriotism and to the desire for profits. Unlike the average Belgian merchant, Leopold was willing to take great risks. He had shown considerable skill in developing his own estates, and he had invested large sums in the Suez Canal and similar ventures. Leopold had visions of Belgian grandeur. These could be turned into reality by further developing Belgian ports, extending Belgian railways, improving Belgian cities, and expanding Belgian trade.

The king initially looked to the Far East, especially to China. At first, however, he failed to make financial headway in Asia, and during the 1870s he began to turn his attention to Africa. On the face of it, the monarch's endeavor seemed a forlorn hope. There was no lobby in Belgium comparable to the Kolonialgesellschaft in Germany or the Royal Empire Society in Great Britain. There was no pressure group of settlers looking for new land. The king's supporters comprised only a few special-interest groups. Even Belgian missionaries, later an influential lobby, at first displayed relatively little interest in the Congo. (Leopold had to devote considerable effort to encouraging Catholic evangelists to work in the Free State so that he could counterbalance English-speaking Protestants and non-Belgian Catholics like the White Fathers.) In time, however, Belgian priests and lay workers had a major impact on the Congo; the various Catholic mission societies were especially strong in the Flemish parts of Belgium, which, like Scotland, provided many evangelists eager to serve abroad. Leopold also received aid from humanitarians represented in the Société antiesclavigiste belge, which had been founded in 1888 under the inspiration of Cardinal Lavigerie, the great French advocate of colonial expansion and missionary enterprise. Additional support came from the army, from the Belgian veterans' organization known as the Fédération des anciens militaires, from publicity organizations like the Oeuvre africaine, and from the Congolese section of the great expositions held at Antwerp in 1894 and Tervuren in 1897. Above all, the king was aided by a small number of financiers with personal lines to the court and a penchant for risky speculations that was alien to the rank and file of their colleagues on the stock exchange.

A small number of secular intellectuals also took up the colonial cause. (In 1895 the entire student population of Belgium, comprising the great universities of Brussels, Ghent, Liège, and Louvain—the last important for its religious connections—amounted to only 5,017 persons.) These intellectuals included a number of well-placed journalists and geographers—both military and civil—who were interested in exploration. Among their publications were *Congo illustré*, *Bulletin de la société belge de géographie*, and, most important, *Le Mouvement géographique*—the organ of the Institut national at Brussels (established in 1884)—which was edited by A. J. Wauters and financially supported by Captain Albert Thys, a friend of Wauters's and a leading Congolese financial magnate.

Wauters was perhaps the most important of the early colonial theoreticians in Belgium. An art critic, a man of letters, and a gifted writer, he became passionately committed to the colonial cause. His *Histoire politique du Congo belge* (1911) is still worth reading, although he had no access to archival materials at the time he compiled it. Wauters wrote on every conceivable subject bearing on the Congo: its economic potential, its foreign relations, and its bibliography. He was also an accomplished armchair geographer. He never set foot in the Congo, yet from his study in Brussels he managed to determine the approximate location of the source of the Ubangi River. His calculations were confirmed on the spot by Belgian explorer Alphonse Vangèle. Wauters thereby acquired a substantial degree of authority among professional scholars as well as among general readers interested in Central Africa. He and his friends, including colonial-minded soldiers, scholars, journalists, and administrators, began to meet regularly at the Hôtel de Ravenstein, headquarters of the Société d'études coloniales in Brussels. (The society was a colonial propaganda organization founded with the help of Commandant Charles Lemaire, whose activities will be discussed later. Lemaire also helped to establish the

28

Petit Bleu, a Liberal journal that was transformed into a procolonial organ by his friend Gérard Harry.)

The greatest initial driving force in Congolese colonization, however, was the monarch's personal ambition. Financiers showed interest only when they began to realize Africa's enormous potential. Colonial lobbies were the product more than the cause of royal colonialism. Leopold was well placed to push Belgium's new imperial mission. Able and unscrupulous, he had a personal drive so compelling that it repelled Cecil Rhodes, who was not an overly squeamish man. Leopold also had profound personal convictions. He firmly believed that his country's future was tied to colonial conquest. Colonization would render the little nation more secure by strengthening its resources. Overseas expansion would allay the social struggles in the metropolis, providing Belgium with a pledge of glory and insurance against an uncertain future.

> Surrounded by the sea, Holland, Prussia and France [Leopold wrote], our frontiers can never be extended in Europe. It is far away that we must find compensation for the loss of the two half-provinces of Limburg and Luxemburg. Our neutrality . . . forbids us, outside of our nine provinces, any political activity in Europe. But the sea bathes our coast, the universe lies in front of us, steam and electricity have made distances disappear, all the unappropriated lands on the surface of the globe may become the field of our operations and of our successes.[11]

Colonization, Leopold believed, could not wait. Foreigners were appropriating the last of the world's open frontiers. Belgium must not lose its chance. The nation's civilizing mission, fame, profit, and security all rested on this opportunity. Colonization would provide new markets and new revenues that would help Belgium to strengthen its armed forces and thus to defend its threatened neutrality in Europe. Such issues were of great concern to the monarch who was

29

only too aware of Belgium's precarious military position and of the unwillingness of the Catholic masses to support a large defense establishment. In the more distant future colonial revenues might even "some day, permit the Government, after the example of the Netherlands, to lower the tax rates in the mother country." Meanwhile, colonization would assure "to our middle classes the employment which they seek, to our army a little activity, and to Belgium as a whole the opportunity to prove to the world that it is also an imperial people capable of dominating and of enlightening others." A small country, Belgium was "choking in its narrow limits." The kingdom therefore required "an outlet for her surplus production of men, things and ideas." Belgium had to expand as Athens, Venice, Portugal, and Holland had each done in its own day. "These small states which had but limited provinces in Europe, knew how to create outside possessions and relations which not only extended their commerce, but also procured them the means of paying for their military expenses and maintaining their political existence."[12]

Leopold was particularly impressed with the supposed example of Holland. As the king saw it, Holland possessed a great colonial empire. It was rich and enjoyed a greater degree of social peace, than did Belgium. The Dutch had evidently found the secret of making colonial governance pay. As Jean Stengers has convincingly shown in his lectures, Leopold derived his notions of colonial governance from a eulogy regarding Dutch colonization entitled *Java, or How to Manage a Colony*, by J.W.B. Money (1861). Leopold's notions were crude in the extreme. The Dutch had attained their success by forcing their subjects to raise cash crops and by transferring the surplus accumulated in the colonial treasury to that of the motherland. The colonies should be exploited, not by the operation of a market economy, but by state intervention and compulsory cultivation of cash crops to be sold to and distributed by the state at controlled prices.

30

Leopold's theory of colonial exploitation was archaic by the time he tried to apply it in practice, for Holland's prosperity during the Leopoldine era no longer depended on commerce with its colonies. In 1893, for example, only 13.7 percent of Dutch imports derived from the Dutch East Indies, which took no more than 5.1 percent of Holland's exports. The so-called culture system, so admired by Leopold, had turned out to be inefficient. Officials assigned to supervise production had lacked sufficient knowledge either of agriculture or of the local people. The withdrawal of numerous "hands" from the labor market had conflicted with the demands of private entrepreneurs who were willing to pay the going rate. "Free-wage" laborers had tended to work harder than conscripts. During the so-called Liberal era in Java (c. 1870-1900) the Dutch had largely done away with compulsory labor; state plantations had given way to private enterprise, and alienation of native land to foreigners had been abolished. In effect, this "Liberal" system benefited the planters. It aroused considerable opposition, however, from Dutch trading interests, who considered that the government should stress the role of the indigenous people as customers and not merely as producers. The system adopted at the beginning of the twentieth century, called the "ethical" system, was designed to transform the villages into petty municipalities on Western lines by improving educational, agricultural, veterinary, and other social services, by promoting capital investment, by reforming the administrative machinery, by extending the home market, and also by serving the wider cause of humanity.[13]

Leopold, however, was unaware of the realities in Java. He was swayed by the mechanistic simplicity of a model that took little account of empirical facts. The indigenous people of the Congo were, to Leopold, no more than impersonal units of labor whom a compulsory-labor regime would render capable of yielding profits while it discouraged revolt. There were other advantages to foreign expansion, according to Leopold. Colonial enterprise would cement

31

internal unity in a divided Belgium. "Only on the day when we possess an overseas policy will we be able to cauterize the appalling cancer of liberal-clerical conflict which is eating us away."[14]

The king had a dynastic stake in acquiring a great African fief. Foreign riches would secure the house of Coburg-Gotha in Belgium and would boost the king's revenue and his popularity at home. They would also provide the means whereby Leopold might indulge his dreams of beautifying Belgium by a splendid program of public works—a form of conspicuous consumption that would surely endear the monarch to his subjects. The king would acquire an independent source of revenue, personal power secured by an independent territorial base, and a stronghold from which "Congo-law" companies might labor unrestrained by the restrictions imposed on local concerns by Belgian law. These Congo-style companies, in turn, could operate as far afield as China, where Belgian capital was instrumental in railway development. (Belgian financial intervention in China was in fact resumed after the Sino-Japanese war. These ventures were directed primarily by men with a stake in the Congolese economy, including Jean Jadot, a conservative financier entrenched in the Société générale, Emile Francqui, a "colonial" at the Banque d'outre-mer, and Empain.)

Leopold's thoughts in many ways resembled those of an eighteenth-century prince, a mercantile-minded "projector." However, he had a feeling for the financial methods of his own era. His economic policy was based on the assumption that backward countries could be developed only by means of large-scale foreign investments. But risk capital was scarce. His project required large—indeed, unexpectedly large—investments on what the more cautious kind of financier saw as inadequate security. "Sire," Malou cynically remarked to the king with regard to the latter's Congolese venture, "I have neither faith nor hope, how can you expect me to have charity?"[15] Investors had to be protected. Their interests could be safeguarded only by grants of great territorial concessions and of local monopolies, a practice that soon turned interlopers into enemies and belied Leopold's public declarations in favor of free enterprise.

From Leopold's standpoint, an African kingdom controlled by himself had other uses. Empire building appealed to the romantic and humanitarian impulses of intellectuals like Emile Banning, for a time one of the king's most trusted collaborators. When Banning was a young man his imagination had been set aflame by Bernardin de Saint-Pierre and Chateaubriand. Africa had become to him a sacred battleground where light must prevail over darkness. It was in this spirit that he apostrophized a Europe supposedly sunk in self-indulgence and sloth:

> Tu vis, tu ne crains pas
> t'enivrer de joie,
>
> Quand au front du soleil
> le brigand vend sa proie!

According to Banning, colonization would also help to solve problems concerned with Belgian demographic growth and social mobility. Belgian mothers continued to bear many children, and the Belgian working class especially continued to increase in numbers. Hence social mobility would decline; the ruling elite would cease to be rejuvenated by recruits from the lower orders of society and would therefore become decadent. This process could be arrested, or at least slowed down, by colonization in Africa, one of the world's last open frontiers.

Leopoldine colonialism, at first an ill-sorted collection of nebulous designs, took firmer shape when the discoveries of Livingstone, Speke, Burton, and others became widely known. In 1876 Leopold summoned an international conference that resulted in the creation of the International Association for the Exploration and Civilization of Africa. National committees were set up in many countries, and the Belgian committee first directed its attention to East Africa.

33

In August 1877, however, Henry Morton Stanley (1841-1904) reached the mouth of the Congo after tracing the course of that vast waterway. This turned Leopold to the Congo region, which seemed to offer vast potential riches as well as an opportunity to enlist the idealism of missionary and anti-slave-trade opinion in Europe.

In 1878 Stanley accepted Leopold's offer to return to the Congo to set up stations under the auspices of the Comité d'études du Haut Congo. Its capital was small—1 million francs. The king advances one-quarter of its funds through Baron Léon Lambert, while a Dutch concern, the Afrikaansche Handelsvereeniging, put down 130,000 francs; a number of Belgian financiers including Lambert and Georges Brugmann, also invested some money. The governing council consisted of Barons Lambert and Greindl and two members of the Afrikaansche Handelsvereeniging. Colonel Strauch, the king's representative, acted as president.

A year later the Comité was transformed into the Association internationale du Congo (AIC), which, despite its name, served as the king's personal instrument. The AIC faced a difficult diplomatic task. France was looking toward territorial expansion, while Portugal put forward claims to the Congo, supported by Great Britain. Leopold, however, secured support from Bismarck, apparently through the latter's personal banker, Gerson von Bleichröder, who valued Leopold's stated commitment to free trade in Africa and felt that all civilized states should unite in defense of the social order against Socialists and other international miscreants.[16] The United States recognized the AIC for several reasons. The Americans were interested in the economic possibilities of the Congo; they also felt a sense of national pride in the exploits of Henry M. Stanley, an American citizen and a key figure in "opening" the Congo. Henry Shelton Sanford, former U.S. ambassador to Belgium, played a crucial part as a lobbyist on behalf of his friend Leopold II. Sanford entertained senators and representatives, furnished information regarding the Congo to the State Department, and became

34

acquainted with members of the Senate Committee on Foreign Relations; and everywhere he stressed the philanthropic and humanitarian purpose that supposedly motivated Leopold and the Association members.

The Congress of Berlin (1884-1885) gave international legitimacy to the king's design. The signatories recognized Leopold's claims, agreed to maintain freedom of commerce and navigation in the Congo basin, and set down rules concerning "effective occupation" of colonial territories. The Belgian legislature empowered Leopold to assume sovereignty of a new state to be known as the Etat indépendant du Congo (Congo Free State). On 1 August 1885 the king officially notified the powers of the existence of the new state, which, he promised, would be committed to "perpetual neutrality."

The Congo Free State received support from Dutch and British trading firms established on the Lower Congo; they were counting on Leopold's promise of free trade and navigation on the Congo and regarded the king as a less dangerous claimant than the French or Portuguese. At the same time, Leopold began a skillful campaign to popularize his enterprise. Anxious to dispel domestic opposition to his project, the king had assured the Chamber in 1884 that Belgium would incur no expenses from the vast enterprise in which he had become entangled. Three years later the parliamentary climate had grown more favorable, and the government asked the legislature to authorize a Congolese loan in Belgium of up to 150 million francs. The Liberal left abstained, but the government won a decisive majority—eighty-six to nine, with seven abstentions. A year later the legislature was asked for 10 million francs to build a railway from Matadi to Stanley Pool. Opposition had dwindled further; the government secured a majority of eighty-eight with only six abstentions. In 1890 the Belgian state for the first time was called upon to lend a substantial sum, 25 million francs in all, to the Congo Free State—and the project passed by ninety-five to one. The Socialists and left-wing Socialists continued to oppose royal colonialism, but their objections

35

carried little weight. The Congo Free State had won domestic as well as international legitimacy.[17]

Leopold took steps to obtain further backing from private financiers. Using part of his own substantial fortune (his Civil List alone amounted to 3.3 million francs a year), he set up the Compagnie du Congo pour le commerce et l'industrie (CCCI) in 1886 with a nominal capital of 1 million francs—a negligible sum to carry out the company's vast plans. Captain Thys, the king's orderly officer, managed the company's affairs, and in time the concern became an important holding company. By 1895 its assets amounted to about 35 million francs.

The AIC was a state in embryo, financed and controlled solely by Leopold and his associates. Initially, only a few Belgians were involved; the majority of the king's supporters were foreigners, men like Gustav Nachtigal and Sir Bartle Frere, who were represented on the association's executive committee. Local branch committees derived some backing from geographical societies and from merchants, missionaries, and intellectuals who were anxious to further the cause of enlightenment in "Darkest Africa." All real power, however, rested with the king.

Leopold relied on adventurers to run the AIC, many of them foreigners like Stanley, whose career may serve as a prototype. No African explorer ever raised greater controversy. None had a more extraordinary life. Henry Morton Stanley was born in 1841 in Wales, an illegitimate child. His boyhood, says the *Dictionary of National Biography* with considerable understatement, "was hard and loveless." Indeed, it was worse than Oliver Twist's. After a grim time in the workhouse, Stanley drifted to a farm, to a haberdashery, and to a butcher shop, eventually shipping as cabin boy on a packet bound for New Orleans. A few years later he enlisted in the army of the Confederacy, was captured at Shiloh, and endured unspeakable conditions in a Union prisoner-of-war camp. He obtained his release by enlisting in the Northern artillery but was soon discharged, a sick and broken man.

36

After a few more years of hardship, he managed to make good as a journalist traveling in search of copy to Asia Minor, Tibet, and other distant parts; he also wrote about the American West and acted as military correspondent for an American paper to cover the British expedition against Abyssinia under Sir Robert Napier.

Stanley's great opportunity came when the *New York Herald* commissioned him to look for Livingstone, who was then exploring Central Africa. No news of him had been heard for some time. Stanley's expedition worked its way inland, and in 1871 he found Livingstone in desperate need of supplies. Stanley's story—made public in the racy narrative *How I Found Livingstone* (1872)—was at first received with some incredulity. But eventually the book made his name a household word among European readers thirsting for information about exotic lands, strange tribes, and savage customs.

His second African journey, begun in 1874 and destined to last for nearly a thousand days, accomplished more than any other single expedition. From the East Coast, Stanley traveled to Uganda. Leaving Lakes Victoria and Tanganyika behind him, he struck west for a river locally called the Lualaba, continued on past a series of falls and past the future site of Stanleyville to where the river clearly became the Congo, and then followed its course to the Atlantic. Stanley had fought in two armies without rising above the rank of private; yet he was a conquistador by temperament. Explorers like Carl Mauch and David Livingstone had laid the foundations of their fame by traveling in small parties or alone; they had relied on the goodwill of local African communities and on a small-scale investment in money and men. Stanley headed military-style expeditions that were well equipped and prepared to use armed force. As a strategic and technical achievement, Stanley's march from the East Coast to the West Coast of Africa stands unsurpassed.

From the African point of view, Stanley's enterprises were often disastrous. Stanley never feared a fight, but even a

37

more pacific leader would have faced serious problems in leading a large expedition into the interior with no means of importing supplies from the coast. In backward African societies that produced only a limited agricultural surplus, each major expedition was apt to occasion local inflation and impose a heavy burden on local resources. The invaders' apparent wealth also aroused the cupidity of indigenous warlords. European parties were well supplied with arms and other goods that African leaders were anxious to acquire or, if necessary, to seize by force. Middlemen on the Congo who were determined to maintain their local monopolies saw Stanley's expedition as a threat. When he descended the river in 1877, Kongo and Zumbo traders foresaw the implications of European penetration into the interior. Stanley encountered wide opposition wherever commerce was concentrated in the hands of a powerful, clearly defined group. Yet he managed to overcome all opponents and at last made his way to the sea.

Stanley's reputed toughness was a quality that appealed to Leopold. For several years Stanley ran the rudimentary administration that was set up as the nucleus for Leopold's embryonic African state. With immense effort and great cost in lives, and aided only by a few dozen Europeans and by African laborers who migrated from long distances, Zanzibari workmen, and Kru sailors, Stanley did a remarkable job. From the existing port of Boma, he opened a route that went around the falls and upstream to Stanley Pool. He organized river transport and set up a few small stations, albeit weakly held and ill-suited to resist the advance of Muslim slave traders from the east. His labors earned him the nickname of "Bula Matari"—the breaker of stones—an epithet that was later applied to the Congo Free State's administration as a whole.

Stanley was able to accomplish what he did because his activities at that time seemed to present no real threat to the great mass of African peoples in the region. Political authority among the people of the Lower Congo was far too decentralized—and internecine struggles far too bitter—to permit concerted resistance against the newcomers. Black middlemen might fear white competition, but many other Africans at first looked upon the king's agents in a friendly fashion—as strangers able to command vast wealth by magic means or, more realistically, as a convenient source of trade goods such as mirrors, gunpowder, brass wire, knives, beads, cloth, and liquor. European missionaries likewise were welcomed as strangers whose presence in the country might be useful both for material and for spiritual reasons.

Thus Leopold was able to acquire a local base to serve his ambitions. This stronghold was at first precarious. His administration consisted of a few dozen adventurers from many nations—men like Captain Deane, a former officer in the Indian army. Financially, the king's position was equally shaky. Normal methods of raising money on the stock exchange were not sufficient to pay for the effective occupation of the Congo. International agreements between 1885 and 1890 debarred the monarch from substantially raising import duties; humanitarian opinion embodied in treaty clauses prevented him from selling liquor and guns to Africans; and political considerations at first forbade recourse to subsidies extracted from the pockets of Belgian taxpayers. But Leopold had attained the first of his aims: the house of Coburg-Gotha was entrenched in Africa.

Leopold's new sovereignty, which was publicly dedicated to the pursuit of free trade, international neutrality, and the extirpation of the slave trade, initially enjoyed a good deal of international goodwill. The Free State was exempted, in effect, from the doctrine of "effective occupation" that under the accepted convention of the time required European powers to exercise some kind of administrative control, however tenuous, over any colonial areas that they claimed. To all intents and purposes, sovereignty was vested in the person of the king, who regarded the state as his personal property. The possessions of chartered concerns like the British South Africa Company were subject to some control from an es-

39

tablished government, but Leopold owed no constitutional obligation for his Congo kingdom to any Belgian body. Alone among the world's reigning sovereigns, the king could rightly say, "L'état, c'est moi." Foreign claims, especially those of the Portuguese, which were based on historical precedents and on the stake held by Portuguese traders in parts of the Congo, were set aside. African claims were not even considered. Once Leopold had attained his objective, the mask of internationalism was dropped. The new state was run as part of the king's private domain, a giant fief with a variegated population ranging from Stone Age hunters to Iron Age cultivators and sophisticated craftsmen.

The Congo, Its Land and People

The regions claimed by Leopold were staggering in their immensity. The Congo is one of the world's greatest rivers, longer than the Niger or the Volga. Its drainage basin extends over some 1.4 million square miles—a region larger than the Republic of India—and resembles a shallow saucer of mammoth size set into the tabletop of tropical Africa. The alluvial floor of this saucer is almost completely flat, giving the huge waterway plenty of room to stretch. The three-thousand-mile-long Congo River is wide along most of its length and given to inundation. Great marshes, swamps, and lakes make up a large proportion of the total drainage area. The saucer is only about one thousand feet high at its center; from there it ·rises slowly and often imperceptibly to between three thousand and four thousand feet at the rim. There the vast highlands vary in character from smooth tablelands to deeply cut, sierra-like ridges of dramatic beauty. In the western segment of the rim the unending action of equatorial rain-fed streams cuts deeply into rock and soils. The peripheral area of highlands and plateaus rises progressively toward Katanga (Shaba) in the extreme south of the country. In the east, the region shares in the Great Rift Valley.

The Congo basin, with its multitude of tributaries, forms one of the most important systems of inland waterways in Africa; it provided Leopold with a natural logistic network superior to those available to other colonizers in the African interior. The Congo River is by no means a perfect avenue of communication. It has cut a tortuous channel through the impeding Chrystal Mountains to reach the sea and enters the Atlantic through a true river estuary, its bottom a great canyon extending far out into the ocean. Along the 217-mile stretch between Matadi on the Atlantic and the city of Léopoldville (Kinshasa), its course is broken by a series of spectacular falls and rapids. Yet the navigable parts of the river itself amount to some 1,700 miles, while the system as a whole includes about 7,200 miles of usable waterways. Geographical circumstances thus permitted travelers, soldiers, and merchants greater ease of access to the interior than existed in most parts of the African hinterland, and Congolese colonization became dependent to a great extent on riverboats. Ships' captains were able to navigate on a river distinguished by an unusual evenness of flow; unlike many African waterways, the Congo could be used year-round. As time went on, the Belgians learned to depend on its far-flung tributaries; the roads and railways they later built were largely determined by the specific needs of the Congo and its confluents. The Congo Free State (now known as the Republic of Zaïre) covers 895,000 square miles; thus it is more than eighty times the size of Belgium itself. Yet its initial area was a narrow band of territory along the Atlantic coast, which was adequate to give the Belgians access to the interior but not to build the Congo into a maritime state.

In the imagination of Victorian newspaper readers, the Congo interior was an immense tangle of rain forests—hot, steamy, and impenetrable. Modern geographers report that tropical rain forest actually actually covers less than half the land area, most of it in the northern half of the country. The forest is hard to delimit. The jungle changes in appearance and composition, and its border is not clearly defined be-

41

cause there is a gradual transition from tropical forest to forest-savanna in less densely wooded regions. Tongues of forest penetrate up the river valleys into the neighboring savanna. The true forests, moreover, are diminishing in size. The African practice of shifting cultivation may have cut into the forest land, since the length of time that elapses between successive clearings of the same patch of ground determines the extent to which the jungle can regenerate. The so-called secondary forests that spring up where the original cover has been disturbed usually have denser undergrowth than the original woodlands. They may also contain new species, such as the oil palm, which was introduced by African tillers. In many areas the intervals between cultivation are short, and regular burning of the forest results in its replacement by savanna. In this process, the soil may also deteriorate. Excessive burning hardens the lateritic soils; exposed to tropical downpours, they are then easily leached. The savanna therefore expands as the forests contract, creating new ecological problems.

The natural scenery of the savanna is extremely varied. Its appearance depends on rainfall: where precipitation is high, the savanna turns into splendid parkland; as moisture diminishes, the trees become smaller, sparser, and more stunted. The quality of the soil over much of the Congo is poor, belying travelers' tales of inexhaustible wealth. Only limited regions are truly productive: the alluvial lands in the central basin and along some of the main watercourses, and the volcanic lands of Kivu in the east, which are periodically enriched by wind-borne volcanic ash.[18] There were and are many other obstacles in the way of the Congolese cultivator. Rainfall may be excessive in quantity or irregular; droughts and locusts may destroy crops; and rats, insects, or moisture may ruin stored supplies. Stockmen face a host of veterinary problems for many of which modern science still has found no satisfactory answers.

The settlers who established Leopold's new empire found that horses could not be kept in the Congo. Even where the climate permitted stockbreeding, Africans did not have the skill, the incentive, or the opportunity for training oxen to pull plows or wagons. They remained entirely dependent on the power of human muscle for working the land, digging ore, paddling canoes, bearing burdens, or throwing missiles. They also faced many diseases for which no man knew a remedy (the medical and veterinary revolution that enabled white men to conquer Africa only started at the end of the last century). Indigenous sicknesses included malaria, yellow fever, elephantiasis (which produces enormous swelling of limbs), sleeping sickness, and other insect-borne diseases. There were also water-borne plagues, such as schistosomiasis, river blindness, and the Guinea threadworm. Lice and fleas threatened human health with the infections they carried—afflictions like relapsing fever or the murine plague. In addition, Africans had to cope with killers familiar in the northern hemisphere: tuberculosis, pneumonia, smallpox, influenza, syphilis, and a host of other diseases that were often spread by contact with alien invaders like the Europeans and Arabs.

The image of the hale and healthy savage, spread by generations of writers, had little basis in reality. The indigenous population remained in a state of poverty that would be hard for a modern European to imagine. The so-called traditional African suffered from a host of afflictions. In his struggle against a hostile environment, he depended on a few simple tools—the hoe, the axe, the bow. And as skilled as he might be in carving wood, fashioning pots, weaving cloth, or working metals, his technology could not exploit the country's vast resources in deep-level mineral wealth or hydroelectric power. He had no means of storing large quantities of food; he was unable to transport bulky goods—food, coal, ores—over long distances; and he had no way of counteracting local famines by drawing on supplies from remote regions. He was dependent to an extraordinary extent on his immediate environment.

Not surprisingly, the density of the country's population

remained low. Lack of manpower was a constant problem in the development of agriculture, mining, and industry. At the end of the nineteenth century Stanley made a purely speculative estimate of the population, placing it at twenty-eight million. This and other equally unscientific estimates were frequently cited as facts by political writers, contributing to the widely accepted belief that the population was always small in relation to the immense size of the country. In the early 1920s experts believed that the country contained about ten million people. Although detailed calculations are lacking, we know that the population grew from then on, and supposedly numbered about thirteen million a generation later.

The indigenous people followed many ways of life. Pygmy hunters, who made a scanty living from the forest, differed from the cattle keepers who had imposed their rule on parts of the eastern Congo. The majority of Congolese, however, were farmers whose methods varied as widely as their crops. Indigenous cultivators grew millet, sorghum, cassava, and a variety of vegetables and imported plants that could be adapted to African conditions, such as maize, rice, and tobacco. They were skilled in the arts of pottery, basket weaving, carving, and ironwork. Congolese craftsmen acquired an enviable reputation as makers of beautiful masks, statues, seats and headrests, ceremonial axes, and other objects that are now housed in museums. The Congolese did not know how to read and write, but they developed an extensive oral literature—myths, fairy tales, proverbs, legends, heroic epics—as well as a rich tradition of dancing and dramatic representation. Although their religious beliefs were many, a large number of Congolese held a general belief in the existence of a Supreme Being; most believed in the immortality of the soul and in the ancestral spirits who survived to look after the community and who might be consulted through diviners and other ritualists.

An exact description of the many Congolese economies would require a book rather than a chapter. There were far-reaching differences in the ways of life followed by forest people in the midst of tropical jungle, by pastoralists in the eastern Congo, and by savanna farmers. We have chosen to look in detail at a single example: the Suku of the south-western Congo.[19] Their way of life has many parallels among the savanna peoples. Given the excellence of the anthropological material available on the Suku, they may serve as a convenient paradigm. Like the vast majority of the Congolese population, the Suku are Bantu speakers. Kongo, their tongue, belongs to the Niger-Congo group of languages. Bantu speakers occupy about two-thirds of the Congo; the other ethnic groups speak a variety of idioms, including Eastern-Adamawa, Central Sudanic, and Nilotic languages.

The Suku dwell in rolling savanna country that is broken by occasional stretches of woodland. The soil is sandy and relatively poor, but until recently an abundance of game made meat a valuable addition to the people's diet. (In recent years there have been some changes in their methods of husbandry.) Traditionally, the adult women planted several plots in succession during the rains so that crops would be maturing in one plot while another was being prepared. Cassava was the staple food, but the women also planted sweet potatoes, pumpkins, beans, and peas. The Suku practiced shifting cultivation, which depended on the periodic burning of brushland for fertilization; an area would lie fallow after the crops had been harvested while the villages moved on to prepare another patch. The Suku also maintained small gardens in which they grew such plants as bananas, tobacco, and tomatoes. Cultivated crops were supplemented by wild fruit, berries, mushrooms, and such delicacies as flying ants and caterpillars. Domesticated animals included dogs, goats, pigs, and chickens. Suku agriculture, in other words, was well adjusted to a way of life in which land alone was plentiful but capital and manpower remained scarce.

In the Suku crafts, the division of labor betweeen the sexes was clearly pronounced: the women made pottery; the

45

men wove baskets, mats of raffia, and fishing nets and also carved in wood. All of the men were artisans to some extent, for all built houses, made bows, wove mats, or hammered out crude arrow points. There was some specialization, but even the more highly skilled craftsmen could not make a living from their skills alone and so took part in ordinary activities such as hunting and fishing. Blacksmiths practiced a highly respected occupation that the Suku—like so many other preliterate people—surrounded with special taboos and initiation ceremonies. Other specialists acquired renown in the making of particular objects or as traveling healers, dancers, and musicians. The Suku did most of their work in an individualistic fashion. Women farmed individually; houses were individually built; fishing weirs were individually exploited; and trade, crafts, and animal breeding were carried out on an individual basis. Individuals, however, could not accumulate great wealth. Like their neighbors, the Suku regarded land as a commodity available to all members of the community, just as all members were entitled to water and air. Hunting rights over specific stretches of bush might have been vested in specific lineages, however, so that there was an incipient economic differentiation on kinship lines, and lineage might also determine rights to fishing sites or palm and bamboo groves. The Suku believed that a man could acquire property only because of the supernatural and physical protection received from his kin group. Thus, in a sense, all individual domestic property was viewed as belonging to the lineage as a whole, and there was continuous circulation of household goods and money among its members. Such sharing was especially pronounced when the lineage was faced with special needs, as, for instance, when a member had to find goods to pay bridewealth or to pay a fine. Conversely, when legal compensation or bridewealth was received from another lineage, every adult member could claim a share. Some people did manage to accumulate more wealth than their neighbors, but no Suku questioned the right of the lineage to draw on such property in times of need. A few lineages controlled the office of regional chief and profited from tribute collected in the name of the Suku king, but the resulting differences in wealth were comparatively slight and did not cause profound social conflict.

The institution of slavery likewise did not at first introduce great social cleavage, for slavery initially resembled adoption more than servitude. For all practical purposes, a slave became a full-fledged member of the lineage to which his owner belonged. Slaves did not become a class, for Suku society was stratified according to lineages rather than classes. On these relatively simple foundations, the Suku were able to build a fairly complicated system of political authority: supreme lordship rested with the king, who resided in a large village of his own that accommodated most members of the royal lineage; and royal powers were delegated to regional heads, who in turn controlled local chiefs holding authority over groups of villages.

Indigenous states within the Congo differed enormously in extent, power, and internal composition. An African Aristotle would have found in the Congo every conceivable form of constitution, from small "stateless" neighborhood societies to powerful monarchies that traded in slaves, ivory, copper, and other commodities and that were capable of raising considerable armies and asserting their power over extensive areas.[20] The most powerful of these monarchies were found in the savanna region, where communication was easier than in the tropical rain forest.

The Congo basin became a veritable nursery of African monarchies. Among these empire-building peoples were the Lunda, who were farmers, hunters, and fishermen. Sometime during the fifteenth century the Lunda acquired new ideas concerning political organization from their Luba neighbors in the northeast. Lunda kings came to hold power by divine right; they held extensive ritual functions, as did their headmen, who were responsible for their subjects' supernatural as well as secular well-being. Lunda statesmen established their institutions in fertile river valleys as well as in the savanna.

47

The Lunda were also outstanding conquerors. During the seventeenth century they expanded into what is now Angola, where they came into contact with other trading communities, including the Ovimbundu, who supplied them with guns and other imports in exchange for slaves. Later, Portuguese influence led to the diffusion of new crops such as maize and cassava. The possession of firearms and the expanding commerce with the coast may have helped to strengthen the Lunda so that they could build a great number of satellite states that were subject to an overlord known as the *Mwata Yamvo*. By the end of the eighteenth century the whole of Central Africa was linked by a network of commerce that stretched from coast to coast and supplied the indigenous people with all manner of merchandise, muskets, cloth, and ornaments in exchange for slaves, copper bars, and ivory.[21]

The network of trade and politics underwent further change during the nineteenth century. The demand for ivory steadily increased, both in India and in the West. Wild rubber became a marketable raw material for a variety of industrial purposes. By the 1880s there was an extensive pattern of long-distance trading routes that linked the various parts of the Congo to the Indian and Atlantic oceans. European imports became widely available. One system linked the coast to Malebo (Stanley) Pool. Another went out from there along the main river and its many affluents. A third linked the Portuguese posts in Angola to the Kasai and Katanga rivers. From the Indian Ocean, Swahili-speaking frontiersmen went as far as Katanga and the falls near Stanleyville (Kisangani). Copts (known as *jellaba*) based in Khartum raided south to the middle portion of the Uele River.

The internal balance of power began to shift as the Ovimbundu and other trading peoples sold guns to a great number of new customers. The Lovale, for example, who lived in what is now northeastern Zambia, acquired firearms and turned against the formerly powerful Lunda. The Chokwe (Cokwe, Kioko), a warlike people skilled as traders and hunters, likewise bought new weapons and expanded into the

48

Lunda sphere. Ivory production rested essentially on the skills of hunters, daring men whom established rulers could not easily control and whose travels over long distances in search of elephants often helped to disrupt the existing political order. Chokwe settlers and hunters made their way into the very heartland of the Lunda empire. Swahili-speaking frontiersmen penetrated the interior from the East Coast in search of slaves and ivory. The Lunda empire thus was beset by a number of enemies: its trade decayed; its power collapsed; and new kingdoms came into being. During the second half of the nineteenth century, for instance, a Nyamwezi merchant named Msiri settled down with an armed following in what is now Shaba. He gradually built up his power until he became a great potentate, augmenting his profits earned from trade by tributes in ivory, salt, and copper. Even more powerful was Tippu Tip (Muhammed ibn Hamed), a Zanzibari slave trader who became a great warlord in the eastern Congo.

Commerce in the Lower Congo was even more extensive, despite the geographical obstacles in the merchants' path. Water transport on the upper river depended on canoes, and traders had to rely on the services of porters to carry goods through the cataract region; hence the economic possibilities of the riverine system remained limited. There was, however, a good deal of traffic from the rivers to the northern part of what is now Angola. The staple product was ivory, supplemented by palm oil, palm kernels, beeswax, raw cotton, and rubber.

In economic terms, the effect of this commerce was double-edged. The people of Central Africa acquired a variety of new goods: muskets to add to their arsenals, cloth to improve their wardrobe, knives and hatchets to increase their tool kit, pots and pans to lighten the housewife's lot, and salt to improve their diet. Swahili-speaking men from the coast introduced a variety of new crops. Their caravans brought craftsmen as well as mercenaries, so that commerce helped to diffuse technical skills. Some of the so-called subsistence economies had reserves of land, labor, and enterprise that could be brought into use when new opportunities became available. The export of wasting assets such as ivory and rubber probably stimulated agricultural production in addition to providing employment for traders and porters. Nevertheless, the economic potential of this commerce remained limited. To a considerable extent the prosperity of the new warlords depended on a harsh regime of economic coercion in which trade was accompanied by raiding, looting, and village burning or, more peaceably, by the imposition of tribute. The system had a strongly predatory element. The elephant herds of Central Africa were decimated, for the hunters—whether Chokwe or Swahili—did not think to replenish them. Wild rubber plants were often destroyed. The slave trade debased its victims and impoverished potential customers.

At the same time, traditional methods of production were undergoing considerable changes. The people dwelling along the Congo and its tributaries, as well as those in Kwilu and northern Kasai, began to develop more intensive kinds of farming; some areas specialized in the production of salt, others in the fashioning of canoes or the smelting of iron. There was a good deal of trade between these different regions. All in all, this internal commerce was probably far more important than the more highly publicized traffic in ivory and slaves. Yet the level of technology remained low: the farmer continued to rely mainly on the hoe; the merchant counted on porters; and the riverman depended on canoes. Central Africa remained politically divided and economically backward, a prey to Belgian conquerors who were able to unify, systematize, and ultimately transcend the coercive economies of the area.

At the time when Leopold first began to scheme for a tropical dominion, the task of conquering the Congo seemed to be an assignment almost impossible to execute. European influence was negligible. The Portuguese held claims of ancient standing in the Lower Congo, where their missionaries, soldiers, and merchants had once attempted to impose a form of indirect domination by means of an alliance with Kongo kings. Memories of Portuguese greatness had long since waned, however, and little remained of Portugal's former influence. By the late 1870s a number of European traders—Dutch, Portuguese, and German—had settled in "factories" or trading posts along the lower part of the Congo, especially in Banana and Boma. They dealt in tropical crops like palm oil, groundnuts, and, later, rubber, employing indigenous middlemen and devising an elaborate system of credit. The slave trade with the New World had by this time come to an end, having persisted longer in the Congo than in most other parts of West Africa. The reputation of the Europeans, however, was still besmirched by memories of this commerce, and white expeditions into the interior encountered a great deal of hostility. Access inland was impeded by extraordinary geographical obstacles, by a harsh climate, and above all by disease. No task seemed more difficult than the effective occupation of the huge areas to which the Belgian monarch had laid so implausible a claim.

TWO

_____

THE FORCE PUBLIQUE

THE conquest of the Congo was a long-drawn-out affair that lasted more than three decades. From the military point of view, it was one of the most astonishing achievements in the history of African colonization. Leopold's rumored treasure house was an immense country devoid of railways, roads, harbors and river ports, hospitals, and supply depots—a land of subcontinental size in which every civil or military installation required by the army had to be created by the invader. The Belgian military officers were under constant pressure; Leopold was determined to expand his fief at all costs, lest he be forestalled by the British and the French. His territorial appetite was insatiable. He looked north to what later became the French territory of Oubangui; he looked northeast to the Sudan; he looked south to Katanga. His plans for expansion, however, rested on an inadequate logistical base. The tiny stretch of the Atlantic coast that was the Congo Free State hardly seemed an adequate starting point to gain access to an apparently boundless interior.

Enormous environmental and health problems also faced the newcomers. They had to penetrate one of the world's greatest tropical rain forests, one of a kind no Belgian soldier had ever seen. Belgian columns sometimes had to struggle through dense woodland, its thick undergrowth rising fifteen feet above the ground; from this gloomy tangle emerged giant trees reaching two hundred feet into the sky. Elsewhere they encountered rugged mountain country and dry savanna, while along the banks of the Lower Congo they faced fever-ridden mangrove forests. They made their way through forbidding swamps and through inundated forests where trees emerged from great sheets of water—an astonishing and sometimes frightening spectacle. There was the ever-present

52

fear of falling captive to an enemy who would use the most refined methods of torture imaginable to put a prisoner to death. And then there were the flies, the creeping insects, the rains, the damp, the boils that never healed, the fevers, the heat—and yet more heat.

CONQUEST

The tactical tasks encountered by the Belgian invaders posed problems of a kind never covered in Belgian staff-college courses. They could be overcome only by leaders endowed with imagination, initiative, resolution, and an aptitude for independent thinking. Belgian officers were required, above all, to be skillful diplomatists, capable of finding local allies such as the Batetela, who collaborated with the Belgians for a time in pursuit of their own foreign-policy objectives. So did the son of Msiri, a Yeke potentate who sought Belgian help against his rebellious Sanga subjects. On the other hand, the Belgians found many irreconcilable enemies, especially in Uele, South Kivu, Kwango, and northern Katanga. Luso-African traders were not inclined to accept Free State suzerainty; Swahili-speaking merchants resented their white competitors, as did indigenous conquerors like the Chokwe. The Zande, for example, a warlike people of Central Sudanic speech who lived in the northeastern Congo and the Sudan and who were organized into small independent communities, had worked out an elaborate system of ambushes involving the delivery of simultaneous charges at the head, center, and rear of a marching column. The Belgians were forced to march Indian file in penetrating thick bush, and Zande assaults—delivered in columns from six to eight deep —usually succeeded in cutting their ranks in half.

In the equatorial region the Topoke, a Bantu people situated between the Congo and Lomami rivers, fought in a fashion attuned to the marshy nature of their country. Topoke warriors would wait—standing up to their necks in the mud of a swamp and hiding their heads behind some tuft or tree—until the head of an enemy column appeared, its soldiers holding their rifles above their heads to keep them dry. At this point the *askari* were at the mercy of Topoke spears. Long habit had trained the Topoke to move through the marshes so quickly that the invaders could not easily take defensive action and were apt to suffer serious losses. The Mbesa (Mombesa, Mombassa), another Bantu people, who were renowned for their excellent system of communication by drums, used these drums to good effect to prepare ambushes; the enemy would be attacked by showers of poisoned arrows followed by spear charges. These and similar tactics combined the technology of the early Iron Age with a thorough knowledge of field craft and a flair for guerrilla warfare.

Successful campaigners in Central Africa had to ignore all they had ever learned in military manuals about the tactics, the logistics, and even the ethics of warfare. Their training had dealt with military operations in countries that were well supplied with railways, roads, and river steamers. In Western Europe armies depended on an elaborate network of factories, supply depots, and repair shops. In Africa, on the other hand, soldiers largely had to fend for themselves in the early days. Often they had to fight hundreds of miles away from their bases and were dependent primarily on what they could buy, harvest, loot, or shoot on the spot.

Enthusiastic Brussels crowds that cheered in the streets for successful campaigners had no idea of what their champions had accomplished logistically. Few Europeans ever grasped the scale of the distances involved. In North American terms, the drainage basin of the Congo River—extending over some 1.4 million square miles—would stretch from north to south on a line equal in length to the distance between Ontario and the Gulf of Mexico. In a European context, a column operating on Lake Albert was as far from the main center at Boma as London is from the northern stretches of the Volga River. Military operations had to be conducted far from base in tropical rain forest, in desolate upland plateaus, or in arid bush. Tropical diseases were rampant, and there was no provision for the sick, the wounded, or the dying. Belgian soldiers learned to fight under abysmal conditions: drinking water was often infected and food hard to come by; constant humidity caused boots and belts to mold; rains and heat set men's nerves on edge; and fevers were common, turning dreams into nightmares.

Historians of Belgian colonialism have produced many different military accounts. An enumeration of the countless skirmishes, ambushes, minor "punitive expeditions," and major campaigns would be tedious. Suffice it to say that the Belgians met widespread resistance, but that the resistance was rarely concerted. The diverse states, ministates, and neighborhood communities were often torn by bitter and bloody internecine struggles that were aggravated by the influx of guns and gunpowder, by competition for the commerce in ivory, and by the expansion of the slave trade. The eastern part of the Congo especially was under heavy pressure from Swahili-speaking Muslim invaders who penetrated inland from East Africa in search of elephant tusks and captives. By exploiting these dissensions within their opponents' ranks, the Belgians could always draw on indigenous auxiliaries. Yet some of their most formidable opponents were mutinous black soldiers who had been armed and trained by the Belgians themselves. Rebellious Batetela soldiers (as we shall see later) fought against their erstwhile masters for many years. Their resistance continued until the beginning of the present century, and even long after their revolts had been suppressed, marauders known as "Batetela" (a widely used generic term as well as a tribal designation) infested part of the Congo countryside.

Even more serious was the threat from Swahili-speaking Muslims, a literate people endowed with a considerable degree of political sophistication. Unlike most of the indigenous people, Muslim warlords were well supplied with firearms, sometimes with the most modern weapons. But for Belgian intervention, these Swahili-speaking conquerors would have secured the major part of the Congo. From an economic point of view, much of their influence rested on the trade in captives and ivory. As elephants were "shot out" in one particular region, and as the countryside was ravaged by slave raiding, Swahili-speaking Muslims followed the trade routes to push farther into the interior. They strengthened their commerce by imposing their own political power, often using indigenous chiefs as intermediaries. Such political control over any particular area would yield indirect benefits by enabling the new rulers to levy tolls, tributes, and other imposts. The Muslim system of governance and economic exploitation rested, therefore, on continuous expansion.

Relations between the Belgians and the Swahili-speaking Muslims (commonly, though not usually correctly, described in contemporary literature as Arabs) were at first ambiguous. At one point, Tippu Tip, the most prominent of the Muslim traders, even secured appointment as the official Free State governor at Stanley Falls. His house at Kasongo was an impressive two-story building with a large court in the interior facing his seraglio. But friction between the two groups of invaders was inevitable when Leopold established a state monopoly over ivory, thereby depriving the Muslims of a major source of income.

Militarily, the Muslims were to be taken seriously. In areas where the East Coast men had come as settlers they had built productive agricultural economies based on servile or semiservile labor. Muslim power centered on settlements like Nyangwe or Kasongo in the eastern Congo; these served both as *points d'appui* for trade and and as supply depots. Kasongo, for instance, was built in a corner of a virgin forest; here visitors found splendid plantations of sugar cane, rice, maize, coffee, oranges, and other crops. The Muslim economy, which was based on trade, handicrafts, and farming, was capable of sustaining major military efforts. The Swahili, moreover, had established a relatively efficient system of communication that depended on canoe and carrier transport; they were competent builders and had perfected the art of creating fortified stockades. Furthermore they were well equipped with firearms, including rifles, and they were numerically far superior to the Belgians. According to the standard Belgian history of the Belgian colonial army (the Force Publique), the various Muslim chieftains—had they been united—could have raised a hundred thousand men.

Fortunately for the Belgians, the Muslims, although they acknowledged a vague link to the sultan of Zanzibar, lacked political cohesion, and their rulers were at odds with one another. The Belgians, on the other hand, had a central command, a superior system of logistics, and some artillery. They also had the services of a series of able, determined field commanders—men like Chaltin, Francis-Henry Dhanis (1862-1909), who was raised to a barony in gratitude for his military successes, and Pierre-Joseph Ponthier (1858-1893). All of these men became Belgian national heroes.

Beginning in 1892, local skirmishes between Belgians and Arabs developed into a full-scale campaign that succeeded in destroying the Muslim centers at Nyangwe and Kasongo. Dhanis occupied Kasongo with twenty thousand auxiliaries drawn from the western region of the Congo, who pillaged and burned the town despite his attempts to stop them. Nyangwe, a settlement of some forty thousand inhabitants, suffered a similar fate when the Arabs welshed on a promise of surrender.[1] By 1894 Dhanis had won his war at negligible cost: sixteen Belgian officers and noncommissioned officers had lost their lives during the Arab campaign, six of them through sickness. The ill-coordinated Swahili empire collapsed before it had time to consolidate its power. During the 1890s Chaltin and others fought against Sudanese slave raiders who were loyal to the Mahdist state (an exploitative theocracy misnamed a revolutionary state by its latter-day admirers). The Belgians thus secured their hold on the northeastern corner of the Congo at the cost of much local suffering and disruption.

These campaigns formed part of a wider, ill-concerted, but

nonetheless effective, movement whereby the Belgians, British, and Germans among them established their governance over East and Central Africa. British seapower had previously wiped out the transmarine slave trade in the Indian Ocean, once an important source of Muslim wealth. During the early 1890s the British conquered Nyasaland and crushed the might of local Yao and Arab warlords in the Lake Nyasa region. Farther north, they put an end to the Mahdist empire (1898). The Belgian victories, in turn, helped the Germans to take armed action against the so-called Arabs in German East Africa and to destroy their military power.

The defeat of the Muslims, who had previously fought in loose association with the Egyptian and Zanzibari empires, was inevitable. They had numerous weaknesses: they lacked seapower, were devoid of artillery, and did not know how to harness steam power either for peace or for war. Unlike anticolonial guerrillas of a later period, they could not rely on the support of sympathizers within the metropolitan powers, nor on support from sovereign states hostile to the colonial power, nor on the assistance furnished to many guerrillas of a later vintage through the existence of privileged sanctuaries outside the colonizers' reach. Unlike the Belgians, they lacked unity of command, and their economic strength was limited. In the interior they depended to a considerable extent on the exploitation of slaves and of wasting assets like rhino and elephant tusks—luxury products that were dependent on the fluctuations of foreign markets outside Muslim control. Muslim power was crushed, and the brief period of Muslim domination in East and Central Africa became a matter of history. The success of the Belgian campaign against the slave traders gave Belgian colonialism a brief period of popularity in Europe.

NATIONAL AND SOCIAL ORIGINS OF WHITE CADRES

Before Leopold could embark on the conquest of his new kingdom, he had to create a military instrument. In doing

58

so, he was able to rely on three kinds of volunteers to command the projected force: regular soldiers from Belgium, adventurers, and officers carefully chosen from the armies of lesser foreign countries, especially Scandinavia, Switzerland, and Italy. To these men, service in the Congo offered military experience, the chance of promotion, release from deadening garrison life at home, and an opportunity—as they saw it—to participate in a humanitarian endeavor. Volunteers of a less desirable kind embarked for Africa hoping to make their fortunes by seeking loot and pelf or by becoming lords over the conquered. The Congo Free State therefore managed to draw to a considerable extent on a form of military migrant labor that had largely disappeared in the rest of Europe. Volunteers kept their respective ranks in their home armies, signed on for a specified number of years in the Congo, and normally returned home after the expiration of their terms of service.

A primary foreign recruiting ground was Italy, which supplied at least 112 commissioned and 120 noncommissioned officers for service in the Congo between the founding of the Congo Free State in 1885 and 1922. To these volunteers, most of whom found employment in a civilian capacity, the Congo seemed a land of opportunity. The Italian colonial empire at the time was minuscule; Libya had not as yet fallen under Italian sway, and service in Somalia and Eritrea was harsh and unpopular. Military life in the metropolis was hardly attractive at a time when the Italian army was poorly equipped and beset by many organizational problems. The junior officer's path was a particularly thorny one, as the Italian army had a plethora of senior commanders; the chance of promotion was small, and the pay was so meager that every kind of influence was used freely to reach the higher ranks where an officer might live in decent comfort.[2]

Other officers came from Norway, Denmark, and Sweden which had been at peace since the Napoleonic era. These nations lacked colonies of their own, leaving their soldiers with no opportunity to distinguish themselves abroad. The

Congo Free State, admittedly, did not enjoy a good reputation. In 1896, for example, a Swedish missionary published a widely discussed report in which he accused the rulers of the Free State of resembling the Turks in cruelty and oppression. Men died in droves from sickness and drink. Yet there was no shortage of volunteers, and a substantial number of soldiers decided to seek their fortunes in Africa. Between 1878 and 1914 the Free State and its unofficial predecessor recruited 126 Scandinavian officers—53 from Denmark, 47 from Sweden, 26 from Norway—and 25 NCOs—4 from Denmark, 18 from Sweden, and 3 from Norway. Others served as medical officers, civil servants, and missionaries. Of these volunteers, 38 percent lost their lives, most from disease.[3]

The Scandinavians had always held an important stake in Belgian maritime activities. When Belgium attained its independence in 1830, the kingdom lost access to Dutch ports and, for a time, became dependent on foreign seamen, including many Scandinavians who served as captains, helmsmen, and machinists. They continued to work for Belgium when Leopold's interest extended to Africa. Between 1881 and 1916 approximately 500 merchant seamen—from ships' captains to naval mechanics to ships' carpenters—served in the Belgian Congo; of these, 280 were Swedes (probably including many Finns and Balts), 160 were Danes, and 60 were Norwegians. As a contemporary Belgian observer put it, "the Swedish, Danish and Norwegian sea-captains, helmsmen, machinists and craftsmen . . . in reality made possible the Belgian conquest of the Congo."[4]

By far the greatest number of Leopold's officers were Belgians. In what became the Force Publique there were 648 Belgian officers and 1,612 NCOs between 1878 and 1908; all but 173 officers and 530 NCOs were drawn from the infantry. Incentives for overseas service were psychological and professional rather than financial. To idealists, service in the colonies appeared to be a crusade for humanity. It was not for nothing that General Jacmart, founder of the

Société antiesclavigiste belge, had served as a commandant of the Ecole militaire, the institution that did more than any other to shape the Belgian officer corps. Colonial service afforded danger, but it also supplied more professional opportunities than service in a small army, an army devoid of *gloire*, and one whose purpose and military effectiveness were widely questioned in the motherland. In a colonial campaign a young lieutenant or a captain might still make for himself a nationwide reputation. In the colonies there was still a chance of fighting for glory, for the cause of humanity and civilization. Great churchmen like Cardinal Lavigerie were calling for God's blessing on young soldiers who were ready to risk their lives for Christ in extirpating the slave trade. Instead of worrying about kit inspections, attending roll calls, filling in personnel returns, asking petty favors of the regimental adjutant, and being courteous to the colonel's lady at a garrison dance, a subaltern in the Congo might suddenly be catapulted into a position of power and fame.

For all the misery and hardship suffered by the early pioneers, many enjoyed the authority they wielded in strange and forbidding lands and the release they experienced from the trammels of European convention. The early Belgian colonial soldiers, who were counterguerrillas by profession, likewise experienced at times that romantic feeling of intoxication and triumph described by T. E. Lawrence in World War I: Lawrence felt that he was gaining zest from life while risking it, and that he was fashioning a new world that would be better than the one his ancestors had known.[5]

Lawrence's sentiments were not unique. Emile Lémery, a Belgian junior officer, took part in the Congolese campaign against the Muslims in the 1890s. After the Belgians had won, Lémery had to rebuild the captured town of Nyangwe. He was expected to pacify the surrounding countryside, provide work for ex-slaves, organize river transport, collect ivory and rubber, and act as ruler and judge. In addition, he became the protector and guardian of Arab children whose fathers had been condemned to death for the murder of Europeans. Lémery was as lordly a personage in Nyangwe as the Muslim potentates whom he had helped to overthrow. He wrote enthusiastically in 1894:

> *Vive le Congo*, there is nothing like it! We have liberty, independence and life with wide horizons. Here you are free and no more a slave of society. . . . I hope that later on they [the Congolese] will be grateful for all the efforts I have made here for the good of the State. . . . Here one is everything! Warrior, diplomat, *trader*!! Why not? Whatever they say, I am here for the good of the State . . . and all the means I use are permissible if they are honest.[6]

Above all, service in the Congo offered to subalterns who might otherwise have led an obscure garrison existence the opportunity to achieve public recognition. Belgium was one of the least militaristic countries in Europe! Leopold did not dare to award military decorations as a matter of policy to officers who had done no more than put down an indigenous rebellion.[7] Nevertheless, armed service in the Congo Free State became a means to honor. The king created a series of new orders, including the Ordre de l'étoile africaine, that helped to provide glamour for a new colonial meritocracy. The deeds of fallen soldiers were commemorated in an extensive body of literature that became familiar reading to two generations of Belgian schoolboys. The exploits of these heroes became living legends, and the Belgians' black opponents in battle were relegated to a kind of literary inferno.

There was, for instance, the case of Charles-Eugène de Le Court, a young Belgian lieutenant who died bravely while covering the retreat of a Belgian column. Popular literature turned him into a Victorian stage figure:

> The situation was desperate. All seemed lost. But brave De Le Court sprang into the breach.
> Together with two other Belgian officers and the remnants of their platoons, he immobilized the black demons who had rushed into the pursuit of the column. The rear-

guard action raged with utter fury. Sinister black heads seemed to emerge from every corner, grinding their white teeth. . . . It was a black nightmare, demonical, fantastic. . . .

One Belgian officer had already failed.

And De Le Court understood that his turn too had come. . . .

But, calm, admirable, he continued to smile . . . with the hero's gentle and naive smile. . . .

He fell. . . . He understood the supreme moment of death had come. . . . Smiling, disdainful, sublime, thinking of his King, of his Flag . . . he looked for the last time upon the screaming horde of black demons . . . and . . . collapsed. . . .

Thus Charles De Le Court died in the fullness of youth in the face of the enemy.[8]

Distinctions mattered a good deal to Belgian officers who lacked the social prestige their colleagues enjoyed in countries like neighboring Germany. The Belgian officer corps, though proud of its professional attainments and of the elaborate orders bestowed upon its more deserving members, could not look back on that great array of battle honors that were a source of pride to the armed forces of other European nations.[9] If service in Africa provided an opportunity for fame, it also promised a temporary release from social isolation in a country where the army was subject to bitter attacks.[10] Colonial service did not, of course, break down the army's sense of isolation. Indeed, the Charte coloniale, which was issued after the demise of the Leopoldine empire, specifically prohibited the despatch of drafted men to the colonies. No Belgian ever fought as a private soldier in any colonial war. No Belgian colonial campaign ever aroused the kind of enthusiasm that caused great numbers of young men from Great Britain and the dominions to enlist for service in the Boer War or that induced thousands of German reservists to volunteer in the campaigns against the

Herero and the Nama between 1904 and 1907. Nevertheless, service in the colonies provided volunteers with a sense of purpose and commitment and with opportunities for promotion that they lacked at home.

The officer corps of the Force Publique, the army created to serve in the Congo, reflected the social characteristics of the Belgian officer corps. Aristocratic cavalry officers rarely served in the Congo. The pioneer Belgian officer was usually of bourgeois or lower-middle-class origin. He was rarely a nobleman by birth; if he gained a peerage, it was by dint of merit. He tended to be well educated professionally; quite frequently he had risen from the ranks. His outlook tended to be shaped by the attitudes of a small Belgian town rather than by a big city. If he survived the hardships of early campaigning—and if he resisted the ravages of disease—his career would benefit from a period of service in the colonies.

An examination of the careers pursued by the commanders of the Force Publique will illustrate the point. Between its formal institution in 1886 and the outbreak of World War I, the Force Publique had thirteen commanding officers; the careers of eleven of them have been fairly well documented by the Académie Royale des sciences d'outre-mer (ARSOM) in the *Biographie coloniale belge* (1948-1958). Only four of the eleven had been born in towns as large as Ghent, Namur, or Brussels. Most of them were of middle- or lower-middle-class origin (an exact figure is hard to come by, as published sources do not usually indicate parental professions, and personnel files in the Belgian archives remain closed to researchers). Of these eleven commanders, five began their careers as ordinary soldiers, five joined the army in their teens as cadets, and one was an ex-engineering student. Six of the eleven had left the Ecole de guerre as *adjoints d'état-major*. Six of these officers had to leave the service or died as a result of sickness contracted in the Congo. Of the survivors, four ended their careers with the rank of major general.

64

The social origins of young colonial soldiers of the "heroic period" of imperialism in Africa and those of the guerrilla leaders of more recent times bear some striking resemblances. Baljit Singh and Ko-Wang Mei have investigated the milieu from which the most famous partisan leaders of our time have sprung. In general, the modern guerrilla leaders were reared in country towns or villages; they were members of middle-class or of fairly poor families; they obtained a good education in colleges or military academies; and they began their careers in the armed forces, in administrative employment, or in some profession. Only a small minority came from a proletarian background. They engaged in guerrilla warfare at a period in their lives when they were intellectually mature and physically strong.[11] Given a different historical context, they might have been colonialists.

FUNCTIONS AND CONDITIONS OF SERVICE

The Force Publique was formally constituted in 1886. It began as a small organization serving a multiplicty of purposes. Until 1904 its soldiers were officially required to carry out a variety of nonmilitary duties, from building roads to putting up government stations in remote outposts. Force Publique officers were expected to serve as foremen, architects, engineers, hydrographers, census takers, constables, foremen in charge of collecting wild rubber, store supervisors, and so forth. Above all, they were expected to fight. Their platoons and companies initially differed little in appearance and discipline from the levies raised by indigenous warlords. Much depended on a leader's personality and on his ability to inspire a sense of personal loyalty among his motley collection of men. A number of years elapsed before the followings of individual white chiefs were turned into regular forces within the military hierarchy that were amenable to the orders of any superior officer bearing the correct rank.

By 1914 the pacification of the Congo had largely been

completed, although the Belgians continued to conduct a considerable number of police actions against disaffected African communities as late as 1920. But large-scale warfare within the Congo had ceased. The Force Publique, which numbered about eighteen thousand men, had become a reasonably efficient body. Numerically, it was one of the largest armies in all of sub-Saharan Africa, larger than the armed forces in the whole of German Africa and the peacetime army maintained by the Union of South Africa.[12]

In relation to the large number of Africans in the ranks, the army's white-officer establishment was excessively small; for a long time the Force Publique had to make do with a ratio of officers to soldiers of only one to one hundred, a ratio much smaller than that of the British or German colonial forces. This military deficiency was a result of the constant calls for economy and of the paucity of Belgian administrative cadres. Indeed, a substantial number of officers (often the most enterprising men) were employed as civilian administrators in order to save money. From the administrative standpoint, the position was regularized in 1911, when captains were formally made equal to *chefs de secteur, 1ᵉ classe*, and lieutenants to *chefs de secteur 2ᵉ classe*. The reliance on military officers in the civilian administration engendered serious morale problems. The Force Publique was underofficered and overmanned and thus prone to indiscipline (see Table 5).

The army's lack of discipline led to all manner of excesses. The vice-governor of Katanga reported with disgust the case of one Haesendouck, *agent militaire* at Kilwa, who commanded a post manned by two platoons, about a hundred men in all. Haesendouck was a prime example of the *esprit de caporalisation*—a born bully who taught his soldiers to despise civilian authority and respect none but himself. His soldiers learned their lesson only too well. When Haesendouck had to leave the post one day, the garrison rioted. The soldiers nearly killed a white trader, stole his wares, got drunk, set buildings afire, and raped several women.[13] To

66

THE FORCE PUBLIQUE

TABLE 5

Establishment of the Force Publique, 1910

Category	Personnel
Commandant	1
Capitaines-commandants and *capitaines*	35
Lieutenants and *sous-lieutenants*	121
European NCOs and *agents militaires*	226
Armorers	20
TOTAL NUMBER OF WHITES	403
Blacks, including NCOs and private soldiers	16,333

SOURCE: Belgium, Ministère des colonies, *Annuaire officiel, 1910* (Brussels, 1910).

their credit, the Belgian officers did not sanction this behavior; but there were too few of them, and the Force Publique did not easily shed its reputation for violence.

In its internal structure, the white military establishment was surprisingly egalitarian. Junior officers were relatively well paid. Incredible as it would have sounded to a British or German officer at the time, a junior *sous-lieutenant* received 50 percent of a colonel's salary, and a *capitaine-commandant* in charge of a company earned two-thirds of the amount received by the *commandant* of the entire Force Publique (see Table 6). An able *sous-officier* experienced little difficulty in obtaining advancement. In the Congo, as in the métropole, class differences within the white establishment were less rigid than they were in Great Britain or Germany.

Despite acceptable salaries and opportunities for promotion from the ranks, service conditions were far from pleasant. Initially, the Force Publique suffered heavily from battle casualties, and even more from disease. Between 1877 and 1906, 182 European officers and 460 NCOs lost their lives—nearly one-third of those who served abroad (see Table 7). The rate of loss suffered by the white leaders, which was higher than the casualty rates recorded for major campaigns,

67

TABLE 6

Initial Salaries of the Force Publique, 1912
(In Belgian Francs)

Rank	Salary
Colonel	20,000
Lieutenant-colonel	17,000
Major	15,000
Capitaine-commandant	14,000
Lieutenant	12,000
Sous-lieutenant	10,000
Agent militaire	7,500
Premier sous-officier	6,500
Sous-officier	6,000

SOURCE: SPA, no. 123, Archives africaines, Brussels.

TABLE 7

Death Rates of Belgian and Foreign Officers
in the Congo, 1877-1906

Branch of Service	Officers		NCOs	
	Total No. Serving	Died	Total No. Serving	Died
Infantry	475	138	1,082	318
Cavalry	62	15	209	71
Artillery	65	18	180	55
Engineers	21	6	52	15
Transport	5	1	20	1
Miscellaneous	20	4	69	20
Foreign volunteers (officers and NCOs)	163	59		

SOURCE: Emile Wanty, *Le Milieu militaire belge de 1831 à 1914* (Brussels, 1957), p. 161.

suggested that many officers must have signed on from a sense of adventure or idealism rather than for the purpose of self-advancement. The pioneering venture also attracted many plebeians; the Belgians employed a far higher proportion of white noncommissioned officers than the British or the Germans.

Gradually, however, the Congo ceased to exercise the attractions of a remote, romantic land of wild adventure. By 1914 the European officer's or sergeant's existence had become much safer as sickness and combat had ceased to take a major toll. Junior officers had become military instructors and store supervisors more than leaders of armed men on campaign. They were concerned with kit inspection, rifle, drill, and parade-ground maneuvers rather than the more spectacular task of chasing rebels and slave raiders through the bush. Their superiors had to worry about administrative problems familiar to all large organizations: budgets, equipment schedules, personnel and matériel lists, and such.

The problem of finding suitable officers became more difficult. Belgium was a small but highly industrialized country, and it lacked a substantial military class; there was no military unemployment. Experts began to complain of the Congolese army's chronic disease, *la pénurie des cadres*. Promotion in the Force Publique was slow, making recruitment of European officers more difficult; for a long time the highest rank attainable in Africa was that of colonel. After World War I the personnel problem remained so serious that the Belgians were unable to maintain the desired minimum ratio of one European to forty-three Africans, compared with a ratio of about one white officer or NCO to ten *askari* in the German colonial forces. This numerical imbalance imposed a heavy strain on the white officers in the Congo, so that discipline remained a major problem throughout the colonial era and in its aftermath.

The officers who joined the Force Publique differed in ability and background. Dependence initially was on the straightforward fighting man, such as Louis-Napoléon Chaltin (1857-1933), a simple soldier who had started in the ranks. Chaltin joined the Force Publique during the early campaigns of the Congo Free State. A man of great personal courage, he was shot in the leg, then lost two fingers, and finally was injured so badly in a riding accident that he had to retire from the army. When Belgium faced its first German invasion in 1914, Chaltin again volunteered for service and formed a unit composed exclusively of Belgian ex-colonials, 350 in all. His unit took part in the defense of Namur, where the volunteers suffered heavily and where most were taken prisoner. Chaltin, who had risen to the rank of colonel, became associated with numerous commercial companies. He served as president of Belcoma Cafegas, manager of the Société coloniale belge du Congo Oriental, and director of the Compagnie du Kasai, the Société minière du Kasai, Unatra, and the Société minière du Aruwimi, among others.

Chaltin, however, was a person of minor significance in comparison with a great military entrepreneur such as Major General Albert Thys (1849-1915). Thys, a physician's son, joined the army at seventeen, soon advanced to the rank of sergeant, graduated from the Ecole militaire, and was commissioned in the infantry. His fortunes rose when Leopold II admitted the young lieutenant to his military household. He worked for the Comité d'études du Haut Congo, acquired highly placed contacts, and later played an important part in the organization of the Association internationale du Congo (AIC). As competent a financier as he was an administrator, in 1886 he helped found the CCCI, which was set up to develop trade and railways in the Congo. This company in turn established ties with numerous associated concerns, including the Société anonyme belge pour le commerce du Haut Congo (SAB) and the Compagnie du Katanga (CK), and it participated in other major enterprises, such as the Banque d'outre-mer and the Union minière du Haut Katanga. The CCCI likewise became one of the principal stockholders of the Compagnie des chemins de fer du Congo Supérieur aux grands lacs africains (CFL, founded 1902) and of similar concerns.[14]

Thys achieved his greatest fame as a railway builder. Riverine transportation and porters alone could not solve the logistic problems of the Congo. Acting on behalf of the Compagnie du chemin de fer du Congo (CCFC, established in 1889), Thys took in hand the enormously complicated task of building a line from Matadi to Léopoldville. The railway builders had to make do with relatively small amounts of capital to pay for transport systems that covered huge areas and provided only a limited amount of freight. Some 80 million francs—just over 2.6 million pounds sterling—had been invested in the Congo by 1914. This was a considerable sum compared with most other private investments in the Congo, but it is insignificant when matched with the funds raised by great private corporations in the metropolitan countries.

The railway pioneers had to cope with extraordinary geographic obstacles; they lacked the most rudimentary technical information; they had no reliable charts and maps; they faced tremendous supply problems; they had to labor in an oppressive climate; and they were decimated by sickness. Within four months during 1891-1892, some 900 men —17 percent of the black workmen engaged in railway building—died of disease. Africans came to dread construction work; the CCFC had to recruit migrant laborers from the Antilles and Chinese from Macao, newcomers who fared even worse than the native-born Congolese. The death rate among European technicians, managers, and engineers was equally high. By the time the Matadi-Léopoldville line opened in 1898, some 1,800 nonwhite laborers and 132 whites had perished, according to a published account. Probably an even greater number had died in fact.

Thys attained his goal by using his organizing ability, his ruthless determination, and the exertions of his African workmen. As he explained to a meeting of the Société Royale de géographie d'Anvers: "In actual fact, the railway from Matadi to Stanley Pool has been built entirely by blacks. . . . The Negro race is eminently suited for labor. . . . We have even applied the piecework system, the highest form of free labor, for the completion of the last 250-kilometer stretch."[15]

In the long run, however, the military bureaucrats proved as important as the builders. Jules Joseph Van Dorpe (1856-1902), a one-time commandant of the Force Publique, is at

71

characteristic example of one of those little-known military specialists who never acquired fame in battle but whose professional ability helped to lay the foundations of the Belgian empire. A Fleming by origin, Van Dorpe was born in Menton. At seventeen he joined the third regiment of Chasseurs à pied, and a year later he had advanced to the rank of sergeant; at twenty-two he was a *sous-lieutenant*. In 1884 he entered the Ecole de guerre, and in 1888 he volunteered for service under the flag of the Congo Free State.

When Van Dorpe arrived in Africa, the Belgians faced an apparently insoluble logistic problem. Much of the enormous drainage basin of the Congo River lay within the borders of the Congo Free State. This area has since been made accessible by a combined system of river, rail, and road communications, but eighty years ago the logistic infrastructure built by the colonizers did not exist. There were no river ports, no maintenance yards, no boat-building facilities; neither were there railways or railway repair yards. Transport managers had to rely largely on a few river steamers, on canoes, and, above all, on porters. Between Stanley Pool—just below Léopoldville—and Matadi, 217 miles of the Congo River's great length is cut by a series of thirty-two falls and cataracts. Van Dorpe thus had to organize carrier transport, then the indispensable prerequisite for conquest and commerce alike. Steamers were brought to the Congo in separate parts to be assembled. By 1894 forty-three of these craft were plying the river, and transport along the Matadi-Léopoldville stretch was in working order.

Van Dorpe returned to the Congo several times, first as a district commissioner, later as commandant of the Force Publique and director of transport (1895-1898), and finally as *commissaire général* (1898-1901). He never led a regiment into battle, but he lived during an era when tropical disease had not yet been conquered, when malaria-bearing mosquitoes were more perilous than the enemy's muskets. He returned to Belgium in 1901, weakened by disease, and died the following year.

The Blacks

When Leopold first proclaimed his sovereignty over the Congo, the means of coercion available to him were negligible. The forces of the Free State consisted of a few hundred black mercenaries recruited from the West Coast of Africa and Zanzibar for a seven-year tour of duty. The Force Publique was at first composed of Hausa, who were to become the elite of the new force of Zanzibaris, Somalis, Gold Coasters, Dahomeans, and a substantial number of Sierra Leoneans.[16] These mercenaries, who were used to conditions in the bush and familiar with the ways of white men, adjusted to the tropical climate and played a major part in the Belgian occupation. They were also among the first labor migrants in the Congo, a territory where military service was an important early source of long-term wage employment.

In addition to recruiting Africans from abroad, the Free State authorities began to enroll native-born Congolese, especially riverine peoples using the Lingala tongue. Lingala, accordingly, spread through much of the Congo territory and became a military lingua franca of great significance in the subsequent history of the country. In levying recruits, the Congo Free State relied both on volunteers and on impressment, using the same coercive techniques in the military as in the economic field. Chiefs were forced to supply soldiers for the army, as well as porters and supplies. Hence the upkeep of the army alone put a severe drain on impoverished rural economies.

A fighting column of the Force Publique in the early days was little different from the military force that might be levied by a Swahili-speaking freebooter. It would contain volunteers as well as men who, to all intents and purposes, were slaves. The soldiers were followed on the march by a train of wives and attendants who were apt to loot supplies and terrorize villagers. When Dhanis occupied the Muslim stronghold of Kasongo, for instance, twenty thousand auxiliaries recruited from the eastern Congo followed in his train.

73

Despite his attempts to stop their depredations, his motley crew of warriors pillaged and burned the settlement.[17]

From a serving soldier's point of view, the logistics and tactics of the early Belgian forces bore an even more striking resemblance to those of their indigenous hosts:

> We camped about noon, having marched some six hours, ample in the climate and through such thick jungle. . . . We had marched for the first hour or so through native clearings, where the trunks of large trees lay by hundreds across our paths. Over these we had to climb, the trail seeming to lead to the top of every white ant hill within range. The carriers had an especially hard time of it, for many of them were chained by the neck. . . . They carried our boxes slung on poles, and when one of them fell he usually brought down all his companions on the same chain. Many of the poor wretches became so exhausted by this kind of marching that they could be urged forward only by blows from the butt-ends of rifles.[18]

In the same way, the Belgians became habituated to using Arab-style stockades to protect their forces on the march and to serve as tactical pivots. As soon as a column had closed up, the soldiers were formed in a circle with rifles still in hand, while the carriers were sent out into the surrounding jungle to cut stout poles. These were stuck in the ground by the soldiers and bound together with small creepers to form a circular stockade. Within this barricade the soldiers and carriers arranged rough shelters of poles and leaves under which they lay, rifles at hand, prepared to repulse the enemy.

Belgian fighting soldiers gradually systematized these methods, blending the skills of African warriors with the techniques developed by an industrial economy. Chaltin led a major expedition in 1897 against Muslim forces in the northeast. His advance guard consisted of two companies of 250 men each, advancing single file and covered by 500 Zande spearmen moving about five hundred meters away from the flanks of the vanguard. The main force of artillery and four companies of infantry, also moving single file, followed at a distance of two hundred meters. The rear guard of one platoon and a supply column was escorted by spearmen of the auxiliary force. Chaltin prohibited the usual retinue of women and camp followers from accompanying his forces and thus avoided the complications experienced by other leaders. When his men set up camp the advance guard built the frontal defenses, the main guard constructed the two sides, and the rear guard the back. The camp was surrounded by one, and sometimes two, lines of palisades, guarded by outposts stationed some five hundred meters away, and reinforced by Zande warriors. In combat, Chaltin placed the spearmen behind the wing designated to outflank the enemy, making sure that the defeated forces would be pursued and destroyed.[19]

In the early stages, Belgian commanders, like their colleagues in other pioneer colonies, had almost no trained men at their disposal. They had to create their cadres from motley forces of African adventurers, conscripts, and cutthroats. The officer who succeeded under these conditions had to be an all-rounder—as knowledgable about ships' engines as about training riflemen, treating malaria, drawing maps, and building palisades. He succeeded only if he could accommodate himself to a country in which large expeditions were apt to starve and small parties might be massacred.

Seen in African terms, the Free State soldiers at first looked rather like the Muslim warlords they were paid to fight. Pioneer commanders such as Major H. J. Lothaire headed soldiers dressed in the local fashion rather than in regular uniforms. He relied on Africans who had often been press-ganged or who had enlisted for loot and women. These professional soldiers were supplemented by African spearmen who were useful for reconnoitering difficult country, for looting enemy grain stores, or for pursuing a beaten opponent. Their columns were followed by a train of auxiliaries and porters whose collective depredations during a lengthy campaign might ravage an entire countryside. Only a man of iron nerve could hold such a force together and weld them into an army. Lothaire, known to Africans as "Lopembe," was just such a personality. A ruthless fighter, he acquired a reputation for the ferocity of his punishments, for his soldierly skill, and for personal bravery. He managed to inspire an extraordinary degree of personal loyalty among his warriors, who "looked to Lopembe as their chief, and the other whites as mere 'boys' of Lopembe."

During the early years of Belgian rule, life in the army was widely unpopular with the Africans:

> As the State established its authority . . . a regular system of recruiting was instituted, each district being called upon to furnish a certain number of conscripts. . . . The *commissaires de district* have orders to see that their quotas are promptly forthcoming, and each naturally enough delegates the duty of recruiting to his *chefs de zone* who, in their turn, call upon the more subordinate *chefs de poste* to levy upon the local chiefs for the men required. The native chieftain usually makes his selection from the worthless and recalcitrant slaves of the village, who, when they reach the station, are promptly placed in the chain, or *"collier national"* as the Belgians call it, so that they cannot escape.[20]

These unpromising recruits were subjected to a harsh discipline, enforced if need be by flogging; in the beginning, punishments ranged from a dozen to a hundred lashes for serious offenders.

In addition, the Belgians managed to enlist a variety of African allies, among them the Batetela, who were later, as we shall see, driven to revolt. The Belgians hesitated to recruit Africans and made a point of limiting the number of members of any one ethnic community at a military post to a maximum of 25 percent of the total. Many tribes, such as the warlike Zande, at first would not serve; since the Free State was initially unable to enforce its authority over the various Zande communities, they remained exempt from military service. Recruits could be obtained from weaker tribes, such as the Mobangi, a people who had previously paid tribute and other marks of deference to the Zande. The Mobangi accordingly sent as many young men as they could into the Force Publique in order to shake off Zande suzerainty. But the Belgians relied more commonly on impressment. Guy Burrows, a former district commissioner in the service of the Congo Free State, observed:

> The chief who fails to send the number of men required of him soon gets into trouble. . . . He certainly would refuse if he dared, and those tribes who are strong enough to refuse do so. It is an enormous drain on the resources for they know well that most of the young men who go to the State army never return.[21]

Burrows's book was a general indictment of Leopold's administration. A patriotic Briton who heartily despised Belgians and other foreigners, Burrows probably exaggerated the evils committed by his one-time employers, but even by official figures, life for the average recruit in the early days of the Force Publique was incredibly grim. Newcomers had to put up with poor food, unsanitary conditions, and a totally foreign way of life. The trainees' mortality rate approached that of troops in battle. Ironically, the life expectancy of a Congolese recruit greatly improved once he left his training camp and joined an active field company. The soldier was far less likely to be killed in a campaign than he was to perish from the privations of an early boot camp—hardships exceeded in peacetime perhaps only by the glittering professional army maintained by Great Britain in the early nineteenth century.[22]

The Force Publique, dispersed over a huge territory with a large percentage of unwilling recruits and a small percentage of officers, resembled in many ways an eighteenth-century European army composed of mercenaries and commanded by genuine or would-be gentlemen. The Force Publique was naturally prone to desertion, indiscipline, and mutiny.

In 1897, for example, an advance column sent out well in advance of an expeditionary force commanded by Major Dhanis rebelled. The mutineers, about thirteen hundred Bakussu and Batetela soldiers, killed most of the whites in the force, seized all rifles and munitions, and appointed a private soldier named Mulamba to be their chief. (The terms "Bakussu" and "Batetela" were widely used by the Belgians in a generic fashion, referring to military men recruited in the general Lomami-Sankuru-Maniema area.) Among their many military grievances, the Batetela complained of excessive marching and inadequate rations. Their resentment was indirectly linked to Dhanis's practice of permitting his army on the move to be followed by a large number of women and servants, thereby tripling his requirements for provisions and imposing a heavy burden on the countryside.[23]

An even more serious outbreak occurred in 1895 in the Kasai district, where Force Publique soldiers—many of them Batetela—took to arms. Before joining the Force Publique many of them had served in the personal bodyguard of chief Ngongo Lutete, whose force had acquired a reputation for toughness and reliability.[24] A former Muslim slave who had managed to become a warlord and slave raider on his own account, Ngongo Lutete first sided with the Muslims, then switched allegiance to the Belgians. When he wavered in his loyalty, the Belgians executed him for treason. His former warriors then turned against their new paymasters. Batetela mercenaries in many parts of the eastern Congo joined the rebels, and there was widespread fighting. Another group of mutineers inflicted heavy losses on the Belgians, captured and looted the fort of Shinkakasa, and for a time even threatened Belgian headquarters at Boma. Although the Belgians eventually destroyed the mutineers, the conquest was bloody and slow. As late as 1900 a detachment of Batetela and other soldiers manning a fort on the Atlantic estuary of the Congo, a thousand miles from their home, opened artillery fire against a moored Antwerp liner. The mutineers, however, lacked mass support among an ethnically divided population; the rising collapsed, although the last of the rebels were not apprehended until 1908.

During the 1890s the army expanded rapidly. As the Belgians extended their effective sphere of influence, they also gained new recruiting grounds. The Force Publique amounted to 3,186 men in 1891; three years later its strength had increased to 10,215 soldiers. By 1898, 19,028 men were under arms, vastly outnumbering the armies of the German and Portuguese empires. Between 1892 and 1914 a total of 66,000 men passed through the ranks of the Force Publique. Accordingly, far more Congolese had their first experience of the Western world through the army than through the mission stations during this period. Although the military share of the Congolese budget gradually decreased, the military element continued to play a decisive role in shaping the modern Congo.[25]

The Belgians employed their new army for a wide variety of tasks, including the enforcement of local *corvées*. Native soldiers were deliberately posted away from their own areas, lest they be swayed by local sympathies. Small detachments of the Force Publique were called upon to enforce the power of the Free State in isolated spots. Such outposts superintended the collecting of wood for steamers on the Congo River and helped to enforce levies on rubber, ivory, and food. Frequently they usurped the power of local chiefs, demanding food and women, and sometimes setting themselves up as local tyrants.

MILITARY MODERNIZATION

Despite the Force Publique's unprepossessing start, gradual improvements made it a highly effective army. The commissariat expanded, communications were rendered more efficient, and the armed forces became less dependent on requisitioning local supplies. The soldiers paid for what they needed, looting lessened, and the army grew accustomed to receiving pay and rations punctually. The death rate declined, and the number of genuine volunteers increased, especially as the children or boy-servants of soldiers decided to follow in the footsteps of their fathers or patrons and join the army of their own free will. The Force Publique ceased to resemble an indigenous African levy. Discipline was tightened, and the soldiers came to be regarded as part of a new black elite whose status and privileges were the envy of ordinary villagers.

The soldiers became used to a life of punctuality, ordered by the blare of the bugle. Reveille sounded at 5:30 in the morning, and from then until 9:00 at night the soldiers were kept busy with drill parades, inspections, weapons training, and tactical exercises up to company level.

> The first thing that the native has to be taught is to distinguish his left hand from his right, plurality from unity, and other elementary ideas. . . . For hours the recruits will stand in detachments doing nothing but holding out alternately their right hand and their left to the raucous shouts of *"Droit!"* and *"Gauche!"* Within a few days an extraordinary change comes over even the most primitive of these recruits. They seem to acquire an art of turning themselves into automats, and before six months' training are up they perform the most complicated evolutions and drill in large bodies with a precision and a uniformity which no other European troops could vie with. . . . Besides the ordinary routine of drill the native soldiers are trained in various physical exercises. . . . In most training camps a mid-day bath is compulsory, and all life in these camps is regulated with the most minute precision.[26]

The training was based on a simplified version of Belgian infantry drill, and the task was both astonishingly easy and extraordinarily difficult. The men of the Force Publique needed no one to teach them how to march for long distances, how to find their way in the bush, how to distinguish poisonous from edible plants, how to identify the sights and sounds and smells of the forest. Many of them had been at war; all were inured to hardship. But warriors had to be turned into soldiers with a sense of discipline and time, obedient to every word of command, capable of marching in formation, well turned out on parade with buttons polished, with rifle barrels that gleamed to the inspecting officer's eye, and with packs ordered according to military regulations.

They had everything to learn about new weapons and tactics. To a warrior habituated to the use of the spear, skill in wielding a bayonet—with parries, thrusts, and butt strokes —was a new and exhilarating, though in practice a useless, military art. Archers and owners of Arab flintlocks had to learn how to load an Albini rifle. Surprise attacks in darkness had to be practiced by men who had been taught in childhood that only witches and evil spirits chose to walk at night. Belgian officers, in turn, became familiar with African tactics. They learned how to put up obstacles such as log barricades on forest paths, to avoid camouflaged pitfalls lined with sharp wooden stakes, and to build barricades of timber and tangled thorn. They became accustomed to leading a column in tall grass, in dense bush country, and in tropical rain forest. They acquired knowledge about building canoes, preserving venison, and a host of other skills that made the difference between disaster and victory.

As time went on, the Force Publique came to resemble a European-style force with a tight bureaucratic structure. At its head was a *commandant* who resided at Boma and who was often an *inspecteur d'état*. He was assisted by a headquarters staff through which he communicated with the local *commandants*. Each province had assigned to it a detachment of the Force Publique, which was under the supervision of a *commandant* who was responsible for the military operations of his detachment, for its distribution throughout the region, and for its regular discipline. As far as active service was concerned, the *commandant* had to hold his men at the disposition of the civil head. Depots at various centers served as training quarters for recruits and as stations for the maintenance of sufficient reserves.

Most of the soldiers were infantrymen, and a *peloton* of fifty infantrymen was the basic tactical unit. Training was conducted up to company level. Just before the outbreak of World War I, the bulk of the Force Publique was grouped into twenty active field companies—mobile, self-contained units whose strength varied from 250 to 750 men. As the organization became more standardized, a "reenforced" field company comprised up to 250 men, including three European officers, three European NCOs, and twelve African NCOs.

The Force Publique became almost a state within a state, in which ties of kinship and traditional rank were replaced by a new military hierarchy with its own NCOs. In the early days, these "foremen" within the military establishment were drawn from the ranks of West African volunteers, especially the Hausa. The Belgians later increased the promotion of local men. In the larger centers these black NCOs were housed with their families in barracks or huts. Each wife received food allowances and accommodations for herself and her children; she was also paid a regular wage after her husband's first term of enlistment.[27]

The Force Publique also provided a new ladder of social advancement. Under the Belgian dispensation, the *sergent major*—proudly wearing four red and gold stripes on his uniform—stood a world apart from both the *milicien* and the ordinary villager. He was a true professional; he drew higher rations and much higher pay than the African private. He also enjoyed great respect. He was more influential and sometimes more highly regarded than any African trader or African evangelist. The African ranker, on the other hand, was one of the most poorly paid fighting men in colonial Africa. The Belgian military establishment, like its civilian counterpart, therefore depended to a considerable extent on the coercive use of labor—much more so than did the British (not to speak of the Germans), the best military paymasters in sub-Saharan Africa. The Belgians thereby saved themselves a great deal of money, but at a high price in terms of discipline and efficiency.[28]

82

For all its unpleasant features, the army to some extent acted as a purveyor of technical skills. Instruction was formalized in two military schools that were set up to provide three-year courses to selected students. Belgian instructors taught French, military theory, arithmetic, and even Western military music. The most competent students were promoted to become noncommissioned officers; the less successful became artisans or clerks in the administration. The Force Publique also had an artillery establishment whose size would have astonished British colonial officers and whose maintenance required a high level of competence.[29]

Belgium's domestic preoccupation with positional warfare and the art of fortification caused the Congo authorities to build a modern fort, called Shinkakasa, near Boma. This military absurdity was designed to defend the Congo Free State against the Portuguese. Built by a pupil of the famous Belgian engineer General Brialmont, it was heavily armed with 16-cm. guns, 4.7-cm. rapid-firing pieces, and machine guns, all of which had to be serviced and repaired. From the military standpoint, the army was burdened with too much heavy equipment. But the Belgians—unlike, say, the British —were willing to train black armorers and artillerymen, just as they were prepared to train African engine drivers, a policy then unknown, for instance, in the Rhodesias.

The Belgian colonial forces, as constituted in 1914, were organized for the purpose of maintaining internal security and were ill-suited for operations outside the borders of the Congo. A small contingent immediately joined the British and French in the conquest of Cameroun. Operations against German East Africa required more complex preparations. After the Belgian homeland had been overrun by the Germans in August 1914, no reinforcements could be expected from the métropole. The Belgian military authorities had to create a self-contained force—divided into brigades supported by artillery and a squadron of airplanes, sustained by medical services and by supply columns with munitions, tools, wireless, provisions, and all the other appurtenances of war—that would be based on the eastern Congo, some two thousand kilometers from the sea. Provisions had to be sent inland by water and thence several hundred miles by carriers. By April 1916 the Belgians were at last ready to take the offensive in concert with British imperial troops. By September they reached their objective. In purely military terms, this operation formed but a minor chapter in the East African campaign. Politically, however, its effects were far from negligible. The campaign provided a fillip for Belgian morale. For once, Belgian troops had taken the offensive. They occupied an area of nearly 180,000 square kilometers, including Rwanda-Urundi, which subsequently passed to Belgian trusteeship. In a very real sense, the Congo had assisted the defeated "motherland" in holding its own overseas. When Belgium was again overrun by the Germans during World War II, the colony would once more render a similar service to a demoralized métropole.

THREE

THE BEGINNINGS
OF CIVIL ADMINISTRATION

THE Congo Free State was Leopold's personal creation. It functioned as an absolute autocracy in theory as well as in practice. In drawing up the formal instruments of government, the sovereign profited from the advice of a number of well-known scholars, including Sir Travers Twiss, an Oxford man, and Egide-Rodolphe Arntz, a German-born jurist who had fled Prussia because of his revolutionary activities and who had later risen to high academic honors in Belgium, where he backed the king's colonial endeavors. In creating his new domain, Leopold initially acted through a professional soldier, Colonel Maximilien-Charles Strauch, who was the head of Leopold's military household and president for a time of the Comité d'études du Haut Congo. Later the royal dictatorship was put on a more formal footing. In Belgium the sovereign was assisted until 1901 by a chief secretary of state with his own cabinet; this cabinet dealt with the organization and functions of the different services, controlled the appointment of officials, and thereby played an important part in dispensing royal patronage.

Belgium lacked commercial links to Africa and thus had no reservoir of civilians willing to shoulder the task of administering distant tropical possessions where a man seemed more likely to lose his life than to win a fortune. The solid Liberal and Catholic bourgeois were at first little inclined to send their sons to serve in a colony beset by scandal, plagued by disease, and supposedly overrun by foreigners. When Leopold began to look for administrators, he was forced to draw his volunteers from among army officers, both

Belgian and foreign. The spirit of the administration was therefore military and royalist.

Promotion within the colonial hierarchy depended on royal favor. Advancement came to those, both Liberal and Catholic, who were trusted by the king. Governor-General Baron Théophile-Théodore Wahis (1844-1921), capable soldier, was a Catholic, as were most of his successors.[1] The Congo Free State's administration nevertheless had a reputation for anticlericalism and impiety. Membership in a Masonic lodge seems to have been helpful to many an aspiring civil servant. Colonel Charles Liebrechts, for example, started his career as a rifleman in the Belgian army, was later commissioned in the artillery and attached to the Institut cartographique, and then volunteered for service in the Congo. If one is to believe *Le Patriote*, a Catholic journal hostile to Leopold, Liebrechts was introduced to the Loge des amis philanthropes while serving in Brussels; he became an *apprenti* in 1886, a *compagnon* in 1887, and later a *maître*.[2] He played an important part in persuading Belgian industrialists to take an active interest in the Congo, and he was finally promoted to *secrétaire général du Département de l'intérieur* of the Free State, with his office in Brussels.

THE SUPERSTRUCTURE

The *secrétaires généraux* (originally known as *administrateurs généraux*) headed the administrative establishment. Each was in charge of a major department or group of departments, and each was selected personally by the king, who insisted on both proven ability and political dependability. The first *administrateurs* were: Strauch, who was in charge of international questions; Edmond van Eetvelde, a Belgian diplomat concerned with foreign affairs; and Hubert-Jean van Neuss, who directed the finances of the Free State. Any civil servant who disagreed with his sovereign on major policy matters had to resign (rather like a British parliamentary undersecretary). When the king decided to entrust vast concessions to private companies, Van Neuss would not go along with Leopold's design. He sided with Emile Banning, *directeur général* at the Ministry of Foreign Affairs and one of the king's most devoted supporters until he broke with Leopold over the question of free trade. Van Neuss sent in his resignation and rejoined the metropolitan administration, where he ended as *secrétaire général* at the Ministry of Finance.

By the beginning of the century the number of Free State *secrétaires généraux* in Brussels had risen to four. The treasurer-general was responsible for the general accounting of income and expenditure and for the public debt of the Free State. The secretary-general for foreign affairs looked after international relations, consular and diplomatic services, shipping, education, religion, and a broad range of commercial questions; thus he held a key position in the earlier stages of the Congo Free State. A good deal of power was also wielded by Liebrechts, the secretary-general of the interior, who was occupied with general administration, defense and police, public health, public works, agriculture and plantations, commercial exploitation of the state forests, and other developments. In 1904, moreover, Liebrechts set up a separate propaganda department known as the *bureau central de presse*. The bureau was nominally run by the Comité pour la représentation des intérêts coloniaux en Afrique, located in Frankfurt, where it was known as the Komitee zur Wartung der Interessen in Afrika, but it operated under the direction of Liebrechts. It used the services of Belgian consular officers to make a case for the Congo Free State, and it dispersed subsidies to encourage newspaper editors and politicians to give Leopold a favorable press abroad.[3]

Below the *secrétaires généraux* was an elaborate hierarchy of *directeurs généraux, directeurs, chefs de divisions,* and *chefs de bureaux* who provided Belgium with what was probably the best-staffed metropolitan colonial administration of the time. According to *Le Moniteur belge* of 4 November 1908, the central administration at the time of the *reprise* (that is, the Belgian annexation of the Congo) comprised the officials listed in Table 8. By comparison, the German service—for all the charges of *Assessorismus* made against it—was small. Its senior officials included one *Direktor*, ten *Vortragende Räte*, and five *Ständige Hilfsarbeiter* (qualified experts on a particular subject).

TABLE 8

Central Administration of the Congo Free State, 1908

Title	Number of Officials	Salary (In Belgian Francs)
Secrétaire général	1	9,000-10,000
Directeurs généraux	4	7,500- 8,500
Directeurs	8	5,500- 7,500
Chefs de divisions	17	4,000- 5,000
Chefs de bureaux	21	4,000- 5,000
Sous-chefs de bureaux	25	3,000- 3,800

SOURCE: *Le Moniteur belge*, 4 November 1908.

The central administration of the Congo Free State was relatively simple; after the demise of the Congo Free State it became increasingly complex. Correspondence was placed in files that were divided by *direction générale* and subject. Documents had to be drafted, copied, minuted, and collated before they could be sent from Brussels to the governor-general. A routine communication concerning, say, personnel might take two months to be drafted, processed, and despatched. In the manner of the time, considerable attention was devoted to form and precedence. During this process a good deal of information was accumulated on the way from official to official, so that the center became increasingly well informed with regard to developments in the Congo itself.

The link between this central structure in Brussels and the Free State's administrative headquarters in Boma was the *gouverneur général*, known originally as the *administrateur général*. The early administrators were non-Belgians, whose appointments showed the semi-international character of

Leopold's original enterprise. Henry Morton Stanley, Leopold's chief agent from 1879 to 1884, was replaced by Sir Francis de Winton (1853-1901), who served as the first *administrateur général*. Leopold would have much preferred General Charles George Gordon of Chinese fame, whose name alone would have been an invaluable asset in gaining the support of British humanitarian opinion, but the British needed Gordon at Khartoum. Leopold settled for de Winton, a British army officer with impeccable social connections (he ended his career by taking charge of financial matters for the Duke of York).

Leopold's initial instructions were simple. The *administrateur général* was to reside at Vivi and serve as the monarch's chief agent.[4] He was entrusted with absolute powers of command. His task was strictly to maintain free trade in a manner laid down by international agreement. Expenditures were to be kept to the irreducible minimum; incompetent officials were to be sacked on the spot; no government monopolies might be set up; and no import or transit duties might be sanctioned. The *administrateur général* was to confine his principal efforts to taking possession of the Lower Congo, but he was enjoined to maintain at least two posts on the upper river. De Winton was thoroughly in accord with these notions of limited government. He saw no point in alienating the Africans, either by direct taxation or by the imposition of tolls on trading caravans. The Free State, in his view, ought to wipe out the slave trade, settle freed captives near its stations, possibly promote Indian immigration, and use captured ivory to pay for its military expeditions.[5]

Once the Berlin Conference had recognized Leopold's sovereignty over the Congo, the king's need for British support declined. He therefore selected Camille Janssen (1837-1926), a *docteur en droit* from Liège who was clearly acceptable to enlightened public opinion at home, to succeed de Winton in 1886 as the first *gouverneur général* and the first Belgian-born head of the Congo administration. Janssen had served in the Belgian consular service and had represented Belgium in the international tribunals set up in Egypt. An able and humane man, Janssen was pro-African in sympathy and keenly interested in African customs. He was one of the cofounders of the International African Institute, and he traveled widely in the Congo. But he was too honest to continue for long in Leopold's employ. He preferred to resign his appointment, which was worth forty-five thousand francs a year, rather than carry out decrees of which he disapproved.

The appointment of his successor, Théophile-Théodore Wahis, a man of a very different stamp, symbolized the increasingly exploitative nature of the Free State's administration. The scion of a military family, he had entered the Belgian army as a cadet and later fought with distinction in Mexico in defense of Maximilian's ill-starred venture. He subsequently served in the Congo, where his indefeasible loyalty, his military record, and his reputation as a rough diamond caught Leopold's eye. Wahis took an active part in defending the record of the Congo Free State in Europe, and he was rewarded with a barony and the rank of *lieutenant général* for his services. Nominally, he was in charge of Congolese affairs longer than any other man—from 1891 to 1912, with extended interruptions.

Wahis's career reflected both the Belgianization of the supposedly "international" Congo state and the military orientation of pioneer governance. His real powers, however, were strictly limited. "The Governor-General . . . is nominally head of the local government," wrote a British observer, "although . . . it has been his custom to reside principally in Europe and to act chiefly as an intermediary between the local administration . . . and the Sovereign in Belgium." During the governor-general's absences from Boma, the actual work of running the colony was entrusted either to the *vice-gouverneur général* or to an *inspecteur d'état* like Félix Fuchs, who eventually succeeded to Wahis's office. The vice-governor-general ranks "personally with the Secretaries-General but functionally is subservient to them."[6] Hence his position was in fact greatly inferior to that of a British or a German governor.

The governor-general was assisted by a *comité consulta-tif*, which was set up in 1887 and consisted of senior civil servants. The governor-general or his substitute was encouraged to consult them before acting on a matter of general policy, but he was not obliged to do so.[7] The vice-governor-general communicated with his subordinates through the medium of a state secretary, who supplied an important element of administrative continuity.

In addition, the Belgians, like the French, exercised supervision over the various departments through a highly trained group of senior officials known as *inspecteurs d'état*. These men might tour the country as a group or might supervise particular departments. Their visits usually were un-scheduled and were apt to be detailed and searching—all the more so since these top-level surveys were supplemented by an elaborate system of additional inspections carried out by the immediate superior of a functionary under scrutiny and by the *adjoint supérieur* of a province. The inspector would check returns, books of account, stocks of trade goods, and produce received from the Africans as imposts; he would examine buildings, listen to complaints, and even make sure that the toilets were in working order. This painstaking investigatory system gravely slowed the administrative machine, but where it functioned as its makers had intended, there was little room for personal dishonesty or slackness.

THE DISTRICT OFFICIALS

The Congolese district administration, one of the most elaborate in early colonial Africa, reproduced many of the hierarchical complexities of the administrative system in the métropole. Governance was expensive; hence the indigenous people were forced to bear a heavy tax burden (see Table 9). The Congo administration employed far more Europeans than did the neighboring British and German territories, and

TABLE 9

Congo Budget, 1906
(In Belgian Francs)

Revenue	
Products derived from domain land and taxes paid in kind	16,100,000
Customs duties	6,350,000
Income derived from transport and similar services	6,400,000
Income from stock	5,000,000
Direct and personal taxes	600,000
Miscellaneous	1,425,000
TOTAL REVENUE	35,875,000

Expenditures	
Central administration	159,000
Administrative services	6,415,000
Force Publique	5,935,000
Navigation	2,373,000
Health	619,000
Public works	1,870,000
Religion and education	873,000
Agriculture	1,935,000
Domanial cultivation	6,572,000
Repayment of loans	4,167,000
Justice	1,387,000
Postal services	140,000
Miscellaneous	3,315,000
TOTAL EXPENDITURES	35,760,000

SOURCE: Belgium, Sénat de Belgique, *Rapport de la commission spéciale, 1908* (no. 11) (Brussels, 1908), pp. 22-23.
NOTE: The *domaine privé* does not appear in these calculations.

as the king tried to turn conquest into cash, the European personnel increased in numbers.[8]

The Formal Organization: An Overview

Belgian power originally centered on the Lower Congo. The Free State headquarters was situated at Boma, once a great slave market. By the late 1880s the port facilities at Boma had been extended, and a road led from the wharves to one-storied houses belonging to senior Congolese officials, which were surrounded by warehouses and gardens. At the governor-general's residence hall, which was built of corrugated iron, visitors might get a drink at the Cercle de Boma, which overlooked the Congo River and its scattered islands. The township was defended by a small earthwork fort that was furnished with five small cannons and garrisoned by a few hundred soldiers.

As the Belgians pushed inland they created new districts, later known as provinces, which numbered fourteen by 1906. These were split into *zones* or districts, each supervised by a *commissaire de district*. The *zones* were further divided into *secteurs*, each of which was run by a *chef de secteur* who in turn supervised the local *chefs de poste*.

This brief sketch does not do justice to the complexity of the Belgian hierarchy and its variability from one time or place to another. There was an intricate order of rank. The highest provincial officials were the *commissaires généraux*; next were three classes (first, second, and third) of district commissioners. Together, these officials constituted the *personnel supérieur de district*, that is, the higher functionaries. The lower functionaries—the *personnel inférieur*—were the *chefs de secteur*, again in three classes, and the *chefs de poste*. The distinction between these two groups was comparable to the gulf that separated commissioned officers from other ranks in the army; it had no equivalent in the British colonial administration, where every district officer was supposed to be a gentleman by definition. Under the Belgian dispensation, a civil servant could be promoted from the *personnel inférieur* to the higher strata of the administration, just as a sergeant was eligible for promotion in the army. Nonetheless, class differences between the two ranks remained severe; on the higher level, rank was personal, but a lower-grade official held his rank only as long as he carried out certain specific functions.

Once the pioneering days were over, the Free State came

to depend on this elaborate administrative system and on an equally cumbersome and intricate method of reporting. The Belgian arrangement, like that of the French, was based on the assumption—inspired by military and bureaucratic notions rather than by the ethos of the gentleman—that no man was to be wholly trusted. Belgian administration, as we have seen, contained a *corps d'élite*—the *inspecteurs d'état*, who toured the colony and enjoyed far-reaching powers of supervision. But every superior officer was also expected to maintain an unceasing surveillance over his subordinates; in turn, each administrator had to report the most minute details of his work to his immediate superior. The *chef de poste* therefore wrote to the *chef de secteur*; the *chef de secteur* reported to the *commissaire de district*; and the latter communicated with his superior, who then conveyed his observation to headquarters at Boma. Every detail of routine work was closely regulated by written instructions that gave explicit guidance regarding the most trifling transactions that might engage a civil servant's attention.

The Belgian system was distinguished by the operation of an independent judicature. The government of the Free State had its own minister of justice at Boma, ranking with the vice-governor-general and answerable at first to the governor-general and later to his sovereign in Europe. The magistracy was totally separate from the administration at large and reproduced the complexities of the judicial system in the métropole. At its apex was a supreme court composed of three independent judges who heard appeals. Below the supreme court was a high court consisting of one judge who resided at Boma. The judges were professional lawyers of high legal reputation; indeed, the Free State magistracy, like the *inspecteurs d'état*, turned out to be a reservoir of liberal theory and reformist practice.

The judicial authorities were not afraid to tackle individual abuses. In the Congolese archives are many dossiers assembled by the *procureur d'état* (public prosecutor) concerning outrages committed by individuals. For example, the *pro-*

cureur d'état insisted that disciplinary action be taken against a police officer who had arrested and whipped two Senegalese without proper cause. Another European was accused by anonymous informers of having murdered two Africans. The suspect fled the country, but the *procureur d'état* took charge of the matter and persuaded Governor-General Wahis to write to the colonial authorities at Dakar, Sierra Leone, and Tenerife requesting that they arrest the fugitive.[9]

Despite its reputation for integrity, Belgian justice suffered from excessive formalism, a serious failing in a frontier community. According to Wahis, the complexities of the *tribune d'appel* were such as to bring the judicial system into disrepute. He cited the case of one Van Cacklen who apparently had been guilty of all manner of excesses. But Van Cacklen and his "forest guards" were acquitted on a technicality. The court's decision persuaded the Africans that the accused had been granted a license to kill.

The Belgians were not often able to surmount the law's delay. That the high court was separated from the main Belgian centers in the Congo by the river's great cataracts was itself a major handicap. There were also weaknesses at the lower levels. In each of the main government posts a *juge substitut* performed functions corresponding roughly to those of an examining magistrate in the French system. These judge substitutes had executive powers in ordinary cases, and in more complicated matters they acted as substitutes for the *procureur général* (crown prosecutor). They were usually young men, lawyers sent out from Brussels, newly qualified, without any previous experience of Africans or, indeed, of legal administration of any kind. Justice was administered in an even rougher fashion at the lowest level, where ordinary administrative officials could act as magistrates in simple cases.

The administration had other weaknesses that it shared with every pioneer system in tropical Africa. The early civil service suffered from a heavy rate of sickness and mortality; postings were necessarily made frequently, so that local administrators could not easily acquire thorough familiarity with the customs and dialects of their regions. Individual Belgian administrators did make valuable contributions to the study of ethnography and linguistics in the Congo, but judging from a technical publication like C. F. Witterwulghe's *Vocabulaire à l'usage des fonctionnaires se rendant dans les territoires du district de l'Uele et de l'enclave Redjaf-Lado* (1903), the general level of linguistic competence was low. This is hardly surprising, though, given that few Congolese tongues had been reduced to writing before 1900.

The Free State also had vices peculiarly its own. It was the only colonial state in Africa whose administration was designed for the purpose of extorting a direct profit from the colonial treasury to the motherland. This objective was not even attained by the British South Africa Company, an overtly commercial body that was unable to pay its stock-holders a single penny in dividends as long as it had charge of the two Rhodesias. Unlike this company, the Congo Free State began to circumscribe freedom of trade and to enforce local monopolies. It did both too much and too little. By interfering with domestic and foreign merchants, the Free State restricted economic enterprise and inhibited the emergence of an indigenous trading class. Yet it lacked the experience, the resources, and the trained personnel to undertake large-scale development. Though it was large in relation to the resources of the country at the time, the governmental machine could not effectively administer a country extending over more than 900,000 square miles. By the end of the 1890s the Free State maintained about fifty posts, each of which was expected to oversee an area of some 15,000 square miles. One government station was responsible for a region as large as the state of New Jersey or the kingdom of the Netherlands.

In the Congo, as everywhere else, pioneer officials had to cope with danger, loneliness, disease, the fear of death, and a sense of culture shock. There were the vagaries of the climate, including humidity and heat; there were mosquitoes and hookworm, bad food and infected water, recurrent attacks of malaria and of enteric infections. And there were the strange dreads of the jungle, with its uncanny sounds and unknown perils, and the long nights when the rain poured down and sleep would not come. The sense of isolation engendered by the enormous distances also had to be surmounted. The average Belgian youngster, explained a soldier, had been spoiled by the tramway; if a Belgian were asked to walk all the way from Brussels to Paris, he would laugh at the request. Yet, in the Congo, treks of that magnitude were nothing out of the ordinary and had to be undertaken in a grim climate.[10] Before completion of the railway a traveler needed eighteen days to proceed from Matadi to Léopoldville.

Successful administration in the bush required a man of a peculiar stamp—a born loner capable of coping with any conceivable problem. A pioneer official had to be his own builder, his own transport manager, his own physician, and his own entertainer. Above all, a Free State officer was always under pressure from the center to get more "results"— to see that more roads were built, that more ivory tusks and more rubber bales reached the Free State stores, that more taxes were collected, that more labor was forthcoming for porterage, for railway building, or for cutting the wood required for fuel by river steamers. Many a civil servant stuck in some lonely bush post tried to cheer his life by taking to women, drugs, or drink. Some seem to have oscillated between depression (*nostalgie*) and manic rage (known to the Germans as *Tropenkoller* and to the British as *furor africanus*).

The exact way in which men would react to the pressures of a lonely existence was hard to predict. The higher functionaries in particular seem to have taken some satisfaction from the immense power they exercised and the social prestige they enjoyed. Among them, Burrows wrote, the expression " '*je suis officier belge*' is an ejaculation so frequent that . . . one would fain believe such a rank to be the highest honour on earth." The more subordinate officials, men willing to risk their health and renounce their accustomed way of life for a pittance, probably faced even greater psychological difficulties; having been reared, as often as not, in the atmosphere of the barracks, they were apt to respond to difficulties by imposing swift punishment for real or imaginary offenses. Others, suddenly transplanted from a village background or some lowly occupation, were aghast at the difficulties and privations of a life of which they had never even read. The petty annoyances that were inseparable from contact with African villagers often became to them terrible transgressions to be suppressed with severity.

Once the pioneer military officials had set up a regular routine, they were apt to run their stations with military precision. Belgian civil servants maintained in the Congo their vaunted reputation for punctuality, hard work, and attention to detail. Military men like Lemaire attached much importance to formalities and regulated their stations by the sound of the trumpet and tom-tom. Days began and ended with a formal salute to the Congo flag; all agents dined in an official mess presided over by the *commissaire*; and Lemaire personally supervised the kitchen garden and the cuisine. Government stations became local markets and centers of small-scale industry. Uvira station, for example, gave jobs to five African blacksmiths and ten carpenters; 120 workmen were employed to construct fortifications. The station grew its own food: half a hectare was planted with maize, and two hectares with sown pasture. The monthly station reports were replete with details concerning farming, construction work, and road building. Great emphasis was placed on cleanliness, punctuality, and economy.[11] Drunkards there might be aplenty, but for better or for worse, the Belgians desired to rule in a spirit of Prussian efficiency.

Social Origins and Conditions of Service

Assessments of the civil service in the Congo Free State differ. A perusal of contemporary accounts concerning the

Congo might persuade a reader that totally different countries are being described. Captain Guy Burrows, for example, was convinced that both the Belgian and the foreign employees of the Free State were a worthless crew. Belgian officers, he said, tended to be plebeian in origin and insolent in demeanor. Even the judges were a dubious lot:

> I have seen some very "queer fish" among the judges, many of whom have a failing for absinthe and other strong liquids. Their principal ambition seems to be to make the sum total of the fines they impose as large as possible. One of the agents of the Mongalla Company was fined £8 for boxing the ears of an insolent cannibal policeman at Matadi. The judge appointed to make inquiry into the atrocities committed in the Mongalla concession is said to have obtained his information by sending his "boy" among the native staff of the "factories," and, on his reports, to have arrested a number of white men. . . . [Also] he engaged in a little quiet trading for ivory. . . . In short the entire judicial system is a farce.[12]

Burrows's strictures, though widely accepted abroad, must be treated with caution. He was clearly guilty of exaggeration. E. D. Morel, a Congo reformer, wanted nothing to do with him. Colonel Liebrechts sued Burrows in a British court and secured a conviction for libel.[13] The Free State administration was able to mobilize in its support not only disreputable journalists but also respectable men who would never have dreamed of selling their pens to the king. These included, for instance, Father Castelain, a Jesuit, a former chairman of the Belgian Society of Economy, and a scholar of repute. The entries in the *Biographie coloniale belge* do not bear out Burrows's general description of an ill-educated service composed of philistines. Rather, many Belgian officials made a considerable contribution to the study of Congolese geography and ethnography, developing a real sympathy for the people whom they were called upon to govern.

The king, moreover, was anxious to find good applicants.

Volunteers intending to serve in the Congo, he insisted, must apply in writing to the *secrétaire d'état*. The candidate's "morality, antecedents and physical condition" were to be investigated by the *secrétaire général* of the department concerned. Each recruit, the king continued, should have a general knowledge of geography, hygiene, and the law. Officers of the Force Publique had to pass an examination.[14] Despite these requirements, the personal caliber of the early applicants varied. There were cultured men and ignoramuses, men of honor and men fit for jails. A substantial number were foreigners, although their ratio gradually declined as conditions of service improved and as colonial employment lost some of its initial unpopularity in Belgium. Even so, by the end of Leopold's personal rule in 1908, more than one-third of all Free State officials were not of Belgian nationality (see Table 10).

TABLE 10

Nationalities of Free State Officials, 1908

Nationality	Civil Officials	Military Officials	Artisans	Total
Belgian	486	339	74	899
Danish	12	13	2	27
Swedish	69	63	34	166
Norwegian	13	23	3	39
German	—	—	13	13
Italian	57	44	7	108
Finnish	3	—	49	52
Lagos	1	—	—	1
Swiss	92	—	1	93
Dutch	9	—	—	9
Russian	2	—	7	9
Argentinian	1	—	—	1
Luxemburgian	7	—	—	7
Austrian	1	—	—	1
French	2	—	—	2
Bulgarian	1	—	—	1
TOTAL	756	482	190	1,428

SOURCE: SPA 116, no. 46, Archives africaines.

Most of these foreign volunteers were hardly the ragamuffins of legend. They included men like Dragutin Lerman (1863-1918), who later advanced to the rank of *commissaire général*. Lerman was born in Pozega, a small Croatian township within the Austro-Hungarian empire. The son of a wine grower, he obtained a good education at the local *gymnasium* (high school with a syllabus emphasizing Greek and Latin). He subsequently traveled to Budapest, Brod, and later to London, and he worked in a number of jobs—as an assistant on his father's farm, as a salesman, and as a builder. In his spare time he became an ardent reader of travel books, especially about Schliemann's archeological expeditions. He then began to take private lessons in English, and in 1882 he signed up with an expedition organized by Stanley. Subsequently, he returned home and served for two years in the Austro-Hungarian army. Lerman, however, could not escape the lure of Africa. In 1888 he decided to join Leopold's administration, and he accepted an appointment as *commissaire adjoint de district* at twenty-four hundred francs per annum.

Lerman did not go to Africa for money. He envisaged the Congo Free State as a humanitarian enterprise and felt proud to represent his Croatian fatherland in a benevolent adventure designed to help a hitherto neglected people. He was quite free from the vulgar prejudice—widespread among colonials at the time—regarding educated Africans, and he displayed considerable intellectual interests. In Liberia, Lerman made a point of calling on Dr. E. W. Blyden, a famous West Indian scholar, who struck him as a most intelligent and kind person, the "prototype of a true African." Blyden, Lerman recalled, helped him to understand the realities of Liberia, and he made a considerable impression on the young Croat. Educated Africans, Lerman continued, were unfortunately few in number, but they were pleasant, serious, well-mannered, and excellent company.[15] Once in the Congo, Lerman took part in several military expeditions against Arab slave traders and participated in the conquest of the Kwango region. He was not a hard-liner; in fact, he got on well with foreign missionaries, including the Reverend George Grenfell, a prominent Baptist. But his health gave way, and in 1894, before the Congo Free State had acquired an international reputation for rapacity, he returned to his native Pozega. His pension helped him to marry the daughter of a local landowner and start a business of his own, but his firm failed to prosper, and he ended as a prospector for a Belgian mining company in Bosnia.

Lerman was not unique in his enthusiasms and attitudes. Viscount Mountmorres, an English scholar and clergyman—Balliol College to the core—went to the Congo in 1905 to conduct an independent inquiry that was paid for by Sir Alfred Jones, a Liverpool magnate and a friend of Leopold's. Mountmorres nevertheless had a mind of his own. He rather liked the Free State officials he met, and his general impression of the colonial administration was surprisingly favorable. Foreign-born employees made up just under one-half of the European personnel, who numbered slightly less than two thousand at the time. The Belgians, he decided, were the best officials within the administration. Italy had an excessive supply of poorly paid officials willing to serve abroad, and a considerable number of Italians served in the Congo Free State, including such able specialists as Giovanni Trolli, the one-time head of the Congolese medical service. Mountmorres was impressed by some of these Italian labor migrants. But, he said, "almost every unsatisfactory State official whom I have met was an Italian, and . . . they are far from satisfactory even in the capacity of military officer." The Scandinavians were largely drawn from the Swedish officer corps and were inclined to be overly military in their approach; otherwise they were perfectly acceptable. "During the whole course of my journey," he wrote, "I was struck by the fact that I scarcely met with a single government official who could definitely be described as undesirable." The officials were hard-working, more so perhaps than those of any other colonial nation. Mountmorres was clearly impressed by people who worked unstintingly from 5:45 in the morning to noon, and then again from 2:15 in the afternoon till 6:00—and in many cases for an extra hour in the evening just to cope with clerical duties.

> It is astounding to witness the whole-hearted zeal with which the officials . . . devote themselves to their work. Each one seems to make it a matter of personal pride to surpass all his predecessors in the amount of work which he can accomplish during his three years. He spends his spare time in devising methods for making bricks in a district where clay is unknown, inventing a substitute for mortar where lime does not exist, or studying the latest publications on tropical botany.[16]

Whatever the personal qualities of Belgian administrators, they could not easily escape the vices of the Free State system. Their personal positions were insecure, for they enjoyed neither administrative tenure nor pension rights; before embarking for the fever-ridden banks of the Congo River the more cautious among them took out life insurance policies—if they could get them—to protect their next of kin. Like the pioneers of other nations in the tropics, the Free State administrators were under heavy emotional pressure that sometimes led to serious disorders. Yet they were expected to make good as jacks-of-all-trades. The district officer had to be an understanding judge, capable of hearing complaints and petitions from Africans. He was expected to maintain government stations, to wage local wars, to attend to, supervise, and pay African workmen, to enforce labor and food imposts (a subject to which we shall return), to recruit labor, and to organize transport. In many smaller *postes* he would take charge of the collection of rubber—an activity that was to give rise to bloody scandals—and also to oversee state plantations of rubber, cocoa, coffee, and other crops. At the same time he was fighting a constant war against red tape, since elaborate records had to be kept of every transaction and returns had to be furnished in duplicate.

The job could be done only by delegating authority to

African subordinates. The average African probably did not identify Bula Matari—the Congo Free State—with the *chef de secteur*, whom he might never see, as much as with the policemen and *capitaos* (African supervisors) whom the government placed in the villages, where they formed a new elite. "The soldier promptly imposes himself on the chief. He takes unto himself a wife at the chief's expense, and as a rule the chief consents in order to curry favour with the soldier, who has as much power—and uses it indiscriminately—as an Irish constable at a League meeting."[17] The subordinates varied in origin. In the Province Orientale, for example, the Belgians employed Swahili-speaking coastmen or partly Muslimized Bakussu warriors to serve as auxiliaries.

> Each of these Arabs . . . has a band of cut-throats, armed with muskets, belonging in part to the State, which also furnished ammunition, and to them is entrusted the duty of compelling the native to furnish rubber. This task . . . they perform with great zeal, for it affords them an opportunity . . . of massacring and pillaging [and] . . . with the levying of tribute on the natives for their own individual benefit.[18]

The dissimilarities between different areas of the Congo go far to explain the contrasting impressions of foreign observers of equal integrity. In the beginning, the Congo Free State did not fully control the huge territory that was nominally under its charge, and indigenous states continued to function within the interstices of Belgian rule. Even on a purely formal level, the Free State was far from all-powerful. The Comité spécial du Katanga (CSK), founded in 1900, maintained its own civil administration; it was divided into a number of administrative areas, with only the magistracy subject to the Free State. To protect the borders of Katanga against the designs (real or imagined) of the British South Africa Company in Rhodesia, the CSK had its own police force, and it set up its own stations designed to collect rubber.

Whether officials served the CSK or the Congo Free State, there were no fixed rules with regard to recruitment or promotion. Commissioned officers employed by the state continued to remain in the military establishment, but sergeants had to leave the army upon entering the Free State administration. Definite criteria for salaries were nonexistent; there was no career structure. As a Belgian critic commented: "Le fonctionnaire congolais n'est jamais sûr du lendemain"; hence subordinate officials were unwilling to criticize their superiors and thereby jeopardize their careers.[19] The system accordingly produced the widespread abuses that we shall discuss at greater length in subsequent chapters. Even defenders of the state like Liebrechts agreed that there was oppression. Often local chiefs attempted to escape from Free State exactions by moving into an area that was still free from Belgian occupation.[20]

Nothing in the selection of the personnel, however, could account for their abuse of power. In 1888, for instance, Leopold commissioned a group of twenty officials as district commissioners. We have traced the careers of eighteen of these early pioneers (Table 11 is a breakdown, with some overlapping in the descriptive categories employed). The majority—ten of the eighteen—came from small towns. They were reasonably well educated (there were three Belgian staff-college graduates and three former engineers), and they gave the early administration a strongly military flavor (thirteen of the eighteen were army officers). Two of the civilian engineers had been trained in the military. Some of these men came from military families; only one—Philippe-Maurice Le Clément de Saint-Marcq—was of impeccably aristocratic origin. For many others, colonial, like military, service afforded a means of social promotion.

Belgian officials were relatively well remunerated. After the turn of the century they accumulated pension rights at home while serving overseas. They had a reputation for being well turned out, and dressing for dinner was a widespread rule even in remote stations. Above all, the Congo

105

TABLE 11

Career Information on Eighteen Early Officials, 1888

Description	Number
Origin	
Small towns	10
Large towns (3 from Brussels, 2 from Liège,	
1 each from Antwerp, Rotterdam, and London)	8
Army Officers	
Ex-sergeants with commissions	5
Members of the Institut cartographique militaire[a]	3
Adjoints d'état-major	2
Graduates of the Ecole de guerre or its Swedish	
equivalent	3
Civilians	
Engineers (railways, roads, mines)	3
Ex-clerks	4
Cause of Death Related to Colonial Service	
Fever	3
Killed in action or assassinated	2

[a] The Institut cartographique was at one time an important reservoir of officers with colonial inclinations.

Free State made astonishingly elaborate provisions to keep its officials supplied. Even a lowly *chef de poste* would receive in his quarterly food consignments

a bottle of red wine a day, a plentiful supply of flour, of cake, of plain biscuits and dessert biscuits, sardines, pâtés and potted meats of various kinds (foie gras, pheasant, larks, etc.) preserved tinned meats, bacon, marmalade, jams, pickles, sauces, condiments, preserved soup, tea, coffee, butter of two qualities for cooking and table purposes, sugar, rice, preserved fruits and vegetables both dried and tinned, candles, matches, soap, milk . . . whilst all that is sent is of the best quality obtainable. The pâtés came from Fischer's of Strasburg, the marmalade from England, the jams and preserved fruits from St. James, Paris, the table butter from the Danish Creamery Co.[21]

This life attracted applicants from the lower middle class as well as the middle class. Ethnic origins are now hard to trace; twelve of the twenty district commissioners had Flemish or Dutch rather than French names, but in Belgium this meant little. Of the eighteen for whom we have information, five were ex-sergeants who had been commissioned in the Belgian army before transferring to the Congolese administration, and four were ex-clerks who had previously worked in banks or in overseas trading firms. One Jules-Marie-Jean De Kuyper, a Dutchman from Rotterdam, had started his career as a clerk and subsequently worked for the Nieuwe Afrikaansche Handelsvennotschap in Banana before joining the Congolese service. Camille-Théodore-Joseph Van den Plas, the son of a teacher, attended a small-town *école moyenne*, later volunteered for the army, and reached the rank of *sergent major* before being commissioned. He later transferred to the Congolese service.

The risk was high: five of the eighteen perished on the battlefield or on an early sickbed.[22] In 1890 the annual mortality rate among officials stood at 15 percent; in 1895 it was still 8.7 percent. Conditions did not improve until about 1905, as Europeans gradually learned to protect themselves against malaria and other tropical diseases; between 1905 and 1920 the death rate dropped from 5.42 percent a year to 1.34 percent.[23] A young Belgian who enlisted in Free State service took his life in his hands, but if he survived the hardships of life in a young colony, he stood a reasonable chance of reaching senior office and even national fame. Lieutenant Colonel Liebrechts ended his official career as *secrétaire général du Département de l'intérieur*; Dhanis became known to his contemporaries as a Belgian hero.[24]

Thus the abuses that made the Congo Free State infamous in international opinion were not occasioned by the choice of personnel. As Jean Stengers has shown, they were caused less by men or local circumstances than by a system that pushed the production of wild rubber by all available means.[25] The very virtues of the Belgian system—its methodical punc-

107

tiliousness, its insistence on conformity to rules and regulations, the efficiency of its accounting system—were themselves apt to become vices. The penal code prescribed punishment for cruel conduct, and the courts were far from inactive. But although the magistracy had good intentions, its numbers were far too small in relation to the size of the territory to act as an effective brake on wrongdoing.

THE BEGINNINGS OF CIVIL GOVERNANCE

The face of Belgian rule varied from region to region. The military aspect of the Belgian conquest was discussed in Chapter Two, and Chapter Four will deal with civilian oppression derived from a primitive form of *Raubwirtschaft*—an economy based upon the forcible appropriation of wealth. *Corvées* designed to extract ivory, rubber, and other forms of natural wealth were so common that in many areas Africans took to arms or offered passive resistance by destroying rubber plants in an effort to force the whites to leave.[26]

Belgian rule, however, did not universally depend upon brute force. The coercive powers of the Free State were limited. And it must be remembered that the area of the Congo stretched from north to south along a line equal in length to the distance from Ontario in northeastern Canada to the Gulf of Mexico; the distance from the Atlantic shore to Lake Tanganyika—some 1,200 miles—is as great as that from London to Tunis in North Africa. This vast region contained many peoples, and their forms of political organization ranged from tightly run monarchies to stateless societies. A few hundred Belgian district officials clearly could exert no more than the most tenuous control over such a huge and diverse area. Exploitation, however ruthless, was limited by local considerations of *Realpolitik*.

When the Belgians were about to enter the Congo region much of the country was in a state of turmoil, and the local balance of power was being changed by the introduction of imported firearms. The agents of change included traders from Angola, some of them Afro-Portuguese, and especially the Umbundu people. The Umbundu, who had already made a name for themselves as slave traders during the 1700s, greatly enlarged their traffic in the nineteenth century. Like the Arabs, they gradually pushed farther and farther into the interior in search of ivory and slaves. In the 1870s ivory was supplemented as an article of trade by wild rubber, and a new incentive was added to inland penetration. The imported guns and gunpowder used in trade helped to build up the power of warlords such as Kakenge, a great Lovale chief, and Msiri, an East Coast magnate. To defend themselves against alien raiders, the victims in turn acquired new weapons and new tactics; they then hit on the idea of selling their captives. The trade in rubber, ivory, firearms, and slaves spread like an epidemic.

The beneficiaries of the new commerce included not only the Swahili and the Umbundu, but also indigenous raiders such as the Lovale and Chokwe. The Chokwe, who were skilled hunters and slave traders, were so successful that they managed to overturn the balance of power throughout western Katanga, the Kasai region, and the southern parts of Kwango; by the time the Belgians arrived in the Congo, the Chokwe and the Lunda were locked in fierce battles for supremacy. Another conquering group was the Yeke. (The term "Yeke" originated in local designations of the hunting and trading caravans led by Msiri, whose followers were from the Nyamwezi country, near Tabora. These hunters and traders acquired Kisanga-speaking women, who passed on their indigenous tongue to the offspring of these unions.) The Yeke fought for land and riches both on their own behalf and in the service of other warlords.[27] One of the best-known of these adventurers was Msiri (Msidi or Mwenda), a Nyamwezi from East Africa who set up a warrior state of his own in Katanga. Msiri cooperated with the Swahili from the east; he also assisted the Yeke armies against the existing Lunda monarchies. He and his Yeke allies were far from being mere parasites. They introduced the sweet potato to

109

some of their neighbors and brought new techniques of divination, vaccination against smallpox, new insignia, new titles, new political ceremonies, and a new technique for making copper wire. However, they were unable to create a truly united state, and their governance rested precariously on the barrel of the musket.

In the eastern Congo the balance of power was shifting in favor of Swahili-speaking invaders, men like Tippu Tip who came as traders and ended as conquerors. Between the Lomami and the Lualaba rivers—north of the Luba kingdom of Kasongo Kalombo—Tippu Tip was powerful enough to replace inconvenient chiefs or to confirm leaders in office. He imposed a monopoly on the shooting of elephants; he enforced tolls, built roads, constructed fortifications, and organized plantations, and he established his own Pax Arabica around the Swahili centers at Nyangwe and Kasongo. South of the Lukuga River, however, there was nothing constructive about the penetration by ill-coordinated bands of Swahili speakers who preyed on the indigenous people, murdering, looting, and raiding for slaves.

The Belgians initially had little insight into the complexities of local politics. They were content to send out expeditions to reconnoiter the country, distribute flags, and establish a vague claim to suzerainty. These early expeditions often failed to achieve their purpose when they encountered a powerful potentate. In 1892, for instance, Lerman made his way to the country of Mwene Putu, a Yeke king who controlled the region between the Kwango and Kingushi rivers with an army of two thousand warriors whom he employed to raid for ivory, rubber, and slaves. In exchange, Mwene Putu purchased guns, gunpowder, liquor, and cloth to distribute to his followers as reward for their services. His rule was harsh. Criminals were physically mutilated for small offenses. Inmates of the royal harem—he had a hundred wives—had to submit to the ordeal of boiling water when charged with unfaithfulness, and they were executed if they cried during the ordeal.[28] In Mwene Putu's eyes, the Bel-

110

gian expedition was no more than a traders' caravan, and when the strangers refused to pay tribute, they were expelled. In the end, however, the chief submitted. According to Lerman, Mwene Putu's warriors would not have been in a position to resist a second Belgian expedition of three hundred well-armed soldiers. The monarch, moreover, believed that he could no longer rely on the loyalty of his subchiefs; nevertheless, the Belgian takeover there proceeded in a troubled fashion.

The Kivu district had a bloodier history. Government by Belgian-trained troops began not under the auspices of the Congo Free State but under the flag of mutineers against Belgian authority. The soldiers whom Dhanis had attempted to lead to the Upper Nile revolted against his orders, marched south, and tried to establish a state of their own between Lake Tanganyika and the Luama River. Leopold's colonial forces fought several campaigns against the rebels. The battles were long and bitter, and the Belgians suffered several defeats; but in 1899 they succeeded in establishing the Congo Free State's authority north of Lake Tanganyika. The mutineers were cut off from reinforcements. They lost their chief and finally sought refuge across the border in German East Africa. By 1900 the Kivu area had partially passed under Belgian administration.[29] However, the bulk of the area was not fully controlled by the colonizers until the 1920s.

Belgian authority was weak at first. Between 1900 and 1907 the Kivu district was headed by eight different officers in succession, most of them soldiers of ability who made names for themselves in Belgian colonial history: J. A. Milz, Charles Tombeur, F. V. van Olsen, and P. Costermans. None of them stayed long enough to acquire thorough familiarity with their Kivu subjects, but they did try to govern their charges with a light hand, lest the local Africans lend their support to the neighboring Germans. Belgian posts were instructed not to interfere with indigenous politics except for the purpose of settling quarrels and maintaining the general

111

authority of the Free State. Station heads were enjoined to enforce a strict discipline over their men and to punish all breaches of order with due severity. The district head prohibited the imposition of *corvées* or food imposts. Full compensation was to be paid for all wrongs inflicted upon local denizens by the occupying power.[30] The local administration did not entirely stick to these principles. (In 1913, for instance, a Belgian inspector reported the case of an African soldier who had been killed by the indigenous people while trying to recruit porters.)[31]

Belgian power in the area was strictly limited. The military force available to the station head at Kalembelembe, for example, amounted to only fifteen men, and the *chef de poste*, a civilian, bitterly distrusted the military and all its ways. Given such scanty military resources, the Belgian administration had to tread carefully. The *capitaine-commandant* of Ruzizi-Kivu stated in a circular:

> We must treat the indigenous people in a circumspect fashion. When we begin to impose taxes, we should first levy imposts on African communities who live a long way from our stations, so as not to alienate our immediate neighbors. We should endeavor to group people of the same stock, following the same customs, under recognized chiefs. But we must do so in a pacific manner.[32]

The Belgians did nothing to interfere with indigenous social stratification. In the Bugoye area, a region disputed by Belgium and Germany, the majority of the people were Hutu cultivators who supplemented their incomes by hunting and fishing. Most of the local Belgian administrators believed that the ruling class consisted of Tutsi pastoralists who levied tribute in kind—cattle, banana wine, hoes, and food—from weaker communities and enforced their authority by occasional raids. The Hutu, for their part, were divided by intertribal vendettas and were unable to resist their overlords. The Belgians essentially accepted the situation. Their military force in the entire area was limited at first to two detachments totaling seventy-two men. The *commandant supérieur* thus decided that the existing regime should be left undisturbed and that the Tutsi should be used as intermediaries of Belgian governance, for no indigenous Hutu possessed the authority to act as chief. The Belgians were content to limit the tribute imposed by the Tutsi and to insist that tribute should no longer be sent to the Tutsi paramount who lived in Ruanda under German protection.[33]

Indigenous chiefs benefited from collaboration with the Belgians. The *plaques de chef indigène* awarded to them were widely regarded as marks of distinction. Cooperation with the whites also entailed more solid political benefits. The Belgians backed their supporters against domestic rivals. Hence a traditional chief like Lubisha, a magnate among the Fulero people in the Luvingi region, increasingly relied upon the support the government might provide. Lubisha did not start out as a Belgian appointee. He ruled, in the accustomed fashion, through a council of subchiefs who had to be consulted on all major matters and whose assent was required for policy decisions. He posted his various wives in the villages within his domain, where they acted as his representatives and took precedence over the local headmen. Lubisha's economic power depended on tribute in kind and on labor services provided by the villages under his sway. Tributary wealth and cattle, in turn, were redistributed among the subchiefs. The Belgians, however, subtly changed the system by superimposing their own *corvées* on those exacted locally by subchiefs. They also provided the chief with a reserve of externally controlled military power, and Lubisha's power began to depend primarily on white support.[34]

Belgian expertise increased with time. Their soldiers became better disciplined and better fed; the military no longer depended upon local exactions for their rations. By 1912 a private stationed at the Goma post in the Kivu area received six kilos of meat a week, in addition to a substantial daily ration of banana flour, sorgho, or beans. The Belgians grew familiar with the manners and customs of their subjects.

Local reports from about 1910 increasingly dealt with such subjects as the nature of bridewealth and with anthropological problems of a kind that had been ignored by the pioneers.

Nevertheless, the Belgians' hold over their territory was often slight. Rebellions persisted, even in areas never touched by rubber scandals. The warlike Zande people in the northeast proved hard to subdue. Potentates like Mopoie, a member of the Vongara clan, continued to resist. A tall, handsome man with a pleasant countenance and a natural gift for leadership, Mopoie had acquired substantial wealth by obtaining firearms and cloth from the Sudanese Arabs in exchange for ivory and slaves. He built a stronghold by the Sili River, an affluent of the Gurba, and conducted extensive raids, determined to seize control of the entire Gurba region. For arms he relied on Arab, Greek, and Portuguese traders; for advice, he depended on two Egyptian councilors. The Zande would, in fact, have liked peace with the Belgians, but they were determined not to submit to rubber *corvées*. Mopoie therefore continued to enjoy a good deal of popular sympathy. In 1911 the Belgians finally despatched a strong expedition against him. The chief fled into the French Congo but continued to agitate against the Belgians and against Boeli, his younger brother, whom the Belgians had installed as their nominee. When Mopoie raised the standard of revolt again in 1916, it took a composite Franco-British-Belgian force to subdue him at last. Mopoie was captured and "shot while trying to escape."[35]

The Belgians were no more fortunate in the Costermansville area. In 1901 they sent out an expedition to conquer the country. As was their practice, they set up a fortified post complete with a mess and quarters for the white personnel, a military camp, workshops, sheep enclosures, cattle kraals, and gardens. They sent out detachments to enforce obedience from local chiefs, and they carried out larger-scale operations against Chief Kabare, the local potentate, who was guilty of having burned villages and stolen cattle from chiefs who had submitted to the Belgians. Kabare submitted

114

for a time, and the newcomers recognized his chiefly dignity in return for a promise to supply them with men and materials for the building of roads and fortifications. Under the new dispensation, lesser headmen tried to make themselves independent from their indigenous overlords, and numerous internecine quarrels necessitated armed intervention by the *chef de poste*. Chiefs loyal to the Belgian regime were murdered, and by 1911 the political situation had taken a disastrous turn. "Le secteur tout entier retombe dans l'insoumission," anxiously reported a Belgian official. "C'est l'anarchie complète dans tous les groupements."[36]

FOUR

THE ECONOMICS OF COERCION

THE Congo Free State was ostensibly conceived in a spirit of international philanthropy. Its creation seemed to be a triumph for missionary enterprise, abolitionism, and free trade—all causes for which nineteenth-century humanitarians struggled with much conviction. The signatories to the General Act of the Berlin Conference in 1885 agreed to respect the neutrality of the Congo Free State and to maintain complete freedom of commercial intercourse "in all the regions forming the basis of the Congo and its outlets." They pledged themselves to "watch over the preservation of the native tribes and to care for the improvement of their moral and material well-being, and to help in suppressing slavery and especially the Slave Trade." Freedom of religion was to be assured; the navigation of the Congo and the Niger was to be open to flags of all nations. The cause of "commerce and Christianity" seemed about to win a decisive victory. The battle against Islamic freebooters, slavers, and African savages—the enemy appeared in a confused image—was to be won by an all-European, endeavor. Soldiers and officials drawn from many nations would reform a backward land in a manner comparable to the way in which European intervention would later try to bring about reforms in the Ottoman empire, in Macedonia, and in Crete.

Congolese realities turned out to be very different from European expectations. The Congo venture was much more expensive and much more speculative than Leopold had anticipated. The administrative and military edifice set up by the Congo Free State was far costlier to maintain than those established within their respective spheres of influence by the "Arabs," most of them Swahili-speaking freebooters from the East Coast. The Muslims lived on the land; their institutions, however brutal, were better adapted to low-cost governance in the bush than were the hierarchical structures of a Western state.

International agreements initially limited the ability of the Free State to obtain revenue by means of customs duties, although Leopold later found means to circumvent the treaty rights. At first the Free State would not countenance traffic in liquor, although this would have been a profitable source of revenue. No serious attempt was made to develop the existing trade in tropical products such as palm oil, peanuts, and sesame; an enterprise of this kind would have been difficult even for experienced traders at a time when world prices for such crops were falling sharply.[1] In any case, the Belgians lacked an established infrastructure capable of coping with the complexities of the commerce in oil products, which involved the provision of credit to middlemen and the risks in storage of perishable goods.

RAUBWIRTSCHAFT AND IVORY

The Congo Free State initially took to trading in ivory, just as had the Arabs whom the Christians had vowed to subdue. Ivory, a product of high value and low bulk, was one of Africa's major exports; by 1870 the continent was supplying about 85 percent of the world's total ivory requirements. Elephant tusks were used for knife handles, billiard balls, piano keys, and a host of knickknacks that cluttered fashionable Victorian parlors. In addition, elephant teeth were imported by India—their major purchaser—to be fashioned into women's bangles and other ornaments. The desire to capture a share of the ivory trade was one of the motives for the partition of Central Africa. Dutch, British, and French firms located at the mouth of the Congo had purchased ivory from African caravans. Arabs from Zanzibar—including Tippu Tip, the great Swahili magnate—intensified the exploitation of the upper Congo basin and gradually extended their sphere of influence nearer to the West Coast.

117

The existence of large, untouched ivory resources between Stanley Falls and Stanley Pool—an area that might easily be opened to river traffic—had been revealed by Stanley's journey. After the Mahdi set up a militant theocracy in the Sudan and Europeans were no longer able to send vessels down the Upper Nile, the Congo River appeared to be the most serviceable route to the equatorial province of the Sudan, which was supposedly populated by boundless herds of elephants. The prospect of finding ivory helped to push Leopold in his thrust to the Nile, and the profits derived from the sale of ivory helped to finance his colonization plans and the pioneer administration. Between 1889 and 1895 ivory accounted for more than half of the Congo's exports, as Table 12 indicates.

TABLE 12

Congolese Ivory Trade, 1888-1900

Year	Value (in Belgian francs)	Percentage of Total Exports	Weight (in kilos)
1888	1,096,240	42.0	5,824
1889	2,270,640	52.8	45,252
1890	4,668,887	56.6	76,448
1891	2,835,508	53.0	59,686
1892	3,730,420	67.8	118,739
1893	3,718,668	60.0	223,384
1894	5,041,660	57.5	185,558
1895	5,844,640	53.4	273,287
1896	3,826,320	30.9	246,125
1897	4,916,480	32.4	280,117
1898	—	—	201,240
1899	—	—	292,193
1900	5,253,000	11.0	330,491

SOURCE: Max Büchler, *Der Kongostaat Leopolds II*, part 1 (Zurich, 1912), pp. 232-33.

The ivory economy of the frontier imposed its own style on the pioneer administration. Like Arab chiefs, Belgian administrators were concerned with expanding their spheres of influence so as to obtain more of the supply. In doing so, they frequently came to blows with African middlemen who were determined to prevent foreigners from interfering with local trade monopolies. The most brutal methods imaginable were used by the Free State administration and the concessionary companies to enforce the collection of tusks, and commerce often led to war. Yet an ivory economy also depended on good relations with the Africans. An African elephant hunter was a highly skilled craftsman who needed experience and courage of the highest order—a man supremely fitted to be a warrior, and sometimes a conqueror. The pursuit of the great, dangerous beasts was not a task to be left to unwilling conscripts, and the Belgians were disposed to cooperate with local chiefs involved in the ivory traffic in order to profit from their expertise. A local administrator at the time wrote:

> In this country dwell princes and chiefs with far-reaching family ties and power; these are the lords (*mfumunsi*) over great regions. They have influence, not merely over their own fiefs and their own dependents, but to a certain extent over the freemen within their country; they are able therefore to induce these people to work on specified tasks. With chiefs, it is possible to arrive at agreements, according to which a chief obliges himself to carry out specific tasks in exchange for European trade goods. It would be especially advantageous if the chief, as already often happens in trade, should personally take service with the Europeans in the capacity of "lingster," . . . should live in a European settlement, and should personally supervise the way the work is carried out.[2]

The requirements of the ivory trade accordingly contributed to the formation of shifting alliances with the Africans, as recognized in an official "instruction":

> When we shall found our stations on the upper Congo, we shall be able to buy ivory at lower prices than we are now able to do at Léopoldville.

119

Hence, we shall be able to compete with the natives at Stanley Pool, and this may trouble our relations with these people.

But we cannot do without an alliance with them, especially at present, and far from inflicting injuries on them, we must endeavor to make our presence economically advantageous to them.

Perhaps we can link our interests with theirs by, for instance, developing other forms of trade. . . .

At Mr. Stanley's request, we have sent a great amount of goods, valued at 197,000 francs, into the Congo in order to buy ivory.

These include textiles of different kinds, rifles, gunpowder, muskets, brass rods and brass wire, pots, and such. . . . We request that Dr. Pechuel should instruct his officials to buy as much ivory as possible.[3]

The Belgians at first negotiated temporary arrangements with the very Muslims they had vowed to suppress. Tippu Tip was induced to collaborate as a local governor. Belgian officers such as Jérome Joseph Becker actually considered Muslim rule a positive good and believed that Muslim slavery was well adjusted to the African temperament. (Becker later fell into disgrace over the question of Arab policy and in the end resigned his commission.) In the long run, however, Belgians and Muslims could not work together. They were competitors in a declining ivory trade, and they clashed over the wider questions of slavery and sovereignty. As the Belgo-Muslim alliance broke down, war became inevitable—and the Belgians won. For a short time, Belgium became the world's most important trader in ivory; during the 1890s Antwerp took the place of Liverpool and London as the greatest ivory market in existence.

Nevertheless, the export of ivory was a self-destructive industry. Neither Belgians nor Muslims made any provision for the preservation of the elephant herds on which the traffic in tusks depended. By the late 1890s many of the great

beasts had been "shot out," and the greater proportion of the
exports consisted of old teeth that had long lain in store, a
source of supply that would soon be exhausted. In 1897 the
tusks sold at Antwerp already included 21,446 *ivoire morte*
as against 8,539 *ivoire vivante*. Moreover, the expenses of
the ivory trade were heavy. The commerce in elephant tusks
required the maintenance of a considerable administrative
and commercial superstructure on a tiny and uncertain base.
The total value of Congolese ivory exports in 1895 was just
under 6 million francs—a little more than one-third of 1
percent of Belgium's total imports during the year, or just
over one-sixth of the expenditure of the municipality of
Brussels in 1895. In perspective, the revenue from the sale
of gas alone during the year in the Brussels municipality—
5.2 million francs—approached the total value of ivory exports by the Congo Free State. Thus it is no wonder that
the Congo venture seemed dangerous and speculative and
that many experts anticipated that Leopold's African enterprise would end in disaster.

THE RISE OF THE RUBBER ECONOMY

With ivory supplies dwindling, the Belgians increasingly
turned to exploitation of the Congo's wild rubber. Unlike
elephant tusks—a raw material that was useful only for
fashioning luxuries—rubber commanded an ever-growing
market for the manufacture of hoses, motor tires, and other
industrial products for which there was a constantly increasing world demand. Among the first pioneers of the wild-
rubber industry were Congolese Africans, who had offered
wild rubber for sale to Europeans as early as 1867.[4] For a
short time the Africans found sales of rubber so profitable
that this trade was said to have "killed" the commerce in
palm oil and kernels. The collection of wild rubber required
little financial outlay and could therefore be adjusted not
only to the purposes of indigenous African cultivators but

121

also to those of warlords or of foreign concession companies operating with scanty capital.

Raubwirtschaft (ruinous exploitation) of the kind used to produce wild rubber, however, depended on primitive methods that were destructive to rubber-bearing plants; hence the liane *landolphia*, whose milky juice produced wild rubber, was soon destroyed in the coastal regions. When Free State authorities began to realize the value of this trade, they were obliged to push even farther inland, despite the growing hostility of African middlemen. Leopold acquired a quasi monopoly of the Congo's foreign trade in wild rubber, which in 1897 accounted for 16,309,944 francs of the Congo's total exports, which were valued at 23,427,197 francs. Great Britain came second that year with 2,847,870 francs, and Germany was third with 1,284,870 francs. Not surprisingly, foreign opposition to the Free State regime centered in the United Kingdom and the German Reich.

By 1896 rubber exports had increased rapidly, reaching their highest point in the first years of the present century (see Table 13). The value of rubber exports in 1904 stood at 43,478,451 francs, about 83 percent of the Congo's foreign trade—at least, of that portion of the Congo's external commerce that statisticians managed to count. Corresponding recorded figures for ivory had dropped to 3,839,000 francs (about 7.4 percent of Congolese trade), and for palm oil, 1,042 francs (2 percent).

Of itself, the wild-rubber trade need not have turned into an economic disaster for the Congolese Africans. As we have seen, they were willing to produce rubber in return for trade goods, and indigenous production did respond to rising world demands. The Free State administration, however, was under heavy financial pressure to pay the costs of administration and war, and at the same time to produce profits for the king and his associates. Many, though not all, Free State administrators also labored under the misconception that Africans were by nature idle and would never respond to economic incentives alone, a prejudice that was

TABLE 13

Congolese Rubber Exports, 1887-1909

Year	Weight (in kilos)	Value (in Belgian francs)	Value per Kilo (in Belgian francs)
1887	30,050	116,768	3.70
1888	74,294	260,029	3.50
1889	131,113	458,895	3.50
1890	123,666	556,497	4.50
1891	81,680	326,720	4.00
1892	156,339	625,356	4.00
1893	241,153	964,612	4.00
1894	338,194	1,472,944	4.35
1895	576,517	2,882,585	5.00
1896	1,317,346	6,586,730	5.00
1897	1,662,380	8,311,900	5.00
1898	2,113,465	15,850,987	7.50
1899	3,746,739	28,100,917	7.50
1900	5,316,534	39,874,005	7.50
1901	6,022,733	43,965,950	7.30
1902	5,350,452	41,733,525	7.80
1903	5,917,983	47,343,864	8.00
1904	4,830,939	43,478,451	9.00
1905	4,861,767	43,755,903	9.00
1906	4,848,930	48,489,310	10.00
1907	4,529,461	43,982,748	9.20
1908	4,262,531	30,770,550	5.80
1909	3,492,392	38,416,312	11.00

SOURCE: Büchler, *Der Kongostaat Leopolds II*, pt. 1, p. 219.

reinforced by some of their leading intellectuals. Henri Rolin, a distinguished jurist and a professor of colonization and colonial policy at the University of Brussels, maintained that the Commission congolaise d'enquête described the situation perfectly when it stated:

The native, by reason of atavistic leanings and by reason of the country's natural conditions, does not want to work. He does only what is absolutely necessary for his subsistence. The fertility of the soil, the vastness of the territory, the scanty amount of labor that needs to be done,

123

the clement nature of his environment, all this reduces to the minimum the efforts needed. A few branches and a few leaves suffice to shelter him; he wears only a few clothes or no clothes at all; hunting, fishing, and a rudimentary agriculture suffice to satisfy his needs. . . . No allurement will make him do serious work for any length of time.[5]

Rolin's views were in no wise peculiar. Even after the worst abuses had been stopped, many academicians, journalists, and administrators continued to believe that backward Africans were noneconomic men, that they would not respond to economic incentives, and that they would only labor under the threat of force. This doctrine did not necessarily rest upon racist premises. *Le XXᵉ siècle*, a most respectable publication, polemicized on purely utilitarian grounds against the advocates of free labor in the eastern Congo. Admittedly, the journal argued, free African labor had been successfully used in the construction of the Matadi-Léopoldville railway, but Sierra Leonians and Senegalese were much more advanced than the primitive denizens of the Province Orientale. Forced labor was fully justified for public purposes; free labor could only be introduced gradually—and this was, in fact, being done. Many foreign newspapers concurred. The *Frankfurter Zeitung*, representing the liberal tradition of a great German banking and mercantile community, argued on somewhat similar lines. Although it had always manfully censured the atrocities committed in the Congo in the name of civilization, this paper too considered that forced labor could not be abolished immediately. If coercion were to be done away with at once, it contended, the Congo would be deprived of all of its revenue. A system of free contractual labor would have to await the introduction of a money economy.[6]

Coercion of Africans was applied in several distinct steps. First, the right of Africans to trade freely with foreign merchants, including Greek and Portuguese bush traders, was gradually diminished. The state entered directly into competition with private dealers, a policy that led to bitter opposition from both foreign and Belgian private interests, including concerns such as the Société anonyme belge pour le commerce du Haut Congo (SAB) founded by Albert Thys. Statism of the Leopoldine variety was strongly attacked by many who had previously been among the king's most steadfast supporters, including Janssen (who resigned), Van Neuss, Emile Banning, and Auguste Beernaert—all of whom protested loudly against what they regarded as a departure that was as unwise in economic terms at it was contrary to the king's engagements in the political field. Leopold, however, continued on his course and, for all practical purposes, largely eliminated free trade from his dominion.

The king put his trust into large-scale concession companies that were meant to attract private capital to a region that was as yet little known to financiers. This policy derived in part from the monarch's economic prejudices, and even more so from the weakness of the existing firms. (The value of Congo Free State exports during the 1890s was but a fraction of that from British West Africa.) The concessionary regime also permitted direct royal participation. The king claimed for himself a *domaine privé*, a huge area in the basin of Lake Leopold and the Lukenie River that was about ten times the size of Belgium. In this area he imposed *corvées* on the indigenous people and levied taxes in kind—ivory, rubber, and food; the profits thus derived were devoted to pensions for royal relatives and to public works in Belgium. In addition, Leopold established a regime that linked state capitalism with private monopolies in a manner that had no exact parallel in any other European colonial empire: he acquired a half interest in a variety of concession companies —the Société anversoise du commerce au Congo (Anversoise), the Anglo-Belgian Indian Rubber Company (ABIR), and other concerns—controlled by interlocking directorates that were linked to the king. Much to the disgust of trading companies that did not have ties to the royal clique, private trade in rubber and ivory was largely eliminated after 1891.

In some ways, the British South Africa Company's regime in the Rhodesias might be compared with the Free State, but the company's power was held in check to a certain extent by the British Colonial Office, and even more so by local settlers, who were represented in the legislative council of Southern Rhodesia, where the Colonial Office intended them to serve as a check upon the company. The company's administrator, Cecil Rhodes—for all his prejudices and failings —regarded Africans as real people. He had made his money in Africa, and he was willing to risk his life by personally negotiating with rebellious Ndebele chiefs in the Matopos.

To Leopold, however, Africans were a distant abstraction —savage phantoms rather than persons of flesh and blood capable of experiencing joy, grief, or suffering. He was not influenced by the Belgian antislavery lobby, which was incomparably weaker than that of the British, which had managed to turn free labor into a popular cause. Thus in its labor practices the Congo Free State went far beyond the then-accepted standards that sanctioned the use of African conscripts for such "public" services as the construction of roads or the porterage required by civil officials on government duty. The Free State also used forced labor for the production of goods—mainly wild rubber—following the supposed practice of the Dutch in the East Indies. This policy seemed to make good sense in economic terms.

Leopold's financial support was initially slender. Unlike Rhodes, he did not enjoy a stable financial base built upon the command of gold and diamonds. Even the resources of the Belgian state and of foreign as well as Belgian financiers were not enough to meet the demands of Leopold's nascent empire. Like Jules Ferry in France, Leopold lacked widespread metropolitan support for his colonial venture. He had founded his empire at a time when most Belgian bankers were disinclined to risk their clients' savings in what

126

appeared to be a highly speculative undertaking. He therefore had to rely on a relatively small number of capitalists, such as Alexandre-Jean-Marie-de Brown de Tiège (1841-1910), an Antwerp financier. In return for financial favors to the king, these men were able to obtain vast territorial concessions where they were allowed to raise armed forces of their own or to secure the assistance of the Force Publique for the purpose of extorting wild rubber and other natural products from the indigenous peoples. Among the principal concession companies were the Anversoise and the ABIR —which were united in 1911 under the name of Compagnie du Congo belge—the Compagnie du Kasai, the Comité spécial du Katanga (CSK), and Tanganyika Concessions, Ltd.

These concerns were initiated with little capital. ABIR, one of the most notorious early concessionary enterprises, was floated with an initial capital of less than £ 8,000; even the Compagnie du Katanga (CK) and Tanganyika Concessions, Ltd., two of the larger companies, began their operations with an investment of no more than £ 100,000 each. Such ventures made a special appeal to speculators. ABIR's president was Arthur-Constant van den Nest, an Antwerp senator, a financier who had founded the Volksbank at Antwerp, and a keen supporter of Leopold's project. Apart from the Free State government, shareholders in ABIR included men like Count d'Oultremont, a military man who had done well on the stock exchange and in court society.[7]

Another important figure was John Thomas North (1842-1896), a British adventurer whose career symbolized the demimonde aspect of Leopoldine capitalism. An unlettered Yorkshireman from Leeds, young John North had started life as a mechanic. He later emigrated to Latin America, obtained a job on the Chilean railways, became the manager of a nitrate plant, and was soon trading on his own account. He had remarkable organizing ability, and his schemes prospered. He built his own fleet of lighters for loading nitrate onto ships. He returned to England to advertise the advantages of his fertilizers and easily obtained support for the companies he founded, being a man who "breathed sympathy and security." He invested money in railways, coal mines, agricultural lands, and other enterprises that helped to sustain his nitrate empire. His opportunity came during the war between Chile and Peru (1879-1884). Experts predicted that Peru would be beaten, that it would lose its rich nitrate deposits to Chile, and that the victors would then expropriate all existing mines. North, however, decided to gamble on the Chileans' financial orthodoxy. He bought as many Peruvian nitrate deposits as he could, paying rock-bottom prices at a time when Peruvian mines were going cheaply. His speculation paid off. Intimidated perhaps by the sight of the Union Jack that floated over North's company headquarters, the Chileans recognized the titles to his deeds.

North moved back to London, acquired a country seat in Kent, a colonelcy in a Volunteer regiment, and a fine racing stable. These marks of distinction gained him entry into the world of fashion; he also entered that circle of speculative financiers whose money and parvenu life style had such a particular appeal for Leopold.[8] In 1892 North helped to found ABIR. In addition, he placed money into other concession companies, such as the Société de culture in the Congo; he also invested in a luxury hotel in Ostend, an enterprise that aroused some unfavorable comment in the Belgian legislature, where anxious senators feared that the colonel would corrupt Ostend's morals by opening a gambling saloon. North's affairs, however, were apparently of a kind to afford him some anxiety, and he died of apoplexy at the age of fifty-four.[9]

The concession companies of the various financiers were closely tied to the Free State, which either held half the shares in these ventures or became entitled to a fixed portion of their profits. The companies were also tied to the state through the appointment of senior officials to their boards, a practice that was frowned upon in the British and German colonial services. They were further bound to one another

128

through interlocking directorates. Browne de Tiège, the founder of the Caisse hypothécaire anversoise, served as Leopold's financial adviser. He was president of Anversoise and of the Société générale africaine, and he served as *administrateur* of ABIR, the Société internationale forestière et minière du commerce (Forminière), the Société belge de crédit maritime at Antwerp, the Société minoteries et elévateurs à grains (Molinos) at Buenos Aires, and other companies. Browne de Tiège likewise represented the *arrondissement* of Saint Nicolas in the Belgian parliament.

The *administrateurs* of Anversoise included Baron Constant Goffinet, who was also an *administrateur* of the CK, of the Compagnie du chemin de fer du Congo (CCFC), and a senior member of the king's personal household. Another *administrateur* was Edouard-Gustave Bunge of Antwerp, founder of the Compagnie Royale Belgo-Argentine and of the Compagnie cotonnière congolaise, and a president of the Antwerp chamber of commerce. The president of the CSK was Hubert Droogmans (1858-1938), who became *secrétaire général des finances* of the Free State in 1894, and later *secrétaire général* at the Ministry of Colonies, which was formed in 1908. Nicolas Arnold became *directeur des finances* in 1896, *directeur général* under the Free State administration in 1904, and *secrétaire général* at the Ministry of Colonies in 1911. Arnold also sat as the government representative on the boards of the Sociéte du Kilo-Moto, Forminière, and other companies; in addition, he served as president of the Union coloniale belge, the Commission de propagande coloniale scolaire, and other bodies. A third government member was Emile-Joseph de Keyzer, a member of the financial administration of the Free State and a *directeur général*; he served as secretary of the Société financière des caoutchoucs and as *administrateur* of the Société minière de la Luama, the Société minière du Congo septentrional, and other concerns. Major Raymond-Pierre Lombard, who was *secrétaire général* of the Département de l'intérieur of the

Free State and later *directeur général* at the Ministry of Colonies, was also a government member on the directorate of the CSK.

The Free State administration, and later the Belgian Congolese administration, became linked with commercial companies to a much greater extent than did the British colonial administration; former governors of the latter might occasionally join the boards of commercial companies *after* they had retired from the colonial service, but never during their terms of office.

CONSEQUENCES OF THE CONCESSIONS ECONOMY

Having parceled out territory to the concession companies, the Free State administration proceeded to exact goods and services from the Congolese Africans in order to make government profitable.

> A district, having furnished its levy of soldiers and contract workers, is "taxed" for its quota of rubber, porterage, paddlers, and wood or food. (*a*) The villages nearest the white stations are usually drawn on for transport service and for food supplies; the riverine villages for paddlers, fish, and wood; and the interior villages for porterage, and for *chikwanga* (or cassava bread), bananas, game, and other products of agriculture or the chase. (*b*) The more distant villages are called on for rubber. In the case of all these "imposts," no individual can be called on to devote more than forty hours a month to the Government service. Naturally in the case of food, wood, and rubber requisitions, the quantity of produce which this will represent is largely a matter of individual opinion on the part of the local administrators, but there are elaborate regulations governing the method by which in each district the calculation shall be made, and providing for its periodical revision. Payment must be made for all work done at a rate which varies in different districts—absolutely in accord-

ance with the local conditions prevailing, and relatively in accordance with the changing value of the commodities in which it is made. That is to say in one district the native's time may be estimated as worth 5c. an hour; whilst in another it is reckoned at 3c. an hour, and at the same time in the former neighbourhood the cloth or salt, or other merchandise, in which payment is made, may be 33.3 per cent. cheaper than in the latter; so that for forty hours the native in the one place will receive, say, three fathoms of cloth as the equivalent of two francs, and in the other only one and one-fifth fathoms as the equivalent of fcs. 1.20 at the dearer rate.[10]

The severity of these imposts varied widely. Some districts escaped lightly; in others, government exactions were so heavy that the entire local economy might be disrupted. A local producer observing the Leopoldine rubber regime noted:

> The Congo native, when about to gather rubber, generally goes with his fellow-villagers far into the jungle. Then, having formed a rough, shelterless camp, he begins his search for the creepers. Having found one of sufficient size, he cuts with his knife a number of incisions in the bark, and, hanging a small earthenware pot below the vine, allows the sap slowly to trickle into it. Should the creeper have already been tapped, the man must climb into the supporting tree . . . and make an incision in the vine high above the ground . . . and here he will remain, perhaps the whole day, until the flow has ceased. Not infrequently, the natives slumber on their lofty perches, and falling to the ground, become victims to the white man's greed.[11]

Coercion was accompanied by widespread cruelties. The worst outrages occurred in concessionary areas in which the companies imposed their private jurisdictions. Armed African "sentinels" were stationed in the villages to enforce the collection of rubber. In addition, *capitaos* (African supervisors) chosen within the various villages commonly set themselves up as representatives of the state, claiming women and food for both themselves and their followers, terrorizing the population, and displacing the local chiefs. These *capitaos*, who were often former slaves or ex-soldiers, owed their position to the new regime and counted themselves among its most loyal supporters. They were commonly a scourge upon the country. Within Anversoise territory, in an area known as the Mongalla concession,

> Each post had established in the principal villages capita-chiefs—men selected generally on account of their superior intelligence and audacity. These capitas assumed great state among the natives, and had under their command scores of assistants recruited from the scum of the native population. They were supposed to see that the natives collected the rubber, and they ensured this generally by means of blows, and occasionally by a bullet from their "gas pipes." The manager of the "factory" entrusted to the capita-chief a quantity of merchandise, sufficient to pay the natives for their rubber at a rate not exceeding threepence per pound; but the capitas usually appropriated the goods to their own use, and took the rubber without any payment whatever. Some of them had, as the result of these peculations, become the possessors of dozens of wives and many slaves. They literally "ate up" the country by forcing the natives to bring them goats and fowls and other provisions. . . . Some of the capitas had hundreds of armed followers, who went about in bands devastating the villages, ravishing the women and shooting down the men on the slightest provocation. Several of the capitas who had been soldiers had fortified posts, where they assembled their bands and put them through a regular course of drill.[12]

The Congo soon became infamous in Europe as a land where abuses were commonplace. The worst, from the villagers' standpoint, were not the individual outrages—however contemptible—but the steady, unrelenting pressure to which tillers were subjected in rubber-producing districts. The ravages of the rubber collectors were probably worse than those of any indigenous warlord, for an armed host would simply pass through a district, plunder the land, and disappear, whereas the rubber collectors stayed. Congolese serfdom, which was dependent on the use of unskilled labor obtained by conscription, was probably more exploitative than outright slavery, since the "employer" did not own the manpower he used and was under no necessity to maintain his human "capital" in working order.

The fact of widespread atrocities in the Congo is undisputed. The only question concerns their extent and their impact on the many African communities. The question is hard to answer, for the impact of coercion varied immensely. For all the polemics concerning "red rubber," uncoerced trade continued in a variety of products, especially in palm oil and palm kernels. In terms of volume, though not in value, rubber accounted for much less than palm produce. (In 1908, exports from the Congo Free State amounted to 126,000 tons. Of this, 73,000 tons consisted of palm oil and palm kernels, only 45,000 tons consisted of rubber.) By the standards of the late colonial era, moreover, the commerce of the Congo Free State was insignificant. (By 1959, at the end of the colonial period, the Congo's exports of rubber alone amounted to 401,000 tons, fats and oils, 2,607,000, timber, 1,625,000, and coffee, 934,000—not counting other agricultural exports and a vast Congolese trade in minerals.) Above all, the power for good or evil exercised by the Leopoldine administration was strictly limited. Such atrocities as occurred were regional and local in their impact (see Figure 2). Even at the end of Leopold's rule, many Congolese in the remoter regions still did not know that they were supposedly lieges of an alien king. Moreover, the Africans subjected to the "red rubber" regime varied considerably in their capacity for resistance, open or concealed, and in their exposure to foreign exploitation. Many regions were unsuited ecologically to the cultivation of rubber; others were too inaccessible to be touched. Hence contemporary observers of comparable credibility gave diverse answers. Leopold, moreover, did his best to muddy contemporary sources through a well-organized system of direct and indirect bribery to provide him with a favorable press at home and abroad. He also had a substantial number of honest defenders.

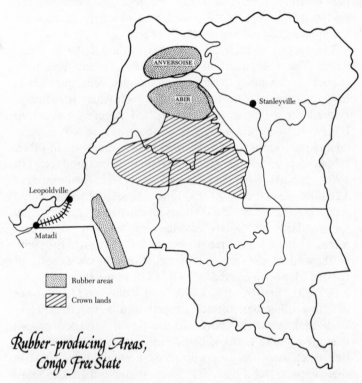

Rubber-producing Areas,
Congo Free State

On the other hand, not all the evidence against Leopold's regime was unbiased. Belgium was not popular; its reputation as a brave little country dates only from World War I. The Belgian record in the colonies became the subject of bitter and sustained criticism of a kind not applied, say, to the Germans.[13] Critics like Captain Guy Burrows of Great Britain, who had himself served under the flag of the Free State and whom we have cited extensively, could see little good in Belgians (or, indeed, in any other foreigners) and condemned the Free State in the strongest terms. His sentiments were common also among British missionaries, many of whom remained totally ignorant of French, had no intention of learning it, and at times referred to the official tongue of the Congo as "the State jargon." Even the most objective evidence—for instance, the type of information extracted by British Consul Roger Casement—by necessity covered only limited areas of the Congo and depended to a considerable extent on secondhand reports that, however honest, did not permit statistical accuracy.[14] (Casement was knighted for his services, but the British Foreign Office was disinclined to alienate Belgium. His Congolese experiences helped to radicalize him with regard to the Irish question; hence Congolese oppression oddly came to be linked with the cause of Irish independence, for which Casement later gave his life.)

Anti–Free State (like anti-Arab) evidence was distorted in other ways. The sight of abandoned villages was a depressing spectacle to an inexperienced European, who assumed that the villagers had fled in terror, not realizing that they might have left to pursue shifting cultivation. Many contemporary observers had well-defined demographic preconceptions, including the assumption that African development was impeded by a fatal manpower deficiency. The future of the continent was supposedly imperiled by a form of inverted Malthusian pressure whereby the capacity of the African soil to produce subsistence greatly exceeded the power of the people to multiply. Intertribal raiding, the practice of polygamy, the atrocities committed by foreign conquerors—Arab, Belgian, Portuguese, or Zulu—were all held responsible in varying degrees for Africa's imagined demographic contraction. These arguments may have exaggerated the loss of human life that was occasioned by conquest, and they probably underestimated the extent to which certain areas might be ravaged not merely by identifiable evildoers like rubber collectors, with their insatiable demands, but also by more impersonal perils such as droughts and locusts, smallpox and sleeping sickness (the latter, in turn, spread by invading armies).

Critics of the Congo Free State, moreover, may also have held Leopold responsible for atrocities committed by indigenous warlords who responded to rising rubber prices by intensifying raids for slaves and rubber. The Belgians did not invent coercive labor in the Congo region. Lovale or Chokwe attacks on the Lunda, for example, led to widespread devastation of a kind that can not be charged to Leopold's greed. Indigenous chiefs had been perfectly willing to benefit from price changes in rubber and ivory by waging new wars or by extorting more goods and services from their subjects. Even within a particular rubber-producing region, the Belgian impact was uneven. The Bolobo area investigated by Anstey, for instance, was first terrorized by a local tyrant; conditions improved when Auguste Dooms, a new man, took over the area and governed in a more enlightened manner. In many cases, abuses resulted from lack of supervision and, indeed, from the very weakness of the administrative machine itself. Certain areas of the Free State suffered little or not at all; the Lower Congo region seems to have been noticeably freer from oppression, although demands for porterage exacted a heavy toll until the railway system was completed.

But however humane the Free State officials might be, they could not avoid the temptations of a system in which official salaries were supplemented by allowances whose size depended on the number of rubber bales or ivory tusks that were collected by local administrators.[15] In 1905, for example, Wahis complained that the Ponthiersville *zone* produced no more than 78 kilos of ivory and 14,382 kilos of rubber; he considered that there was no lack of rubber in the region and enjoined the *chef de zone* to improve his yield.[16] Civil servants were under constant pressure to furnish wealth; their work was evaluated according to their ability to produce revenue. Without any doubt, the worst abuses occurred in areas that were under the direct control of concession companies. According to Mountmorres:

the atrocious condition prevailing in the areas under the control of the Concession Companies has been ably and amply testified to by the missionary witnesses, resident in the district, as well as by Mr. Consul Casement in his able report. On the other hand, many travellers who have visited other parts of the Independent State have unhesitatingly and emphatically repudiated the suggestion that the state of affairs existing in the ABIR and Lulonga territories is to be found throughout the remainder of the State. The deduction so frequently drawn from the vivid and unquestionably true accounts, sent home by missionaries working in the Concessions districts, . . . that their remarks apply to the whole State, is an entirely unsound one.[17]

A mere catalog of atrocities committed by individual company officials, administrators, and their agents in the bush does not reveal the full weight of the economic exploitation that was borne by the villagers. Ernst Vohsen, a German free trader, humanitarian, and businessman, reported that the Belgians were destroying the country's long-term prospects for prosperity. By excluding all competitors and by using methods of coercion, the Belgian administration deliberately depressed the prices that would normally have been paid to indigenous cultivators. Africans were forced to collect rubber and to provide food and labor to government stations and military posts. Under such a regime, Vohsen continued, the indigenous people had nothing left to sell. The Congolese peoples, given this state of affairs, could never develop into "a nation of customers."[18]

Trade statistics published by Belgian statisticians reveal

the exploitative nature of Free State rule more clearly than the most dramatic tales of individual abuses. Infant colonies normally import more than they export; they have to spend money on railways, port facilities, and other investments that yield profits only after many years. In the Congo, however, exports considerably exceeded imports during the early years of the present century (see Chapter Five, Table 15). This pattern, which sharply differentiated the Belgian Congo from colonies such as German East Africa, continued until the end of the 1920s, when mining development in the Katanga and other areas radically changed both the volume and structure of Congolese commerce.

The social consequences of the "red-rubber" regime were far-reaching. Belgian *Raubwirtschaft* widened existing cleavages within African society. Within the dominions of the Compagnie du Kasai, for instance, the company assisted potentates such as King Lukenga, a Kuba monarch who maintained a private army that was subsidized by the company for the purpose of enforcing rubber tributes. In addition, the Belgians created a newly privileged class of *capitaos* and soldiers.[19] There was increased pressure on women, who were obliged to furnish manioc bread to their menfolk working in the forest. Its production required a good deal of labor —extracting the meal from the roots, cleaning, and boiling— and the bread could be preserved only for a few days. Hence the never-ending demand for the labor of men in the forest stepped up the demand for the labor of women at home. Additional requirements included the hauling of produce over long distances to government stations. As villages were taxed collectively, their headmen were placed under increased pressure to put their dependents to work.[20] Free State exactions, moreover, fostered domestic slavery. Domestic industries decayed, and domestic purchasing power probably declined. The impact of the red-rubber regime was unequal even within the rubber-producing forest region. Some communities, such as the Bashilele, were able to resist Belgian pressure to some extent; they insisted on supplying rubber only as part of "legitimate trade" and probably benefited from rising demands. Other groups, such as the Kuba, suffered severely.

Above all, *Raubwirtschaft* occasioned widespread flight or armed resistance. In the Kasai district, Free State exactions led to bitter hostility against Bula Matadi, the Free State regime, which resorted to imprisoning women as a means of compelling their menfolk to work. Indigenous warriors composed new battle songs:

> We cannot endure that our women and children are taken
> And dealt with by white savages.
> We shall make war against Bula Matadi.
> We know that we shall die, but we want to die.
> We want to die.[21]

African resistance was widespread, effective, and caused far-reaching economic damage to the red-rubber administration. A report from the Département de l'intérieur in 1906 sounded a note of desperation:

> Conditions have gone from bad to worse. . . . If nothing is done, rubber production will cease entirely. In the *secteur* of Lilanghi, for instance, the natives are now more hostile than ever before. They have attacked the *chef de poste* three times in succession, and the post will have to be temporarily abandoned. In the Basankusu *secteur*, the Africans are so recalcitrant that payment of taxes has ceased. The situation is no better in the basin of the Lomako river where the entire M'Pussu *secteur* is in revolt. The natives in the Mompono *secteur* refuse to work. The post of Dilolo has been cut off by rebels. Small Belgian parties are being ambushed and slain. The Kioko try to interrupt all communications between Katola and Dilomais; they are probably being assisted by merchants from Bihé who object to the Congolese regime. In the Lisaka *secteur*, many Africans have fled. In the Waka *secteur* in Equateur province the yield of rubber has much declined.

139

The police at our disposal is inadequate. If nothing is done rubber production will further diminish, or cease altogether.[22]

In short, the red-rubber economy occasioned widespread misery, disrupted existing networks of trade, and interfered with the enterprise of African tillers and artisans. Some Africans benefited—primarily the *capitaos* in European employ. Some managed to adjust themselves to new conditions; unemployed African traders, for instance, sometimes found new jobs as sailors on river vessels. Canoemen learned how to reorient their trade to shorter routes or to European requirements. By and large, however, the economics of coercion brought a disaster.

THE *REPRISE*

THE END OF THE CONGO FREE STATE

THE Congo Free State remains a classic example of the evils that beset a coercive economy. Private monopolies in partnership with the state proved efficient as a means of bloody oppression, but they failed even on their own terms as instruments of development. The vast productive resources of the Congo basin—superior to those of any West African colony—remained underdeveloped. By 1912 the worst abuses had been eliminated, and the Congo was exporting more tropical crops than ever before. Yet the colony still lagged far behind British colonies like Nigeria and the Gold Coast. (In 1912 Nigerian exports amounted to twice the value of those of the Belgian Congo: $31.976 million versus $15.858 million, respectively.) Development in British West Africa, and also in the German "model colony" of Togo, depended on a partnership among overseas trading concerns, African middlemen, and African cultivators working for the world market. This model, based on free and noncoercive enterprise and acceptable to missionary and humanitarian opinion alike, worked extremely well; coercion in the Togo and the Gold Coast was restrained to a minimum. British rule in West Africa required far fewer men under arms than Belgian rule in the Congo, while the Germans in Togo retained only a few hundred armed policemen.

The Belgians in Leopold's colony, on the other hand, had acquired a well-merited reputation for brutality. The Congo could easily have become a major source of palm oil and palm kernels produced by free cultivators possessing little skill and almost no capital. Instead, the economic development of the Free State was distorted by the domination of the rubber economy. Rubber accounted for the major part of the colony's exports, but the red-rubber regime represented a form of *Raubwirtschaft* that was bound to be self-destructive. The tapping of wild rubber destroyed the *landolphia* plant on which the industry depended. From 1907 onward, rubber prices dropped. Wild rubber produced by unskilled and unwilling conscripts was usually of low quality and could not compete with the plantation-grown product cultivated by freely contracted workmen under expert supervision. After 1900 Malaya, the Dutch East Indies, Ceylon, and India became substantial plantation producers capable of turning out a raw material that was far superior to the wild rubber obtained in Africa or in the Amazon basin of Brazil. By 1927 wild rubber accounted for no more than 6 percent of world rubber production.

Measured by world standards of a later day, the production of red rubber by coercive means had yielded insignificant quantities. The labor dues exacted from Africans had entailed multiple atrocities; but the impact of such coercion was uneven, and output remained relatively small. Alexandre Delcommune, a Belgian board member of the CSK, calculated that in 1901, when rubber exports were at their highest, the Congo exported only six thousand tons. This rubber was harvested by an estimated five hundred thousand adult taxpayers dwelling within the rubber-producing regions of the Congo. The average yield per worker therefore amounted to no more than twelve kilos per year. Most of the adult population, which was reckoned at two million, produced no rubber.[1]

Red-rubber production, in other words, was economically inefficient. The arbitrary nature of the rubber regime also would have proved incompatible with the needs of a modern mining economy, which the Free State was anxious to promote both for fiscal reasons and for profit. From its earliest days the Free State had attempted to unlock new mineral wealth, especially gold. The mining potential of its fief, especially the copper resources of Katanga, had always been of primary interest. In 1891 Leopold chartered the Compagnie du Katanga (CK), and during the early 1890s Jules Cornet (1865-1929), a much-publicized geologist acting under the auspices of the CK, made several important discoveries concerning the copper deposits in Katanga. The CK joined the Free State in 1900 in setting up the Comité spécial du Katanga (CSK),[2] which received far-reaching—almost unlimited—administrative and economic powers; it became responsible for the entire government of Katanga, except for justice, mail services, and tax collection. At the same time, the CSK conceded a prospecting monopoly to Tanganyika Concessions, Ltd., a British group represented by Robert Williams, whose concern supplied much of the technical expertise in the field of gold exploitation that the Belgians still lacked. J. M. Holland and George Grey (a younger brother of Sir Edward Grey, the British foreign secretary) further explored the region. They realized what Cornet earlier had failed to grasp: from a commercial standpoint the low-grade Katanga copper deposits could be successfully worked. Copper, rather than the hoped-for gold, became the mainstay of the country's mining economy.

Belgian capital rested on two main pillars: the financial establishment of Antwerp and the great Brussels companies. The CK, the CCFC, the CCCI were all centered on Brussels; the ABIR and Anversoise were part of a minor financial complex based in Antwerp. In addition, Forminière began to exploit the diamond discoveries of the Kasai and also moved into neighboring Angola.

In order to mine the copper wealth discovered by Tanganyika Concessions, the Belgians in 1906 created a new body known as the Union minière du Haut Katanga, a powerful trust supported by both British and Belgian capital. Williams served as the company's first vice-president. Its first president, Baron Ferdinand Baeyens, the governor of the Société générale, was succeeded in 1913 by Jean Jadot, a

143

railway engineer with international experience and far-flung mining connections. Jadot was also Baeyens's successor at the Société générale.

Jadot was one of Belgium's financial giants. He had helped to develop railways as far afield as Egypt and China, and he had an important stake in the metallurgical industry of Russia, which he helped to reorganize in 1906. In the same year he restructured the financial establishment of the Congo, and the Société générale began to make considerable investments in Congolese mining and railway ventures. Jadot also succeeded in attracting a good deal of foreign support, and prominent Britons such as Williams and Lord Arthur Butler joined Jadot's board. Foreign participation in Congolese financial affairs was in turn welcomed by Leopold, who looked to these wealthy aliens not merely for cash but also for respectability at a time when the Congo Free State was being bitterly assailed for its administrative abuses.

The formation of the Union minière marked a shift in the policy of the Société générale, which began to take a more active part in colonial investments. Enormous concessions were granted: in all, the Free State allocated a total of twenty-seven million hectares to mining, railway, rubber, and other companies. In return for these favors, foreign capitalists became somewhat more willing to risk their money in the Congo. Mining could at last be financed on a larger scale, particularly the mining of copper, which was becoming increasingly profitable. During the 1890s the demand for copper rose rapidly as electric lighting began to replace gas lighting in many parts of the world, as horse-drawn trams were giving way to electric trams, and as more turbines were being installed overseas. The resultant rise in copper prices made extensive prospecting worthwhile and produced a copper boom that reached its height in 1899. A good deal of developmental work accordingly was done in the Congo, where production on a substantial scale got under way during World War I (production rose from a mere 998 tons in

1911 to 85,570 tons in 1924). At the same time, miners, contractors, artisans, and adventurers—most of them British —began to move into Katanga from the south. These new-comers created their own kind of frontier society, at first linked more closely to the Rhodesias and South Africa than to Belgium and controlled only tenuously by the Belgians, who viewed these immigrants with as much suspicion as Kruger had shown toward British *uitlanders* on the Rand.

Mining in turn depended on additional railway develop-ment. Already in 1891 the CCCI, which was originally set up as a trading firm, had begun to go into the railway-building business when it became associated with the construction of the Chemin de fer Matadi-Léopoldville. Subsequently, the powerful Empain group participated in a railway-building venture designed to serve the eastern Congo. In 1909 the Rhodesian railways linked up with the Katanga system and thereby revolutionized the logistics of Central Africa. Once the line was completed, miners could move heavy ores to the south and ship them overseas through the port of Beira. Stores and heavy mining equipment from South Africa, coal from the Wankie mines in Southern Rhodesia, and maize and beef from Northern Rhodesia could be moved in, providing a double traffic for the railways and indispensable supplies for Katanga.

In 1911 the Union minière began to produce copper on a commercial scale. Elisabethville, the capital of Katanga, turned into a new center of power. John Springer, an Ameri-can missionary, described the transformation:

> The change at Elisabethville was indeed marvelous. Only nine months before I had seen them beginning to fell the trees for the streets. Now we came to a town with twenty miles of well laid-out streets with a population of more than one thousand Europeans, living for the most part, at this stage, in mud huts, wood and iron houses, and many under buck-sails (water-proof canvas). From being

145

a wilderness ten months before Elisabethville had leaped in one year to . . . the largest settlement of Europeans in the entire Belgian Congo.[3]

In addition, African labor migrants began to move to Katanga. The Congo increasingly became dependent on a highly capitalized mining economy.

Even before this economic revolution had been accomplished, however, the Belgian king found himself under severe political and moral attack from a variety of groups, both foreign and domestic, both interested and disinterested. Critics abroad asserted that Free State affairs were not simply an internal matter, that the king, who had obtained his authority under an international mandate, had violated a sacred trust. The Congo might be better off if it were partitioned among the great powers. British and German merchants especially resented Belgian interference with freedom of commerce. Protestant missionaries—British, American, and others—likewise took up the cudgels against an administration they regarded as both oppressive and pro-Catholic. Congo agitation thus acquired religious and ideological overtones as Protestant clerics worked in alliance with anticlericals, both Liberal and Socialist, within the Belgian legislature. The religious conflict spilled over into the Congo, where strong-minded missionaries like William McCutchan Morrisson, an American Calvinist, tried to act like a territorial chief endowed with sovereign powers. In the Kasai province, for example, Protestant and Catholic evangelists accused one another of practicing every kind of sin, original and not so original; fights and affrays were matters of common occurrence. Friction grew so serious that even during World War I American Presbyterians continued to regard the Catholics rather than the Germans as their main enemy.[4]

Whatever the truth or falsehood of the charges and countercharges hurled against the king, the anti-Congo lobbies were well organized, and their attacks proved extremely effective. The Congo Free State, like the Ottoman monarchy, became a major object of humanitarian agitation. The international conscience was highly selective. No comparable indignation raged against German military practices toward the Herero or against British action with regard to the Australian Blackfellows; instead, the "unspeakable Belgian" joined the "unspeakable Turk" in the cabinet of international horrors.

International agitation added to the bitterness of political recrimination within the métropole. The Congo question played a role in Belgium similar to that of the Dreyfus affair in France. The majority of Belgians initially regarded Leopold's critics as a contemptible clique of freethinking or Protestant fanatics, traitors resolved upon depriving Belgium of its African birthright, paid assuredly from secret funds supplied by Liverpool and Bremen merchants. Belgian patriots had destroyed the slave trade; Belgian missionaries were spreading the Gospel; Belgian administrators assured the peace in "Darkest Africa." Belgians need not shy from comparison with any other colonizers. No other power, for instance, specifically enjoined its civil servants to abstain from armed enterprises except in the case of self-defense.[5] No other colonial power laid down in writing that native commissioners must at all times peacefully negotiate before using violence to obtain redress for injuries committed against the state. Leopold had particularly strong support among the kinds of people who backed the army against the Dreyfusards in France: military men, serving and retired civil servants, the bulk of the Catholic clergy, the *bien pensants* in business and the professions. Belgium also developed a number of organized lobbies that continued to be active long after the Congo crisis had been settled. These included the Groupement des pensionnés civiques de l'Etat du Congo (presided over by Major General Richard), the Association des anciens coloniaux (headed by Colonel Bertrand), and the Ligue coloniale belge.

Nevertheless, support for Belgium's colonial mission and support for the king's personal regime were by no means synonymous. In Belgium there was increasing opposition to the Congo Free State from many parts of the political spectrum —liberal Catholics, anticlerical Liberals, and Socialists. Studies such as Professor Félicien Cattier's *Etude sur la situation de l'Etat indépendant du Congo* (1906) and Father Arthur Vermeersch's *La Question congolaise* (1906) made a considerable impression, as did interpretations in the Belgian parliament put forward by men like Emile Vandervelde, Belgium's leading Socialist. After an exhaustive enquiry into the state of affairs in the Congo in 1906, even the king's clerical supporters began to have second thoughts. A critic of the Leopoldine regime wrote that "all those Jesuits, all those White Fathers, all those Redemptorists, all those Trappists, and all those Prémontrés resembled the Saxon Army which had begun the battle of Leipzig fighting on Napoleon's side, and ended by turning their arms against the French Emperor."[6]

The Congo Free State initiated a number of reforms. The Anversoise and ABIR companies were required to relinquish certain of their privileges. Although coercion continued to be applied in a variety of ways, Belgians gradually began to give somewhat greater emphasis to economic incentives in promoting indigenous production. The volume of trade goods imported for African use began to increase. The tremendous gap between exports from the Congo and imports into the country started to diminish with the construction of railways, mines, and other ventures (see Tables 14 and 15).

The new economic order went hand in hand with political reorganization. Except for the two Rhodesias, "private government" by chartered companies or royal potentates increasingly seemed an anachronism in an age of reform. The old arguments for private colonization were no longer valid. Colonial government through a nominally independent Congo Free State had failed to secure Belgium from international entanglements; on the contrary, Belgium had become the object of international odium. The change was all the more threatening at a time when the Anglo-French entente of 1904

TABLE 14

Congolese Imports Destined for Africans, 1893-1912
(In Belgian Francs)

Year	Total Value
1893	3,180,906
1898	7,215,773
1901	9,392,243
1908	11,511,189
1912	14,361,689

SOURCE: Alexandre Delcommune, *L'Avenir du Congo belge menacé: Bilan des dix premières années (1909-1918) d'administration coloniale gouvernementale; le mal—le remède* (Brussels, 1919), pp. 282, 283, 291.

TABLE 15

Value of Congolese Imports and Exports, 1890-1912
(In Belgian Francs)

Year	Imports	Exports
1890	(unknown)	8,242,199
1895	10,685,584	10,943,019
1900	24,724,109	47,377,401
1905	20,075,362	53,032,263
1910	36,846,508	66,602,295
1915	23,453,243	71,994,714
1920	237,543,767	315,245,514
1928	1,624,498,658	1,227,867,419

SOURCE: Louis Franck, *Le Congo belge*, 2 vols. (Brussels, 1928), 1:437.

had prevented Leopold from continuing to play off the British against the French and when German *Weltpolitik* and German designs for a great *Mittelafrika* appeared ever more menacing.

Royal colonialism, moreover, had failed in its promise of economy. In 1884 the king had assured his people that the Congo would never become a charge on the Belgian exchequer. But Belgium had become increasingly involved in

Congolese affairs by lending the taxpayers' money to its sovereign. From the king's standpoint, Belgian annexation of the Free State would allay both foreign criticisms and domestic attacks by Socialists and Radicals. For the first time, moreover, the Congolese enterprise had acquired a certain degree of popularity among national-minded Belgians. It no longer seemed a quixotic adventure. Attacks upon their king by supposedly envious foreigners and treacherous clerics merely encouraged patriotic Belgians to rally to their sovereign. There was no serious alternative to takeover by the Belgian government. No Belgian politician suggested that the Congo be sold to a foreign power. No reformer ever proposed that the Belgians should remove their abuses from the Congo by removing themselves. A straightforward evacuation of the Congo would have left the entire region prey to civil strife; more likely still, other European powers would have partitioned the region among themselves.

In 1906, therefore, the Belgian Chamber voted by an overwhelming majority (128 ayes against 2 nayes and 29 abstentions) in favor of an *ordre du jour* that rendered homage to the Congolese achievement while affirming Belgium's right to the Congo. In 1907 a new treaty of cession was presented to the Belgian legislature, where it met with a good deal of controversy. An additional act was approved in 1908 to modify one of the most objectionable features of the treaty —a clause by which the monarch retained control over the vast regions within the Congo that he had designated as his *domaine privé*. After lengthy negotiations, Belgium agreed to take over the Congo. The Socialists bitterly attacked the deal, but the Right held fast. On 20 August 1908 the Chamber passed a law providing for annexation of the colony. The king still did well on this operation, which was often referred to as *la reprise*. As Bruce Fetter's research shows, the monarch had spent nearly thirty million francs (about one million pounds) on his colonial venture. In the end he profited from his investment.

Belgium undertook to respect financial interests of both the king and the great mining companies. The nation would honor the vast concessions granted under the Leopoldine regime; the small white prospector and the mining entrepreneur, who were to play such a major part in Rhodesian history, were largely kept out of the Congo. Like Northern Rhodesia, the Congo remained a corporate country par excellence, a land whose mining economy came to be dominated by a small group of companies with interlocking directorates. But to a far greater extent than in any British territory under the Colonial Office, these enterprises were closely tied to the state.[7] Mining concerns such as the CSK retained the vast land concessions that had been bestowed upon them during the Free State regime. The Belgian government, for its part, received a large amount of real and personal property belonging to the Free State, together with stock in various Congo companies that had previously been owned by the state.

Excluding the value of residual rights in the unalienated land, the total value of the property that was handed over to the new government by the Free State came to 110,337,000 francs. Within the context of Belgian finance as a whole, this sum was not large; Belgium's total domestic revenue in 1908 was 770,451,000 francs. But in Congolese terms, the nation acquired an enormously powerful position, chiefly owing to mining and railway concerns. In addition, the authorities held two-thirds of the capital of the CSK.

The Congolese taxpayer was left with responsibility not only for the Free State's debt of 110 million francs but also for a "gratitude fund" given to the king "in testimony for his great sacrifice in favor of the Congo created by him," as well as for another 40 million francs for the so-called Niederfulbach Foundation, one of the king's financial instruments, which was ultimately transferred to the Belgian state in 1923.

THE FREE STATE: A BALANCE SHEET

A final balance sheet for the Free State is not easy to draw up. Within less than a quarter of a century the Free State had occupied an immense territory and imposed a uniform government upon most of the region it claimed. The modern state of Zaïre is the unintended creation of Leopold and his ministers. Bula Matadi had largely done away with internecine warfare and had liquidated the independent power of Swahili-speaking adventurers and warlords. The old-fashioned slave trade had ceased. The new rulers had begun a modern transport system, and by 1912, 1,235 kilometers of railways and 3,810 kilometers of telegraph lines were in operation. The Free State had also laid the foundations for many modern cities of the Congo. These included the main port of Matadi, situated about a hundred miles upstream from the mouth of the Congo, the starting point of a rail line to Léopoldville; Boma, then the capital, a river port and railhead; and Léopoldville (now Kinshasa), situated on Stanley Pool along the river, the terminus of navigation on the Congo from Stanleyville (now Kisangani) and of the railroad from Matadi, splendid in its colorful tropical vegetation. A start had been made toward building a modern mining industry, and by 1913 the Union minière was turning out six thousand tons of copper a year. The growing city of Elisabethville (now Lubumbashi), a rough-and-ready diggers' camp in Katanga, ultimately developed into the country's second city.

These new population centers, which were very different from the "agro-towns" built by immigrant Arab and indigenous Lunda rulers, served specialized functions and depended on imported food. Soon they began to attract a growing number of Africans, who dwelt, for the most part, in rough shacks without much supervision from the whites or guidance by tribal authorities. The population of these new settlements included workmen employed by the administration and by foreign firms, domestic servants, women who lived in more or less temporary unions with men who had found work in the townships, street vendors, entertainers, roughs and bully boys—all uniformly referred to as "idlers" or "vagabonds" in contemporary Belgian literature. This urban element, probably numbering no more than a few thousand at the time of the *reprise*, formed a tiny minority among the great mass of Congolese who continued to make a scanty living from the land.

The Free State controlled but a small portion of its territory; many indigenous communities had as yet escaped European control or were in a state of revolt until as late as the 1920s. Nevertheless, the Free State had created the foundations of a Western-style army and a Western-style administration. Missionaries had started churches, schools, hospitals, dispensaries, and workshops. Following the practical and utilitarian bent that was to characterize Belgian administration in later years, the Free State administration had set up a few technical institutions at Boma, Léopoldville, and Stanleyville, where orphan children followed three-year courses designed to turn out noncommissioned officers, clerks, and craftsmen. In addition, the Belgians had created a botanical garden at Eala where they trained African agricultural assistants and carried out research on species of native and imported plants. Soldiers, missionaries, and civil servants had contributed to the scientific exploration of the Congo; they had worked in fields as varied as linguistics, cartography, and ethnography. In Belgium itself, colonial studies were being promoted by a newly founded museum that was transferred to Tervuren in 1897 and was known as the Musée du Congo belge.

In 1906 the Belgians founded the Ecole de médicine tropicale at Brussels, whose graduates later played an impressive part in improving health conditions in the Congo. Although a beginning had been made in the struggle against such tropical disease as smallpox and sleeping sickness, these efforts had not had much effect by 1908. In all probability the demographic explosion that characterized the later colonial period of the Congo was only about to begin. The experts represented on the Commission permanente pour la protection des indigènes were in fact convinced—quite rightly— that the country's demographic situation was worsening rather than improving. In their view, military campaigns had

153

helped to spread sleeping sickness and diseases such as syphilis; labor migrants were apt to contract pulmonary infections and dysentery; and whites had imported new scourges,
such as tuberculosis, cerebrospinal meningitis, and influenza.
Labor migration produced a high death rate that began to
decline only after World War I.[8]

Belgian savants imagined that the institution of polygamy
stood in the way of demographic growth, on the grounds
that elderly men were apt to marry a large number of nubile
young women who were thus denied large families of their
own, and scholars found some evidence in favor of this demographic assumption. The *chef de secteur* in charge of the
chiefdoms of Sakarombi and the Lubunsula chiefdoms of
Mokeke, Moera, Busamba, Kiota, and Kilongozi in Kivu was
convinced that polygamy had a dysgenic effect. Unlike many
of his contemporaries, he believed that women enjoyed a
considerable measure of freedom in African society. Each
polygamous spouse had her own hut, and divorce was common. Wives, moreover, were protected against abuses by their
husbands through the custom of paying bridewealth, which
varied from five to fifteen goats for each wife. However beneficent its social effects, polygamy had untoward demographic consequences. Within the chiefdoms under survey,
some 50 percent of all adult men from fourteen years of age
upward were unmarried. Thirty percent of the marriages
were monogamous, and 20 percent of the married men had
ten or more wives. Chiefs with many wives had only a few
children; Kengele, a great dignitary, had between 100 and
150 wives but only six offspring. The position was made
worse by a high rate of infant mortality; six out of ten children in the area died before the end of their first year.[9]

Faced with an assumed demographic decline, the more
advanced and conscientious Belgian administrators wished
to promote a policy of what they called *moralisation*, the
Belgian equivalent of "trusteeship" in the British colonies
and *Fürsorge* in the German colonies. Designed to improve
working conditions, combat infectious diseases, reduce al-

coholism, and lessen the incidence of polygamy, this policy
was intended to improve the health of the people and to cure
the assumed labor shortage that was suspected of impeding
the territory's economic development.

At the same time, Belgian and foreign lenders had begun
to invest in the Congo, albeit on a moderate scale. In 1906
the total value of Belgian commercial investments in the
colony was estimated at 143 million francs; foreign investments were valued at 40 million. By the standards of the metropolitan economy these figures were insignificant, amount-
ing to no more than a small fraction of Belgium's total trade
(in 1906, Belgium's imports alone were valued at 3,454 million francs). But within the Congolese context, these sums
represented a considerable transfer of capital undertaken at
high risk.

On the other hand, occupation had entailed a great deal
of bloodshed and abuse. The Belgians employed forced labor
not merely in exploiting the country's rubber and ivory resources but also for building roads, and to a lesser extent,
for constructing railways. Conquest had laid an immense burden upon backward agricultural economies, whose precarious surpluses of food and manpower had been used to sub-
sidize the process of white occupation. In addition, the Free
State experiment had imposed a heavy financial burden on
the Congo. It was the most debt-ridden of all European colonies in Africa, carrying a charge more than twice that of
Nigeria, three times that of French West Africa, and more
than eight times that of German East Africa.[10] Alone among
the colonial powers, Belgium, with its strong anticolonial
bent, had refused all financial aid to its colony. Moreover,
according to Jean Stengers's calculations, the Congo Free
State offered the unique spectacle (unique, at any rate, at
the beginning of the twentieth century) of a colonial state
whose public resources were in part transferred to the mother
country. Belgium paid about 40 million francs to the Free
State in direct and indirect disbursements. In return, it
received more than 60 million, thereby violating the then-

accepted rule that a metropolitan power should no longer impose direct tributes upon a dependency.[11] Within the context of Belgian finance, the sum transferred was negligible. In 1908 Belgium's total expenditure amounted to 770,451,-000 francs (at a time when the franc stood at $0.193), so that the surplus transmitted from the Congo to Belgium during the Free State period amounted to less than 3 percent of the Belgian national expenditure within a single year. Nevertheless, for an infant colony the sums involved were considerable—more than half of the Free State's financial receipts in 1908—and they were out of proportion to the benefits obtained by the mother country through these transactions.

In a wider sense, the Congo Free State had created a new society. Twenty years before the *reprise* only a handful of whites were in the Congo; by 1910 the number of Europeans was estimated at 4,003 (exact information is hard to come by, given the enormous size of the territory and the transient nature of the European immigrant group). The white community was itself sharply divided by internal cleavages. The poorest and least-considered stratum consisted of petty bush traders, Portuguese, and later Greeks; their social role was comparable in some measure to that of the Lebanese in West Africa and the Indians in East Africa. Katanga contained a substantial number of British miners, traders, prospectors, and engineers. Their dominant position within the new Katangan economy, their bumptious jingoism and irreverent frontier spirit caused many Belgians to regard them as a threat to Belgian sovereignty. The Belgians would not forget the Jameson Raid (an unsuccessful venture by which Rhodes, in 1895, had tried to overthrow the established government of the Transvaal), and they confused the new spirit of financial respectability that ruled the British South Africa Company's headquarters in London with the old buccaneering manner that had prevailed in the unregenerate days of Rhodes.

The missionaries formed another out-group. The various missionary communities lived in what to the ordinary white resident was almost a separate universe; they had their own schools, their own workshops, their own churches, their own hospitals, even their own villages, and they exercised what sometimes amounted to limited local sovereignties. They were split into different religions, different missionary societies and different missionary orders, and they all too often denounced their competitors as fiercely as they did the heathen. Politically, the Catholics tended to favor Belgian rule much more than did the Protestants, with their Anglo-Saxon orientation. Whereas Protestant missionaries presented a good deal of evidence that rendered the Congo Free State a byword for rapine, most Catholic ecclesiastics went out of their way to defend Leopold and his empire. These included such men as Bishop Victor Roelens, the head of the White Fathers in the Congo, who felt that the abuses committed in the Congo were no worse than those practiced in other European colonies. The bishop had no doubt that Belgian rule at its worst was immeasurably superior to the tyranny of Muslim slave traders, whose depredations he had experienced in the Upper Congo.[12]

The most powerful and the most numerous component of white society consisted of military officers and civil servants, who comprised more than one-third of the white population. Their ethos was to dominate the Congo throughout the colonial era and beyond. But the official structure was far from homogeneous. We have already alluded to the clear-cut divisions in rank, remuneration, and status that divided the official establishment. These were complicated by ideological dissensions. The missionaries stood for a Christian Europe; the ordinary Belgian resident, however, would have no truck with priest or pastor. Out of a hundred whites inhabiting Matadi in 1907, not one would go to Mass on Sunday; in Boma, the capital, only twenty out of two hundred were willing to attend church.[13] To this indifference was added the active hostility generated by the forces of anticlericalism. In 1900 the Grand Orient, a Masonic body, decided to open a Masonic lodge in the Congo for the purpose of countering missionary influence, on the ground that Catholic evangelization constituted neither real progress nor a necessary stage in development.

THE NEW REGIME

On 1 November 1908 Belgium assumed direct administrative powers over the Congo. The Free State regime was ended. "International colonization," which had once been touted by idealists as the sovereign means for introducing backward peoples to Christianity and free trade, had ended in a grubby bargain. The old Free State flag, bright blue with a gold star, continued to float over the Congo until decolonization in 1960, however, when it was hauled down to join that great array of disused emblems beloved by antiquarians but forgotten by the world at large. Free State colonialism became, so to speak, a Belgian national enterprise, and Belgium started upon an unexpectedly short-lived career as a colonial power.

In December 1909 Leopold died; he was succeeded by his nephew, Albert I, a popular and progressive man in his thirties who was far more attractive as an individual than his uncle had been. A new era appeared to open in the Congo, and in the constitutional sphere there was indeed considerable change. Under the Charte coloniale, which had been approved along with the Treaty of Cession and the Acte additional by the Belgian Chamber on 20 August and by the Senate on 9 September 1908, all executive and legislative decisions made in the king's name had to be countersigned by the newly appointed minister of colonies, who was both a parliamentarian and a member of the cabinet—a man who might wield substantial influence, provided his power was not restricted by that brevity of tenure in a particular office that so often distinguished a Belgian minister's career.

The king of the Belgians ceased to be the absolute sovereign of the Congo. Instead, the makers of the Charte coloniale created a system that was designed to exercise centralized rule from Brussels (see Figure 3). Their object was

158

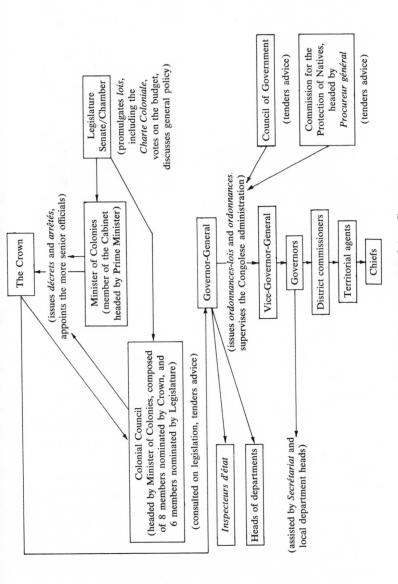

The Formal Structure of Belgian Government

The Crown
(issues *décrets* and *arrêtés*, appoints the more senior officials)

Legislature Senate/Chamber
(promulgates *lois*, including the *Charte Coloniale*, votes on the budget, discusses general policy)

Minister of Colonies
(member of the Cabinet headed by Prime Minister)

Colonial Council
(headed by Minister of Colonies, composed of 8 members nominated by Crown, and 6 members nominated by Legislature)
(consulted on legislation, tenders advice)

Governor-General
(issues *ordonnances-lois* and *ordonnances*, supervises the Congolese administration)

Council of Government
(tenders advice)

Commission for the Protection of Natives, headed by *Procureur général*
(tenders advice)

Inspecteurs d'état

Heads of departments

Vice-Governor-General

Governors

District commissioners

Territorial agents

Chiefs

(assisted by *Secrétariat* and local department heads)

to stamp out abuses in the Congo. They were equally anxious to limit the powers of the Belgian monarchy, whose influence had aroused fears among right-wingers and left-wingers alike.[14]

In actual practice, these changes were not as striking as the new constitution indicated. Opposition papers such as *Le Peuple* pointed out that the new regime did not guarantee, even for Belgian nationals, any of those constitutional liberties—freedom of speech, of the press, of association—to which Belgians had become accustomed at home. From the constitutional standpoint, a British subject under the regime of the Chartered Company in the two Rhodesias thus continued to enjoy a considerably greater degree of liberty than did his Belgian contemporary on the other side of the Northern Rhodesia border. There was no legislative council of the British kind; neither the settlers nor the Africans received any representation. Foced labor was not formally outlawed, and it continued under a variety of guises, albeit in a more humane fashion. The Belgian Chamber refused to accept responsibility for the Congolese debts—much to the chagrin of procolonial groups who would have liked the Belgian taxpayer to take a larger share in developing Belgium's African patrimony. There were no major changes in personnel. De Cuvelier and Liebrechts, the two former *secrétaires généraux* who had been closely associated with Leopold's personal regime, retired, as did the former treasurer general; the remaining Free State officials continued to serve under the new Belgian administration. Droogmans, a man closely linked with the world of chartered finance, became the new *secrétaire général* within the ministry.

Belgium's first minister of colonies was Jules Renkin (1862-1934), a deputy from Brussels who was an admirer of Leopold's work. He believed in Belgium's colonial mission, in Belgian military preparedness vis-à-vis its German neighbor, and in social reforms of a cautious kind at home. The founder of a Christian Democratic group and a lawyer, Renkin had first entered the Belgian cabinet in 1907 as minister of justice; subsequently, he played a major role in the negotiations that led to the *reprise*. Finally, at Leopold's request, he assumed charge of the newly founded Ministry of Colonies, determined to combine administrative reforms with economic development, especially development of the mining industry.

Renkin was a cautious reformer and a convinced advocate of economic progress; he had certain characteristics, in common with Bernhard Dernburg, Germany's reforming colonial secretary (1907-1910). Unlike Dernburg, Renkin enjoyed the confidence of his sovereign and of the Chamber. He set a record unmatched by his successors, staying in office from 1908 to 1918. Under his aegis, atrocities largely became a matter of history; compulsory labor was reduced; indigenous chiefs received more formal powers than they had been granted hitherto; a number of trade restrictions were lifted; and mining capitalists received substantial encouragement. The Congolese administration subsequently extended its political powers more uniformly over the colony, for example, by taking from the CSK its long-accustomed administrative powers and putting Katanga on the same level as the other three provinces. In the economic sphere, however, the CSK received enormous privileges. According to Jean Stengers, "The Compagnie du Katanga received a vast, an enormous present. . . . The parliamentarians of 1908 . . . were of course acting in perfectly good faith. But they were indeed hypnotised by the concessionary companies."[15]

Under the new dispensation, the colonial minister formed the connecting link between the metropolitan and the colonial administrations. Until 1914 he received direct communications not only from the governor-general of the Congo but also from the vice-governor-general administering the key province of Katanga. The colonial minister represented his fief in both branches of the legislature. He drew up the budgets of both the Congo and the colonial ministry in Brussels; he drafted the legislation to be presented to the Belgian parliament. If he received the king's assent, he could provide

161

for taxes and tariffs. He presided over the Conseil colonial, an advisory body set up under the Charte coloniale; he more or less inherited the powers once possessed by the secrétaire d'état of the former Free State; he issued all general instructions to the governor-general; and he countersigned all executive decisions made in the king's name.

The crown continued to exercise considerable powers, at least in the formal sense. The monarch could take executive action in the form of arrêtés, and he could legislate on a great variety of subjects in the form of *décrets*, provided the latter did not countermand the *lois* enacted by parliament. The *décrets* had to be submitted to the colonial council, eight of whose members were appointed by the king, three by the Senate, and three by the Chamber. But under the new dispensation, parliament was supreme: the legislature wielded unqualified supremacy in legislation. Parliamentarians had the right of interpellation, by which a minister could be called upon to defend a policy he had endorsed. Unlike the legislative bodies of Great Britain and France, the Belgian parliament was also able to vote the annual colonial budget. This provision enabled Belgian parliamentarians to debate general questions concerning the Congo; hence Congolese affairs continued to be intertwined with intra-Belgian parliamentary disputes among Catholics, Liberals, and Socialists. This placed an extra check upon the administration in the Congo, but at the price of burdensome delays with regard to the colony's ability to frame its financial policy.

This elaborate system of checks and balances had less importance in practice than in theory. The Belgian parliament rarely made use of its powers; within the space of a half-century the legislature passed only about a dozen laws, apart from technical matters concerned with loans, budgets, and such matters. Belgian sovereigns did not interfere in the work of administration. The Conseil colonial painstakingly scrutinized the draft decrees placed before it in accordance with the Charte coloniale, but it did not provide the administration with new ideas. Insofar as decisions came from

Brussels, they were made by Jules Renkin and his officials in the Ministry of Colonies.

Power centered principally on the local administration, and administrative devolution was facilitated by Renkin's preference for decentralization. On the eve of World War I he initiated a scheme for dividing the Congo into four provinces: Congo-Kasai, Equateur, Orientale, and Katanga. In addition, the Germans unwittingly assisted the process of colonial devolution when, in 1914, they invaded Belgium itself. The Belgian government sought refuge at Le Havre in France, and Belgian civilian and military leaders concerned themselves exclusively with Belgium's very survival as an independent nation.[16] Congolese affairs were left to expatriate officials who ran the country in an empirical fashion—concerned that the economy should be solvent, that the budget should balance, and above all, that no scandal should besmirch the colony's good name.

SIX

BELGIAN SOVEREIGNTY

FORMAL STRUCTURE

Under the old regime, the central organization in Brussels had been composed of four *départements*: foreign affairs and justice, interior, finance, and treasury. After the *reprise* the Free State's central administration became a separate ministry, organized like all other Belgian ministries (see Table 16). It was headed by a minister, who was assisted by a *chef de cabinet* and a *secrétaire général*, and it was subdivided into a number of *directions générales*, whose numbers increased as the state began to assume more and more technical functions. The organization stressed functions, not geographical areas, and reflected the Belgian preoccupation with finance, concessionary questions, economic development, and jurisprudence. None of the *directions générales* was concerned specifically with African matters. Problems with African district administration and chieftainships came under the purview of a relatively minor functionary, a *chef de division* subordinate to an official within the *direction générale* who was responsible for internal affairs. African agriculture and taxes were grouped, respectively, under the *directions générales* that were responsible for farming and finance. Correspondence passed through the *secrétariat général*.[1]

An essential degree of continuity existed between the old and the new regimes. The entire civil service of the central administration was taken over by the Belgian state, and the bureaucracy continued to work in a methodical rather than an efficient fashion. Its complexity meant that the organization continued to be top-heavy and slow in its operations. At the time of the *reprise*, the central administration in Brussels alone required more than fifty senior civil servants (see

164

TABLE 16

Organization of the Ministry of Colonies, 1914

Office	Responsibilities
Minister of colonies	Represents Congo in legislature, prepares legislation and budgets, issues instructions to governor-general, presides over *conseil colonial*, exercises general supervision, etc.
Cabinet du ministre (headed by the *chef du cabinet*, assisted by a *directeur* and a *chef de division*)	Special correspondence, audiences for the minister, and matters reserved for the minister's attention.
Secrétariat général	Personnel, decorations, promotions, pensions, posts and telegraphs, archives, etc. Within certain limits the *secrétaire général* was able to sign for the *gouverneur général*.
1ᵉ Direction générale (justice and public instruction)	Justice, prisons, notaries public, matters concerning education and public worship, relations with missionary societies, etc.
2ᵉ Direction générale (internal affairs)	Internal affairs, district administration, chiefdoms, supplies, transport, health, etc.
3ᵉ Direction générale (finance)	Finance, budgetary questions, currency, concessions, surveys, native taxes, debts—a key position within the administrative structure.
4ᵉ Direction générale (industry and trade)	Commerce, immigration, statistics, trademarks, courses in colonial education.
5ᵉ Direction générale (agriculture)	Government plantations, agricultural research, African agriculture, botanical gardens, laboratories.

SOURCES: Belgium, Ministère des colonies, *Annuaire officiel* (Brussels, 1913), and Germany, Reichstag, no. 1356, 13 Legislature Periode 1 Session, 1912-1914, Anlagen, *Die Kolonialverwaltung der europäischen Staaten.*

Table 17), while the Reichskolonialamt in Berlin made do with a fraction of that number. Far from saving on personnel, the Belgian administrative reform merely provided additional administrative patronage.

TABLE 17

Senior Officials in the Belgian Ministry of Colonies, 1908

Title	Salary (in Belgian francs)	Number of Officials
Secrétaire général	9,000-10,000	1
Directeur général	7,500- 8,500	4
Directeur	5,500- 7,500	8
Chef de division	4,000- 5,000	17
Chef de bureau	4,000- 5,000	21
Sous-chef de bureau	3,000- 3,800	25

SOURCE: Le Moniteur belge, 4 November 1908.
NOTE: The lowest-paid officials, the attachés and commis, were divided into three classes, which received salaries (in francs) of 2,600-2,900, 2,000-2,500, and 1,200-1,800, respectively.

Within the Congo, the hierarchy continued to be headed by the governor-general at Boma (see Table 18). (The capital was not formally moved to Léopoldville until 1923, when the city had become an important river port and a center of the palm oil trade—a boom town reminiscent of the Klondike during the frontier days.) The governor-general was the ceremonial head; he communicated with Brussels and supervised the administration and the preparation of the budget. He could issue decrees, and he was specifically enjoined to further the "moral and material progress" of the indigenous population and to promote mission enterprise. Under the Renkin regime, his functions were further enlarged. Renkin insisted that the governor-general be relieved of all routine work, leaving him time for wider questions relating to African policy, economic activity, and "moral progress."[2] The governor-general's real powers, however, were not nearly as great as those of a British governor; he depended on Brussels

TABLE 18

Functionaries in the Belgian Congo, 1913

Position	Number of Officials		
	Boma	Katanga	Total
Gouverneur général	1	0	1
Vice–gouverneur général	1	1	2
Inspecteurs d'état	1	1	2
Secrétaires généraux and *directeurs*	4	2	6
Sous–directeurs	1	0	1
Commissaires généraux and commissaires de district	11	2	13
Adjoints supérieurs	11	3	14
Chefs de zone	6	1	7
Administrateurs territoriaux	90	23	113
Officiers de la Force Publique	124	24	148
Chefs de section, conducteurs, works supervisors	66	13	79
Medical officers	45	18	63
Pharmacists	9	2	11
Steamer captains	40	0	40
Agents, diverse status	720	135	855
Officials on leave	224	32	256
TOTAL	1,354	257	1,611

SOURCE: SPA 115, no. 44, Archives africaines.

to a greater extent than his British colleague did on London, and he lacked the British governor's social preeminence.

Free State rule disappeared, but the officials stayed in place. Wahis, a king's man, a Catholic, and a professional soldier to the core (he looked like one: sturdy, with cropped hair and a Kaiser Wilhelm moustache), continued to hold office, but he lived in Belgium most of the time and left his duties to others. In 1912 he was replaced by Felix-Alexandre Fuchs (1858-1928). Fuchs was very different from Wahis; he was a civilian, a lawyer, and an *inspecteur d'état*, the kind of man who was apt to represent the new order. He had seen service in the Belgian Ministry of Foreign Affairs before he

167

transferred to the Congo Free State administration, where he soon acquired a reputation for honesty and impartiality by taking his inspectorial duties seriously. During the controversy about the atrocities in the rubber-producing areas, he apparently expressed in a series of confidential reports his disapproval of what he had seen; this indiscretion caused him to be cast into three years of semidisgrace (1904-1907). Later events, however, proved him right; he returned to the Congo and gradually climbed to the top of the administrative hierarchy. In many ways his outlook was similar to that of Janssen: both had obtained the coveted title of *docteur en droit*; both were nonmilitary men. Men of their general orientation—bourgeois, *bien pensant*, French-speaking, urban, and usually Brussels-centered—would come to dominate the gubernatorial office.[3]

In theory, the governor-general was advised by a *conseil de gouvernement*, but in practice it had little impact on administration. Active between 1915 and 1920, this body then became dormant until the 1930s. Only after a series of crises —the depression, World War II, and the subsequent upsurge of African nationalism—was the Congolese administration forced to make use of representative bodies of a more substantive kind, bodies that operated on both the central and the provincial levels to give some means of expression to European settlers and a small African minority.

The governor-general was assisted by specialists who controlled departmental administration or services throughout the provinces. The central administration was organized on lines almost identical to those of the Ministry of Colonies in Brussels. Correspondence passed through the *secrétariat général*, which looked after archives and statistics. The central services were grouped into a number of *directions* (departments) that were organized according to function: justice and public instruction, internal affairs, finances, industry and trade, agriculture, marine and public works, the Force Publique, and surveys. No single *direction* was specifically concerned with African administration as such.

168

The Belgians, like the French, continued to operate a colonial inspectorate, a *corps d'élite* within the administrative structure. The salary of an *inspecteur général* was almost twice that of a *secrétaire général* (thirty-five thousand francs as against twenty thousand, nearly as much as a *vice-gouverneur général*). The purpose of these inspectors was to relieve the governor-general of detailed scrutinies and afford him more time to deal with questions of major policy. They were empowered to take over one or several government departments or, later, to head a province if required. The Belgian inspectorate provided an important element of administrative continuity and also served as an effective means of administration in the sense in which the ancient *missi dominici* had served their kings. Whereas French inspectors came out from France and reported directly to the minister for the colonies, their Belgian colleagues stayed in the Congo and became experts on Congolese affairs.

The governor-general's authority was further diminished by the existence of an independent judiciary that formed a separate body within the wider administrative framework. The judicial hierarchy was a powerful body, reformist in orientation and most often in conflict with the administration. The judicature was headed by a *conseil supérieur* in Brussels that acted as a supreme court and performed certain advisory functions. Within the Congo there were two courts of appeal—one at Boma, the other at Elisabethville—and seven courts of first instance. The judicial officers were responsible not to the governor-general but to the king, and thereby enjoyed a wide measure of independence. The *magistrats de carrière* who staffed the higher courts considered themselves the chosen few; a small body of highly educated men, they formed the only part of the Congolese administration that attracted men of aristocratic background into its service. Unlike most other lawyers, magistrates had to obtain a doctorate in law, which also qualified them for the highest ranks of the colonial hierarchy. Former magistrates were also commonly appointed to the ministerial cabinets, which consisted of the ministers' personal appointees. The lower ranks of the judicial establishment consisted of *juges de police* and *magistrats auxiliaires*. From 1913 on, the more senior officers in the district administration were empowered to act as *juges de police*, while lower officers ranked as *officiers de police judiciaire*.

The intricate nature of the judicial structure further slowed administrative work, which was already impeded by the bureaucratic complexities that beset the Belgian administrative system as a whole. The magistracy suffered from staff problems similar to those afflicting the general administration. There was a high turnover in personnel: twenty-six men passed through five career positions in Elisabethville between 1914 and 1924. Opportunities for advancement were few because service in Africa was not recognized as a basis for promotion by Belgian courts; Belgian magistrates could not, therefore, complete their careers in the Congo. Consequently, instability long remained the rule rather than the exception.

The system was elaborate. The lowest level of the judicial hierarchy consisted of the police courts, which exercised petty jurisdiction over Africans and were difficult to control from above. Cases might be appealed to the next courts in the hierarchy, the district courts, which were presided over by the district commissioner. The third level consisted of *tribunaux du parquet*, each headed by a professional magistrate. At the fourth layer of the judiciary were the tribunals of first instance, which were composed solely of professional magistrates. The fifth and top layer was made up of the courts of appeal. In theory, the Belgian system gave many more privileges to Africans than did the British or the French system. Africans had extensive rights of appeal; compared with the British dispensation, a higher percentage of cases were heard by professional jurists and judged according to a precise penal code. In practice, however, the system was so complex that it was intelligible only to a small group of well-educated blacks. At the same time, it provided a check, however tenuous, on the administration and afforded an element of humanitarian paternalism that may have helped to make the system more workable than it would otherwise have been.

The district administration was subject to frequent reorganization, reflecting a similar measure of administrative instability at the lower levels of the hierarchy. The Congo had originally been divided into *districts, zones, secteurs*, and *postes*. In 1912 the system was reorganized into nine *districts*, each headed by a *commissaire de district* or a *commissaire général* who was assisted by an *adjudant supérieur* and was answerable to the governor-general (see Table 19).[4] In numerical terms, the administration remained minuscule. Those critics who accused Belgium of brutally oppressing its subjects generally forgot to take account of the extraordinary weakness of its administration on the spot. In 1910 the entire *personnel supérieur des districts*, from *commissaires généraux* down to the humble *chefs de secteur*, numbered no more than eighty-six men, an infinitesimally small number to run such a large colony. The districts, however, were filled with a substantial number of officials in lowly positions, despite the constant complaints regarding *la pénurie des cadres*. (In 1913, for example, the German Tanganyika-Moero district contained two hundred European officials, including twenty-nine military officers and twenty-eight noncommissioned officers, twenty-four police officers, twenty-nine senior and sixty-two junior district officials, as well as twenty-eight members of the clerical staff. In neighboring Uganda, the British needed no more than forty-three officials, from governor down to assistant district commissioner, to run the entire colony.)

Burdened with numerous administrative layers, the system worked in a slow and creaking fashion. In order to combat the numerous administrative delays, the Belgians in 1914 began to establish a provincial system to centralize government. Each province was headed by a governor, and specialized services were placed at his disposal. These came to include a secretariat, a financial service, a public works serv-

171

TABLE 19

Administration of Stanleyville District, 1913

Department or Division	Functionaries
	Headquarters
Vice–gouverneur général	
Service territorial	Headed by a *commissaire général*, including 5 senior officials (*commissaires de adjoints supérieurs, administrateurs territoriaux*), and 4 juniors (*agents territoriaux*)
Justice	Two judges, 1 *procureur*, 5 other officials
Secrétariat (*service administratif*)	Two *agents d'administration*, 5 clerks
Force Publique	Eight officers
Public works	Eight officers
Agriculture	One agronomist
Taxes	Four *contrôleurs* and *vérificateurs,* 10 clerks
Postal services	One *percepteur*
Survey	Seven surveyors
Chemin de fer du Congo Supérieur	Twenty-one engineers and *chefs de secteur*; 185 foremen, supervisors, artisans, gangers; 6 physicians; 21 clerical officers; 29 members of the marine department
	District Divisions
Zone (includes postal services and taxes; a military court; registration of births, marriages, and deaths; headquarters of the Force Publique; *service de santé*; and office administration)	*Chef de zone*, normally assisted by an officer
Secteur	*Chef de secteur*, assisted by an officer, 1 or 2 sergeants, and 1 or 2 clerks
Poste	*Agent militaire*

NOTE: Not all of the positions listed were in fact filled.

ice, a service of justice and education (later divided into separate departments), a service of agriculture and forests, a health department, and in some cases a service of commerce, industry, and labor. The provinces in turn were subdivided into twenty-two administrative *districts*, each supervised by a *commissaire de district* whose rank corresponded more or less to that of a provincial commissioner or resident in a British territory. The districts were then subdivided into territories that were headed by territorial administrators. The balance of administrative power lay with the *commissaire de district*, who controlled all the technical services in his area.

Within the district, much more emphasis was placed on the administrative and technical services at district headquarters than on administration in the field. The men in the bush did not carry as much prestige in the Congo as they did, say, in Nigeria or the Gold Coast. Nevertheless, the *chefs de secteur* enjoyed an extraordinary degree of independence. According to a senior Belgian official, the *chefs de secteur* were in permanent contact with the Africans; in practice, Africans could not appeal against any decisions made by a *chef*. A capable man might accomplish much; a laggard might ruin an entire district, letting it go to pieces. The best administrators were men with local experience and a sound practical background. The studies completed by an engineer or artillery officer were of a higher level than those of a *candidat notaire*; capable men tried in the bush were preferred to men sent straight from home with doctoral diplomas in their baggage.[5]

The legal structure of the Congo was as elaborate as its administrative organization. Laws applicable to the Congo were of several kinds; they derived from powers inherent in the crown, the parliament, the cabinet, and the colonial council. The principal *lois* or acts of parliament were the Loi coloniale of 1908, usually called the Colonial Charter, and the annual colonial budget, which normally had to pass both legislative houses. The crown could also issue *décrets* or legislative decrees after they had been discussed by the

173

colonial council and countersigned by the minister of colonies, one of whose functions as the responsible cabinet member was to preside rather than counsel. *Arrêtés*, executive regulations, were executed by the crown in collaboration with the minister and his council.

To the governor-general at the top of the structure in the Congo came these three kinds of directives, and it was his duty to see them carried out by exercising his own power to issue *ordonnances*, many of which were routine administrative regulations that filled in details not contained in directives from above. In certain situations he might have to legislate temporarily by an *ordonnance-loi*, which was valid for six months unless it was confirmed for a longer period or rescinded sooner by royal or parliamentary action. The lives of the great majority of Congolese continued for many years to be regulated by customary African law, or what passed for it, which was dispensed by hundreds of local chiefs until the inroads of industry, commerce, and urbanization imposed other alternatives.

The administration was supported by technicians who far outnumbered the administrative personnel. The number of upper- and mid-level officials employed in the various departments reflected Belgian priorities. The district administration, with its eighty-six officers, was smaller than the so-called *service administratif*, which included the *directeurs* and *sous-directeurs* of the departments, their senior clerks, and others (see Table 20). Medicine did not count for a great deal; in 1910 the Belgians employed only forty-one government doctors throughout the territory. The mining and railway companies had their own doctors, but even so, the medical services barely sufficed to look after the most immediate needs of the administration itself. Given the country's limited revenue and the standards of the time, the "productive" departments—agriculture, mining, and forestry—were well staffed. The strongest services of all were those that enjoyed the smallest prestige. The public works and the marine departments between them employed about three times as

TABLE 20

Occupational Structure of Belgian Administration
in the Congo, 1910

Department	Number of Senior Officials
Upper-Level Personnel	
Justice and public instruction *(gouverneur general, vice-gouverneurs, inspecteurs d'état, juges, magistrats, agents administratifs de la justice)*	105
Personnel supérieur des districts (commissaires généraux to *chefs de secteur)*	86
Service administratif (directeurs, sous-directeurs de département, to *agents d'administration 3ᵉ classe)*	99
Mid-Level Personnel	
Physicians	41
Public works (engineers, foremen, technicians)	142
Marine (steamer captains, technicians)	127
Agriculture (veterinary surgeons, forest inspectors, *chefs de culture)*	67
Survey and mining (surveyors, engineers, prospectors, foremen)	88
Customs *(inspecteurs* and *vérificateurs)*	49
TOTAL	804

SOURCE: Belgium, Ministère des colonies, *Annuaire officiel, 1910.*
NOTE: Officials in the district of Katanga are not included in this table.

many senior officials and technicians as the entire district administration. These men built a network of roads at a time when there were no private firms in the country willing to undertake such work. They put up government buildings and hospitals, drained marshes, and constructed bridges. They controlled navigation, maintained waterways, and took care of dredging and beaconing the more widely used waterways.

The marine department maintained its own flotilla of steamers, dredgers, and flatboats. Without these workers, Belgian rule would have quickly collapsed.

Viewed as a whole, the Belgian administration was tiny in size, cumbrous in procedure, incorruptible in its upper levels, and intensely preoccupied with rank, precedence, status, and dress. Even in the most lonely outstations an officer was expected to maintain a full wardrobe, including a *petite tenue officielle* complete with a dolman, a good civilian suit, and six uniforms—three white, two blue, one khaki. In the higher ranks there was no dishonesty. The senior officials normally were graduates of the universities of Ghent, Louvain, Liège, or Brussels, or, after 1920, the Ecole coloniale. The system required a relatively large number of officials to work it, however, many more proportionately than the British needed, say, in Northern Rhodesia. Financial integrity was bought at the price of a cumbrous system of supervision and reporting. Observations made in the early 1920s by Raymond Leslie Buell, an American expert who visited the Congo, differ little from those made by earlier visitors:

At the present time, each Territorial Agent makes a report upon methods to the District Commissioner and each District Commissioner makes a report to the Governor. The Governor in turn makes a report to the Governor-General. But the District Reports are not sent to Boma. They remain in the provincial archives. The Governor's report merely informs the Governor-General about the development of the province in general terms. Under such a system, the Governor-General has no means of knowing what is actually going on. He may order the Governor to build such and such public works, but he is not, under the system, informed as to the detailed means by which the government secures the labor. Nor does it appear that the Governor-General has much control over native policy generally.[6]

The Social Structure of Administration

In the Congo, as in the remainder of colonial Africa, the governor-general formed the apex of the official hierarchy. He headed the civil service, served as the ceremonial head of government, and had a major part in shaping the social tone of the bureaucracy. His remuneration was greater than that of a high-ranking judge or a lieutenant general in the army. A provincial governor stood at about the same level as the head of a *département* in Brussels, or a *professeur ordinaire* at a university, or a man of high distinction in Belgium at that time. Most governors-general, moreover, were drawn from the ranks of the administration itself. After Wahis left office, no more soldiers were appointed; the military flavor had gradually disappeared from the administration by the 1930s. A few governors-general, such as Lippens, a leading industrialist, came from the business community, and a few were from the ranks of politicians.[7]

Ambitious subalterns who rose from humble circumstances by hard work, initiative, and the ability to pass examinations were replaced in time by diploma-bearing specialists, many of them graduates of the Université coloniale de Belgique founded at Antwerp after World War I. The colonial service continued to provide a ladder for advancement to those young men who managed to obtain scholarships for the colonial university, but its ethos and social composition began to change as service in the Congo gradually became a respectable occupation, one that appealed to sons of the provincial bourgeoisie. The Ardennes region—French-speaking and impoverished, but relatively well supplied with schools —furnished many applicants for the colonial service, as did rural Flanders, where jobs for educated men were equally hard to find. Catholics came to look upon a colonial career as a form of secular mission work, a means of serving God by uplifting the heathen and protecting them against the real or supposed exactions of capitalists.

The average governor-general was a Catholic and, unlike

Fuchs, a Liberal. He was well educated and likely to be city-bred. Of the ten governors-general who held office between 1887 and 1960, five came from larger cities—Brussels, Ghent, Antwerp, and Liège—and three were born in medium-sized towns like Ostend. At least six of the ten retired to Brussels and died there. Seven of the ten were lawyers by training; only three had begun their careers as professional soldiers. Of all the Congo viceroys, only Stanley was of working-class origin; three were sons of professional soldiers, while the remainder were sons of merchants, lawyers, or civil servants. Their parental background ranged from lower middle class (Fuchs's father was an *inspecteur des plantations*, or park superintendent) to upper middle class (Maurice-August Lippens, governor-general from 1921 to 1923, was the son of a burgomaster and senator of Ghent). On retirement several governors-general obtained high positions in industry and finance; Lippens, for instance, became president of the CCCI and of other concerns. But unlike their British counterparts, Belgian governors-general were not normally raised to the nobility. The exceptions were Wahis, who was elevated to a barony by reason of his military achievements, and Lippens, who became a *comte*, more because of his previous service as a cabinet minister than for his work as an administrator in the Congo.

Without exception, the senior officials in the Congo spoke French at home. Judging by their names, however, many of them may have derived from Flemish stock: seven out of ten bore Flemish names, and one had a German name. Their tenures of office ranged from two to as many as twelve years, with an average of about five years. Their religious affiliation was overwhelmingly Catholic. Wahis and most of his successors were staunch adherents of the Church, as were most of the senior officials in the Ministry of Colonies and in the colony itself. Of the ten governors-general who served between 1908 and 1960, seven were Catholic; the exceptions were Maurice Lippens, an anticlerical Liberal who served under the Franck ministry (1918-1924), Eugène Jungers, a man with no religious affiliation, and Hendrik Cornelis, a Socialist and the last of the governors-general. In the lower echelons of the service anticlericals continued to be well represented, but their influence did not become predominant until the final stage of the Belgian regime.

The end of the military era did away with the social promotion that had enabled officers from the ranks to become highly placed civilian administrators. Wahis, for instance, had joined an infantry regiment as a common soldier at the age of sixteen and had advanced all the way to governor-general. Less highly placed officials who had started life in the ranks included Jules-Alexandre Milz, a one-time trooper in the *chasseurs à cheval*, and Camille-Aimé Coquilhat, who had run away from school to fight in a French scout regiment during the Franco-Prussian war of 1870-1871. The new Belgian administration would have liked civil servants of a different kind: well-educated civilians, Belgian nationals with a sound background in law and administration who were capable of running a more complex state than the pioneering administration set up under Leopold. As Renkin wrote in 1910 in a despatch to the governor-general, Belgium aimed at setting up a professional corps of administrators who had educational attainments superior to those prevalent under the *ancien régime*. Terms of engagement would be fixed for at least ten years, with the possibility of subsequent extensions.[8] University graduates would start off as *chefs de secteur 2e classe*, and the trend toward engaging more highly educated men would continue to accelerate.[9]

In drawing up his reforms, Renkin spent considerable time in studying the methods used by other colonial powers. He found that the British placed special emphasis on "character" and on the interview technique. The Dutch preferred applicants with good doctorates to those who were specialists. The French required a *diplôme de bachelier* or a *diplôme supérieur* of their candidates, who were then trained

179

at the Ecole coloniale. Belgian practice conformed to the continental tradition, with its emphasis on specialized training in law and administration, which was the distinguishing feature of the administrative services of France and Germany alike.

In 1911 Renkin set up an Ecole coloniale. Tuition was free; thus poor boys capable of passing the entrance examination continued to make their way in the colonial world, albeit with the pen rather than the sword. The school trained applicants for both the higher and the lower ranks of the administration. Its *section supérieure* turned out officer candidates and officers for the army, as well as youthful civilian agents; the *section inférieure* produced noncommissioned officers and *agents du service administratif* (office personnel). Students took courses in the history of the Congo and in its general organization. Emphasis was placed on Belgium's "civilizing mission," which entailed the abolition of barbarous customs like human sacrifice, the poison ordeal, inhumane punishments such as the mutilation of prisoners, the practice of smoking Indian hemp, and other abominations. The would-be administrators, however, were encouraged to tolerate "inoffensive customs," to respect traditional chiefs (a far cry from the practice of the pioneers), and to maintain strict discipline among their black employees by setting a good personal example. The Belgians also stressed administrative law and such economic questions as labor and taxation. Candidates in the *section supérieure* were required to study jurisprudence and to acquire a detailed knowledge of the penal code. Unlike British administrators, the Belgians were expected to have a knowledge of practical subjects like hygiene and bookkeeping.[10]

Renkin also tried to develop a sound system of promotion. Initially he attempted to handle the matter himself on recommendations from the governor-general; in the end the promotion of senior officials was left largely to the latter's judgment. Promotion of civil servants receiving a starting salary of thirteen thousand francs or more depended on merit alone. Junior officials were promoted according to a system that awarded 50 percent on the basis of seniority and 50 percent on merit.[11]

The qualities that appealed to Renkin were civilian rather than military. He encouraged the promotion of men with a proven record in African administration. One J.P.F.M. Malfeyt, for instance, received praise from Renkin in a personal report submitted to the king for work done in the candidate's capacity as an *inspecteur d'état* of the Province Orientale. Malfeyt, Rankin wrote, was well acquainted with African customs; he was equally expert on economic questions concerning cash crops and taxes. Also, "he has an agreeable nature; and he is willing to work." He deserved to get on.[12]

Similar criteria became applicable at a lower level of government. During the era of the Free State, the *chefs de secteur* had normally been drawn from the ranks of junior officers, all of whom had been obliged to pass an examination upon being commissioned. Under the new regime, the administration began to look for civilians who were capable of passing a general examination rather than for men who had long served in the bush. Only twenty out of a possible one hundred points could be awarded for local experience, including a knowledge of African dialects and evidence of good conduct; eighty points were allotted for a knowledge of accountancy, political and administrative institutions, topography, and similar subjects. Indeed, the Belgians had little interest in attracting accomplished linguists. No advantage was given to candidates with a knowledge of European tongues. Some ability in Flemish was useful, but "distinct preference should be given to candidates speaking French, the national language." Far from choosing classicists, the Belgians preferred candidates who were trained in practical subjects. *Licenciés en sciences commerciales* who were capable of passing the requisite examination would make good *chefs de secteur*; trained engineers would do well as *chefs de section.* The lowest ranks in the civilian service and the Force Publique required at least an adequate elementary school education.[13]

At the lower level of government, the Belgians employed a large number of European clerks, junior administrators, and craftsmen. Although the independent *colon* never attained a great deal of importance within the Congolese power structure, the metropolitan petty bourgeoisie secured a substantial place for itself within the ranks of colonial government and industry. The Congo had more white administrators in relation to its population than any other African colony except perhaps Dahomey and Mauritania.[14]

The large number of lower-ranking white functionaries employed in the Congo administration represented a considerable financial outlay for the colony. The governor-general reported in a despatch to Renkin that the Congo might save money by giving more opportunities to African typists, tax collectors, and mechanics. If office procedures were simplified, more African clerks could be employed. He pointed out that the employment of blacks had many advantages: Africans were content with lower salaries than whites; they had a better knowledge of indigenous languages; they required lower standards in board and lodging; they were better able to stand the climate; and they did not occasion the extra expense of returning to Belgium on leave. Moreover, their position must be ameliorated in the future. Black employees should no longer be treated on the same level as black laborers; if Belgium was prepared to delegate authority to them, they must be regarded accordingly. Renkin thoroughly agreed. He argued that blacks should also be promoted in industry, and in 1913 he insisted that they be trained to drive cars and trucks; whites should be employed only to train them and to maintain the vehicles. If Africans were ever engaged as *agents d'administration*, he stated, their status must be equal to that of their white colleagues.[15]

The conditions of the blacks varied greatly under the several colonial administrations. The Belgians were much more

182

reluctant to employ Africans in high government positions than were the British in West Africa. Nothing like a unified black civil service existed in the colony. Nevertheless, black clerks, interpreters, telegraphists, and such managed to secure some advancement; they became a new subelite of their own, numbering at most a few thousand, dependent for their livelihood on salaries and for their advancement on the civil service, the army, and industry (see Table 21).

TABLE 21

Salaries of African Employees in the Congo Administration, 1910
(In Belgian Francs)

Field of Employment	Salary
Service administratif	600-3,600
Finances	800-1,800
Post and telegraph	1,200-1,500
Industry and commerce	
Clerks	1,200-1,800
Interpreters	1,000

SOURCE: *Considérations générales sur le statut des fonctionnaires* (arrêté royal du 20 juin 1910), SPA 123, Archives africaines.

In addition to improving the conditions of service, the administration tried to remove those Belgian officers who had been guilty of disgracing their country's name. *Moralisation* became a colonial battle cry, and the Ecole coloniale inaugurated a special course in "morals." The personnel of the Congo, wrote an *inspecteur d'état* in 1913, contained numerous officials who should be dismissed because of incapacity or moral turpitude. Twenty-four whites were then being tried before the *tribunal de l'instance* at Léopoldville, nine of them for fraud and embezzlement. Nevertheless, officials were reluctant to give information against their colleagues, and embezzlement and fraud were widespread. Within the framework of an economy in which the state held enormous powers, civil servants were tempted, but never easily, to accept bribes proffered by white merchants in matters bearing on the illegal uses of taxes, the illegal sale of

183

local products, and similar matters. The system of functional decentralization that rendered technical officers subject only to their specific *directions* and outside the territorial officer's authority did not improve matters. Local *agents* could not supervise the technicians' conduct.[16]

Given the legalistic and formalistic nature of Belgian administration, and given the rights secured to Free State officials under the *reprise*, miscreants could not at first be easily removed. Starting in 1912, however, new legislation enabled the government to "purify the cadres." In 1913 Fuchs sent out a circular informing his officials that the governor-general would henceforth remove "without pity" any officer who discredited his country's role as a "moralisateur et civilisateur."[17] Fuchs was as good as his word. The axe fell especially on junior officials, *sous-officiers*, and *chefs de secteur*; in 1914 Fuchs forwarded to the minister of colonies a list of seventeen officials accused of such offenses as embezzlement, fraudulent bookkeeping, illegal ivory trade, and illegal arrests.[18]

Steps were taken to punish officials who were guilty of abusing Africans. A purge struck the department of marine. The great majority of ships' captains and mechanics, wrote the commandant-general angrily, were a disgrace; the department was full of drunkards, "persons without culture or morality." The administration thereafter endeavored to attract a better class of men by paying them higher salaries.[19]

The work of reform was not easy. The Belgian administration was heavily staffed, much more so than the colonial services that administered the British and German colonies. By 1913 the Congo employed 2,480 state officials and 252 officials attached to the state-built Chemin de fer du Congo; by contrast, 1,734 Germans were required to run the entire German colonial empire in Africa and the Pacific. Considering the nature and purpose of Belgian governance, this extensive deployment of European civil servants could not easily have been avoided. The Belgian colonial state had a much greater stake in the colonial economy than did its British equivalent; the work of control and supervision thus required a relatively large number of officials. The Belgians also took their spirit of administrative centralization into the colonies. Centralization discouraged initiative. The system entailed an intricate scheme of supervision, and much time had to be spent in writing reports to all and sundry. Many Belgian *agents* soon regarded paperwork as the be-all and end-all of government, and as paperwork expanded, more officials had to be employed to shuffle the files.[20]

The Belgians used solid economic incentives to attract recruits. Their civil servants in the Congo were reasonably well remunerated, better on the average than their colleagues in German, French, or Portuguese Africa. As an increasing number of competent candidates applied for colonial positions, the quality of the service improved (numerous contemporary accounts survive to prove the point). In a secret report to the kaiser, a German naval officer wrote that Belgian officials compared favorably with their opposite numbers in the French Congo. The Belgian civil servants in general welcomed the end of the *ancien régime* and its abuses, he reported. They worked hard; they were indeed proud of their *système prussien*, which required them to start work in the morning with an early inspection at 6:00.[21]

The Belgian service as a whole was distinguished by a kind of utilitarian Calvinism that valued method, order, punctuality, legality, obedience, endeavor, and respect for official precedence more than for social class. It honored first the judge, next the diplomatist, and then the soldier—all of whom ranked before the district officer in a manner that was inconceivable to British public servants.[22] The Belgian civil administration, like the Belgian army, was not operated on egalitarian principles, but both the military and the civilian hierarchies provided an unbroken ladder of promotion from the lowest to the highest ranks for those who could pass the requisite examinations and who displayed sufficient ability and application to succeed. A great deal of friction existed between military and civilian officers, but there was no military caste divided from the rest of society by special privileges. Instead, the Belgians worked out an all-embracing salary scale to integrate the various social strata. At the bottom was an extensive layer of lower-middle-class employees with the outlook and values of the Belgian petite bourgeoisie; these clerks, army sergeants, and skilled workingmen were all paid according to the same scale. At the top, the *ingénieur en chef* and the *commissaire général* received precisely the same income. The Belgian salariat, military and official, was paid according to function rather than social class. The salary gap between the higher and lower ranks was considerably smaller than in societies with greater stratification, such as Great Britain and Germany. A *commissaire général* received little more than three times the pay drawn by an *agent territorial*, a senior noncommissioned officer, or a blacksmith (see Table 22).

Yet colonial employment failed to acquire much social prestige in the Belgian métropole. Unlike the situation in Great Britain, the Belgian colonial service remained a social enclave, for the colonial mystique in Belgium was confined to a small sector of the population: mostly professional soldiers, missionaries, civil servants, and a handful of intellectuals. Even within the professional ranks of the colonial service a high proportion of officials thought of their work as a job rather than as a mission. André van Iseghem was a well-qualified man, a *docteur en droit* who had reached high office in the Congo, his observations, which may be trusted, were not optimistic. About 50 percent of the ex-colonials, he wrote shortly after the end of World War I, were indifferent to the colonial ideal. On returning to Belgium they wanted to forget their careers in the colonies, regarding them as no more than an interlude. Forty percent of them returned as opponents of the colonial system. "Ils sont revenus pleins de rancoeurs au souvenir de leur vie coloniale; ils confondent dans une même haine l'oeuvre du Congo et les hommes qui la dirigent." Their Congolese reminiscences, which they recounted in offices, clubs, and bars, destroyed the effects of

TABLE 22

Initial Salaries of Military and Civilian Officials in the Belgian Congo, 1910
(Excluding Allowances)

Military Officials	Civilian Officials		Salary (In Belgian Francs)
Colonel	Ingénieur en chef	Commissaire général	20,000
Lieutenant-colonel	Chef de section principal	Commissaire de district	17,000
Major	Chef de section, 1ᵉ classe	Adjoint supérieur	15,000
Capitaine	Chef de section, 2ᵉ classe	Chef de zone	14,000
Lieutenant	Sous-chef	Chef de secteur, 1ᵉ classe	12,000
Sous-lieutenant	Surveillant des travaux	Chef de secteur, 2ᵉ classe	10,000
Agent militaire	Chef de chantier	Chef de poste	7,500
Premier sous-officier	Chef d'atelier	Commissaire de police	7,500
Sous-officier	Stonemason	Agent territorial, 1ᵉ classe	6,500
	Smith, carpenter, artisan	Agent territorial, 2ᵉ classe	6,000

SOURCE: Belgium, Ministère des colonies, *Fonctionnaires et agents de la colonie* (Brussels, 1910).

colonial propaganda. The thirty-four hundred ex-colonials in Belgium, most of them former officials, could not be regarded as a procolonial lobby; only about 10 percent believed in the colonial cause. According to van Iseghem, colonial civil servants had all manner of grievances regarding their living conditions and pay. Above all, they suffered from a feeling of frustration. They resented their lack of prestige and objected to the authoritarian structure of governance and the way they were treated. Having returned to Belgium, they became men without a country (*dépaysés*). Their social position was comparable to that of the military in Great Britain before World War I.[23]

Van Iseghem wrote at a time when civil servants in Belgium and the Congo alike were feeling the effects of World War I. The relative values of official salaries and pensions were declining, and there was widespread discontent. Van Iseghem was pleading the civil servant's case for more adequate pay, and he may have exaggerated a little. However, a great deal of evidence in official files indicates that his assessment was essentially correct. Correspondents never tired of complaining that Belgium lacked the colonial spirit: schools and universities should have cooperated in creating a new sense of mission, a new sense of colonial dedication. This mystique, however, could not be manufactured at will, and within metropolitan society the colonial service remained a social island with its own values and its own set of grievances.

A Changing Ideology

When Belgium took over the Congo Free State, large areas of its new domain were almost devoid of European influence. Many of its indigenous people continued to dwell in stockaded villages, maintained their own military organizations, and owned their own arms. An American missionary observed in 1909:

188

In Rhodesia natives are not allowed to own a gun. And the rule is a good one. But in the Congo State . . . we seldom met a man unarmed, and in the villages [in Katanga] each man's gun was in handy reach, leaning up against the huts or stockades. They are ineffective beyond a hundred yards, but even so by them the game of the country—that is, the eatable animals—had been practically exterminated.[24]

Over much of the country Belgian administrative authority still remained to be enforced, and the future of Belgian rule as a whole still seemed far from secure. Germany might one day attempt to acquire the Congo for itself as part of a great empire to be set up in Mittelafrika. The British, according to the belief of many Belgian colonialists, still nursed ambitions to seize Katanga, where British mining and financial influence remained predominant. As far as missionary and humanitarian opinion was concerned, moreover, Belgium was still on trial, a power with a spotty past. Belgian politicians like Renkin understood these weaknesses. They firmly believed that Belgium had a civilizing mission to perform and that the national mission in turn entailed reform, a doctrine in which most parliamentarians warmly concurred.

The notion of a civilizing mission had not come easily to the pioneers who had braved the fevers, fought the wars, and conquered the country. Among his papers, Commandant Lemaire left a description of some of the hard-bitten *coloniaux* he met on a homeward-bound boat. Their faces were yellow, their beards and hair unkempt. They smoked enormous pipes. They sported trousers and *vestons* whose cut and design appealed to African rather than European taste, and they wore unspeakable ties whose bright colors had aroused the envy of warlords in the bush. They had an exuberant gaiety, but they were just as likely to sink into dark depression. These were marginal men, faced as they had been with the constant perils of brandy, sickness, and death. In-

189

stead of singing heroic tunes about *honneur et patrie*, they sang the sad ditties of the disappointed, composed in the manner of the moralizing broadsheets of that time.

> Y' en a qui font la mauvaise tête
> A leurs parents,
> Qui font des dettes, qui font la bête
> Inutilement;

> Qui, un beau soir, de leur maîtresse
> Ont plein le dos.
> Ils fichent le camp, pleins de tristesse,
> Pour le Congo.

> Dans l'haut Congo, c'est là qu'on crève
> De soif et d'faim,
> C'est là qu'il faut peiner sans trève
> Jusqu'à la fin.

> Le soir, on pense à sa famille:
> Pas rigolo!
> On pleure encore quand on roupille
> Dans l'haut Congo.

> On est méchant, farouche et lâche
> Quand on r'vient de là;
> Mais le plus souvent, d'chez ces sauvages
> On n'revient pas.

> On n'a même pas un'croix de cimetière
> Pour ses pauv's os.
> Une croix de bois, et pis d'la poussière
> Voilà l'Congo![25]

The pioneers were not patient with the Africans. Their language was replete with terms of abuse. According to Congolese opinion, the most common epithet applied to a black man was *macaque* (monkey). The racist component in Belgian thought, however, can be easily overestimated. Victorians of all nationalities were not shy in voicing their disdain of white as well as black foreigners; to the Oxford historian James Froude, the Irish seemed more like tribes of squalid apes than human beings, and Froude's mentor Thomas Carlyle was fond of describing the Irishman's condition as one of unmitigated apehood. White people naturally considered themselves superior to the backward people they met in Africa. Yet a number of soldiers and officials established personal relationships with those whom they grew to know in the bush. Dislike for interethnic contact derived from Africans as much as from Europeans. The *mundele* (Europeans) were initially considered to be ghosts or revenants who were wont to catch Africans, eat them, send them to Mputu (the white man's land), transform them into whites, and return them to the Congo, where the erstwhile victims in turn began a new career as man-eaters.[26]

In the early literature of white colonialism in the Congo there are certain parallels to these African fantasies, born as a result of the grim nature of early culture contacts. These writings tend to stress the grimness of Africa, its travails, and its horrors, from cannibalism to witchcraft executions. Perhaps the most influential of the early publicists was Stanley, an accomplished journalist with a ready pen and a flair for good stories, as well as a sense of the dramatic and considerable narrative powers. Stanley wrote copiously and well. His works, which were translated into French by Gérard Henry, played an important part in shaping procolonial attitudes in Belgium. Stanley had a score of Belgian successors who made their names through their ability to record their experiences in a fashion that was interesting to their readers as well as through their success as explorers. One of the most influential of these was Jérome Becker, a Belgian officer we have already mentioned, whose books reached a wide public.[27] For a brief period Becker was in vogue, but his fame did not last. He hurt his image among a patriotic public by his sturdy conviction that the Belgians should seek an accommodation with the Arabs rather than their destruction; he fell into disgrace and his works plunged into oblivion.

191

Near the end of the century, more specialized publications began to appear. Missionaries made a major contribution to the study of ethnography and linguistics; they translated hymnbooks and both sacred and secular literature into indigenous languages, especially into Kikongo.[28] Publications in French included academic periodicals such as the *Annales d'ethnographie* (starting in 1899). These journals provided scholars and administrators with an impressive body of information collected by professional scholars, missionaries, explorers, and officials interested in human problems as well as in the flora, fauna, and geography of the Congo. Military and civil technicians also contributed to colonial literature. Staff officers, who were highly trained in mathematics, physics, cartography, and the art of expressing their thoughts concisely in staff papers, were particularly well equipped to make their mark in the scientific exploration of Africa. Like Belgian missionaries, they made important contributions to subjects such as ethnography and geography. Others provided more modest and specialized works, such as *L'Art militaire au Congo* (1897), which appealed only to a very narrow circle of readers. Yet some of them can claim literary as well as technical recognition for the clarity and vigor with which they discussed such problems as the *combats relevants à la petite guerre* and for the sociological insight that enabled professional soldiers to interpret indigenous warfare in terms of the African social structure.

In many cases, moreover, the professional soldiers were apt to project to the Belgian public a more favorable image of the African than their colleagues employed in the civil administration or the church. Belgian soldiers, like those of the other colonizing powers, were compelled to endure the dangers and hardships of tropical campaigns side by side with African subordinates. Their military successes depended on the courage and stamina of their *askaris*. Their profession compelled them to make a thorough study of at least the military aspects of African life. Not surprisingly, many white officers acquired a high opinion of the military virtues displayed by both their African subordinates and their opponents.

These assessments were supplemented by a new literature of imperial trusteeship that praised the efforts of physicians, teachers, and civil servants who were determined to lighten the lot of suffering Africans. In 1908, for instance, two Belgian newspapers—the *Etoile belge* and the *Chronique*—sent Emile Vandervelde and Fritz (later Frédéric) van der Linden to write a popular study of the Congo. The two had little in common. Vandervelde, a Socialist parliamentarian and a man of international reputation, had abandoned his party's uncompromising anticolonialism. Van der Linden was then a little-known journalist, a liberal in politics, a scholar, journalist, *conseiller colonial*, and later a colonial administrator. His books, *Le Congo, les noirs et nous* (1910) and *Les Derniers Jours de l'Etat du Congo, journal de voyage juillet-octobre 1908* (1909), were characteristic examples of what might be called the Belgian literature of trusteeship. The old doctrines that stressed the white man's moral obligations cease to be followed; they were replaced in part by a secular creed that justified empire in terms of power held in trust, rather than in terms of religion or profits.

Congolese themes began to be used to a minor extent in literature. Belgium had no Kipling, however, and novels focusing on the Congo appealed only to a limited readership. The undisputed pioneer in the field of Euro-Congolese fiction was Joseph Conrad. Conrad's life was as adventurous as that of any of his imagined characters. He was born in Berdichev in the Ukraine, the son of a Polish landowner with literary tastes who had been sent into exile by the Russians for taking part in the movement for Polish independence. Both of Conrad's parents died young, and he was an orphan by the time he was ten. At a period when other young men of his social class were still in school, Conrad decided to go to sea. He shipped in a French vessel to South America and later became involved with gunrunning in Spain. When he was just eighteen he reached Great Britain for the first time, speaking but a few words of English. It took only a few years for him to obtain a British master mariner's diploma, a certificate of naturalization, a seagoing command—and an astonishing mastery of the English tongue. His journeys took him to far parts of the world, from the South Seas to West Africa. His experiences in the Congo led to his *Heart of Darkness* (1902), a book of immense significance for his literary development. Conrad's story derived from personal experience as a master mariner on a Congo steamboat. It was an indictment of Belgian rule. Conrad's work was followed by a spate of others books, published in Belgium and other European countries, that described real or imagined journeys to the Congo. Among them were Jürgen Jürgensen's *Christian Svarres Congofoerd* (1909) and James van Drunen's *Heures africaines* (1899), a book of reminiscences written in symbolist form and lyrical style.

Once the initial era of conquest had passed, colonial writers began to depict the Congo in a different fashion. There was an end to works like *Africa*, an heroic play cast in verse that depicted the horrors of the slave trade through five acts with a great supporting cast of villains and savages. The tropical rain forest and its exotic denizens became suffused with an air of romance, and so did the new breed of empire builders. Léopold Courouble, a Brussels lawyer and man of letters turned Congolese magistrate, wrote a series of columns that made use of his experiences on the bench. His works, which retain their literary merit today, include *En Plein Soleil, voyage à Bankana: la passe de Swinburne* (1900) and, much later, *Le Lettré*, a eulogy to Félix Fuchs, who had been a personal friend of the author's. Courouble's work blended imagination with realism. He was well aware of the seamy side of empire, but when he wrote of Governor-General Costermans in terms of "le terrible Cosse," he did not depict a villain; instead, he tried to penetrate the mind of a man determined to exercise authority for the common good, yet deeply troubled at the hardships inflicted by compulsory porterage and other apparently unavoidable administrative burdens borne by the indigenous peoples.

The colonial experience was reflected also in Flemish literature. For instance, Alfons Vermeulen's novel *De Pioniersdagen van Chicongo* tells of "Chicongo," a young Dutch pioneer who makes his way into the Congolese interior, where he trades in rubber and ivory and later becomes a big-game hunter. Chicongo is far superior to the ordinary white colonials. Africans come to admire Chicongo's courage, honesty, courtesy, and his prowess both as a fighter and a peacemaker. Chicongo falls in love with Africa and, in an unguarded moment, dreams of being reborn as an African. The story ends in a tragic fashion. He enters into a liaison with Mulekedi, an African girl who prefers the white stranger to her own countrymen. But Mulekedi dies in childbirth, together with her baby. There is no future in a love such as Mulekedi's and Chicongo's.

Udinji: Chez les riverains de Bushimaie (1905) follows a similar tradition. The writer, Charles Cudell, used the notes bequeathed to him by his brother Alfred-Marie, who had served in the Congo as a labor recruiter and company agent. Exploiting this invaluable source material, Cudell produced a *roman de moeurs* that retains a high place in Belgian colonial libraries. Udinji, the heroine, is a complicated character—"strange, full of unformulated aspirations, dreaming of far horizons that she hardly comprehends, with naive notions drawn from the stories told by traders and from old wives' tales." Cudell was more than a novelist concerned with the Congo. He was also one of the first theoreticians of "patient penetration." The Belgians, he wrote, would never succeed unless they approached their task with tact and patience, unless they learned how to understand the manners and customs of their new subjects and to impose their rule by kindness, courage, and intelligence.

The science of ethnography also made a contribution to literature. The *Etudes Bakongo*, published in 1912 by

195

Adolphe de Calonne-Beaufaict, an engineer in the Congolese service, presented original ethnographic research with verve and stylistic elegance. A major study by this author, *Azande*, was published posthumously in Brussels in 1912, further adding to knowledge of the sociology of the Congo and to the wider world of Belgian letters.

The new notions of trusteeship that were diffused by scholars and literary men received considerable support from the more thoughtful members of the Belgian colonial establishment. Many officials had grown disillusioned by what they had seen and done in the early days when living conditions were grim, when disease was unconquered, and when government all too often was synonymous with war. Commandant Lemaire, for instance, had gone to the Congo as an enthusiast, determined to serve the cause of humanity. He was soon disabused:

> I was twenty-five [he wrote in 1907] when I first arrived in the Congo. My only introduction to my work derived from a few books that I had read. Everyone regarded Central Africa as a frightening land. I was all too ready to accept this conventional wisdom. My training began amid the roar of guns, amid burning villages, among all the abuse and excesses that derive from coercion. I also became a ruler of men. For a time I followed the examples that had been set to me. But I came to doubt the value of these proceedings; I reread with horror my first reports; my whole being·revolted; I swore to myself to consecrate my efforts toward the purpose of benefiting the black race.[29]

Lemaire's reflections bore fruit. Louis Franck, an old friend of his, became minister of colonies after World War I, and Lemaire submitted to him a scheme for setting up an Ecole coloniale supérieure. Franck liked the project and appointed Lemaire the first director of the newly established school. The Ecole coloniale supérieure was run as an *internat*. It resembled, in some measure, a British public school. Lemaire was an all-powerful and beneficent headmaster whose personality exercised an immense influence on the students. He stressed honor, duty, morality, and esprit de corps. His was a secular ethos founded upon the notion that the strong must act as trustees for the weak, that the advanced races should protect backward peoples. Unlike a British public school, however, the Ecole coloniale supérieure attracted a number of working-class applicants. Physical exercise and sports were compulsory, as were gardening and handicrafts, skills that would not have counted for much in a great British school. Lemaire and his colleagues tried to undo the evil that they had experienced in the Leopoldine period. Unwittingly, they trained their students for the past—the past as remembered by Lemaire and his colleagues.[30]

THE ECONOMICS OF REFORM

Under the new dispensation promoted by men like Lemaire, the atrocities once associated with "red rubber" disappeared. The Colonial Charter, in fact, specifically prohibited forced labor. There was a progressive decline in the export of other wild products such as ivory and wild rubber, whereas exports of crops such as palm kernels and palm oil increased. In 1910 the Congolese government accordingly abolished the hated labor tax by insisting that imposts should henceforth be paid exclusively in currency. Also, according to a decree issued on 2 May 1910, African men had to furnish an impost varying from four to twelve francs per annum; men who had married several wives were obliged to pay an additional sum that might rise to a maximum of sixty francs per annum. This innovation had the indirect effect of promoting the spread of the money economy into the villages, and it tended to penalize Africans who had contracted polygamous marriages and thereby taken on extensive kinship obligations.

The government imported a large amount of new currency to speed up the flow of cash transactions. A new Direction de l'industrie et du commerce was created at Boma and

Elisabethville to assist trade. Custom duties diminished. In 1910, moreover, the Congo authorities opened the country to the free commerce of all nations. Until 1915, when the exigencies of war caused Belgian policies to harden once again, the Congo enjoyed a brief period of relatively unhampered traffic; small white traders, many of Portuguese or Greek origin, as well as black hawkers operated with little hindrance. There was a rise in agricultural prices and a striking increase not only in investment goods but also in the amount of merchandise—matches, sugar, salt, soap, cloth, and the like—destined for African customers. From 1912 to 1913 alone, the value of imports for African consumption rose from some 14.4 million francs to 20 million.

Simultaneously, the conditions of migrant laborers were ameliorated somewhat. The government licensed a number of labor-recruiting organizations, such as the Bourse du travail du Katanga, which was set up in 1910, and imposed minimum conditions with regard to the food and accommodations. Municipal improvements were also undertaken. Elisabethville, for instance, had begun as a pestilential slum where European pioneers lived in African-style huts if they were lucky and in floorless tents if they were not. Malaria and venereal diseases were rampant; according to data collected by Bruce Fetter, the white death rate was at first stupendously high. The African townsmen were even worse off. Clerks and foremen from Nyasaland, the African elite, managed a living standard superior to that of unlettered workers, but the mass of laborers were in a sorry condition. Conditions varied among the different camps, but in the first year after the opening of the railway, the annual death rate for black people was estimated at 24 percent, and did not decline until the latter part of World War I.

Elisabethville gradually turned into a reasonably well-administered city. Its governance was French-speaking, Catholic, and procapitalist, shaped by the imperialist sentiments of Leopold II. Socially it was characterized by a rigid system of segregation, both within the white community itself and between the European and the African segments of society. Belgian government officials disdained British and South African traders, miners, and mine managers. Well-to-do whites of any origin were contemptuous of the "low" whites—East European Jews, Greeks and Portuguese. The European quarter occupied the central part of the city. Like American cities and like Rhodesian townships such as Bulawayo and Salisbury, the "white" section was laid out on an American-style grid pattern. Adjacent was the African township that housed servants and employees of smaller white firms. On the outskirts large companies such as the Union minière and the Katanga railway built camps for their workmen.

For the new regime, reform entailed a more rapid pace of Belgianization. The Belgians were angered by Britain's refusal to recognize the annexation of the Congo by the Belgian state in 1908, and Belgian colonizers were more afraid of suspected British plots against Katanga than of German Mittelafrika. Elisabethville (now Lubumbashi), which in 1911 already comprised more than seven thousand people, did not fit the Congolese pattern. The new mining township depended on Rhodesia for its traffic, having been connected with the Rhodesian railway system in 1909. (The Bas Congo-Katanga railway, running from the terminus of the Katanga on the upper Congo, did not reach the port of Ilebo on the Kasai until 1928.) British farmers from Northern Rhodesia supplied the Elisabethville compounds with corn and beef. British prospectors and skilled workers from Southern Rhodesia and South Africa thronged the city streets. There was continuous rivalry between Belgians and Britons: British shopkeepers lured customers from the agents of Belgian trading companies; British Protestants competed with Belgian Catholics for pagan souls; and English- and French-speakers quarreled on the board of the Union minière. The few thousand resident Britons made more trouble for the Belgian administration than all the Africans in Katanga. Disdainful of Belgian rule, white Rhodesians and South Africans looked to the British empire, and as late as 1919, the Belgians still feared that the Britons in Katanga might stage a local rising that would provoke another Jameson Raid.

However unjustified these fears, the Belgians took action. They strongly reinforced their military forces and extended their administration right up to the borders of Northern Rhodesia. Sir Robert Williams, the British mining and railway magnate who was a good friend of Leopold's, faced increasing financial and political difficulties as the Belgians strengthened their hold on the Katangan economy. The CSK was made to release its administrative powers in 1910, and the central administration asserted its authority over the still largely English-speaking white mining community of Katanga. In 1911 the Union minière passed completely under Belgian control, and Williams was obliged to close the company's London office. As the mines began to produce more copper, Katanga's financial fortunes gradually improved, and in 1919 the Union minière paid its first dividend. Within the civil service, the foreign element gradually disappeared, first from the general administration and later from the specialist services, although the head and nearly half of the physicians in the medical department were still foreigners as late as the 1920s.

In addition, some attempts were made to encourage Belgian settlement in Katanga. Renkin especially favored Belgian colonists in order to expedite the *mise en valeur* and to counteract "Anglo-Saxon" influence. The Compagnie du Katanga accordingly ceded 150,000 hectares to the Société foncière, agricole et pastorale du Congo for the purpose of providing land to newcomers; the state supplied assistance, but few immigrants came. The company went into liquidation, and the Katanga administration took over its assets, but only a handful of Belgian families managed to stay on the land. The administration also encouraged retired officials to remain in the country on the grounds that the resident white population should not be limited only to artisans and farmers but should also include members of the Belgian ruling class.[31] Nevertheless, Belgians were reluctant to settle in what they saw to be a remote colony on the edge of beyond. Even had they gone, they would have found themselves without influence or power in a state dominated by the dual influence of bureaucracy and the companies.

In general, there was a good deal of continuity between the Free State and its Belgian successor. Free State officials remained in office for the most part, an unavoidable expedient at a time when the Belgians were having difficulty in finding a sufficient number of qualified applicants for their service. The shortage of suitable personnel in turn slowed down the process of civilianizing, which was symbolized by Fuchs's appointment to the highest government position in the Congo. Within the colony, the existing alliance between the state and the companies continued; the relationship between privileged concerns and the administration remained closer in the Belgian Congo than in any other colonial territory. Under the terms of the settlement negotiated between the sovereign and the Belgian state, the nation received a large amount of real and personal property within Belgium that had belonged to the Free State, together with stock—valued at nearly 61 million francs—in several Congo companies that had previously been owned by the Free State. According to Buell's calculation, the total value of the property, excluding that of residual rights in the land handed over to the Belgian government, came to 110,337,000 francs. The government thus held an extensive interest in Congolese concerns.

In metropolitan terms, these sums were insignificant; in 1912 the value of Belgium's imports was 4.958 million francs, and its exports were worth 3.951 million. In the Congolese context, however, the financial power of the state was vast. Congolese exports in 1912 were reckoned at no more than 83,465,000 francs, imports at some 61,864,000 francs.[32] The state did not exercise direct business powers (most state appointees voted with the largest shareholding block within each of the companies with which they were associated), but the state had a direct stake in private profits. As before, state officials continued to be involved in the general direction of great enterprises and therefore had more extensive roles than their confrères in British colonial Africa. The Belgian Congo, in certain respects, became the prototype of the corporate state.

Throughout its colonial history, the Congolese economy continued to be dominated by a few large companies. Even fifty years after the *reprise*, about three-fourths of all economic activity was said to be controlled by five large companies, all but one Belgian-owned. These companies in turn were intimately linked to the state, which owned a considerable amount of share capital in the major Belgian trusts and held a commanding position on the boards of key public services such as transport and electricity, giving it a position much more powerful than that enjoyed by any other African colonial government.

Coercion persisted in the country's economic life, albeit in a much attentuated form. As Albert Thys and Alexandre Delcommune stated in an official communication to the government, the native of the Upper Congo region in particular had not yet reached the state of evolution that induced him naturally to improve his condition by commerce and labor. Hence the application of taxation must remain for a considerable period the chief stimulus for work.[33] Belgian officials, for the most part, thought along similar lines. Although compulsory labor for private profit remained forbidden, the government insisted that local administrators ought to "encourage" Africans to work and that every government official should be "an apostle of labor."[34]

This "evangelism of labor" combined with the need for revenue to shape the colony's agricultural policy. The new Belgian administration had assumed the financial obligations incurred by its predecessor. It maintained an elaborate bureaucratic and military establishment; it was intimately involved in the affairs of major companies; and it had made heavy expenditures in building a transport network. Of all the African colonies, the Belgian Congo accordingly carried the highest debt load.[35] Belgian experts thus considered that African cultivators should be compelled to grow more cash crops in order to right the balance.

In 1908 a new *direction générale* came into being at the Ministry of Colonies; it was concerned specifically with agriculture and headed by Emile Laplae, a firm believer in the merits of the old Dutch system in the East Indies. Laplae tried to persuade Belgian capitalists to invest in the Congo rather than in Southeast Asian plantations. He also attempted to promote European settlement in Katanga. But he met with unexpected difficulties, which increased as the export of wild rubber from the Congo began to decline and the deficit of the Congolese state steadily increased. Belgium would not set up state-run plantations, since they seemed to have failed in other parts of the world. Nor was encouragement given to privately run plantations, as the Belgian establishment, including Socialists like Vandervelde, feared the emergence of an agricultural proletariat.[36]

A system of compulsory cultivation, on the other hand, seemed to allow the best of both worlds. Village cultivators were supposedly idle by nature and insensible to their own best advantage. They had to be guided for their own good. These notions were not entirely the product of racial prejudice; contemporary British literature regarding the Afrikaans-speaking backwoodsmen of South Africa is replete with similar statements concerning the assumed inability of white Afrikaners to benefit from a market economy. Yet a racial note entered into the rulers' deliberations in the Congolese setting: the system of compulsory cultivation would have an "educative effect" on the "children of nature"—a concept that appealed to administrators who were themselves selected in part through a rigid sysem of examinations. Economic compulsion would rouse the villages from their torpor. The cultivation of profitable cash crops would also yield more taxes to the coffers of the state. Backward villagers would be transformed into contented and reasonably prosperous smallholders, a bush-bred petty bourgeoisie of the kind that

203

appealed to Belgian policy makers. Peasant farming would be more crisis-resistant than would plantation enterprise. Peasants, unlike private companies, would not ask for government subsidies.

The *étatiste* trend in the Congo drew added strength from Belgian experiences in World War I. The Germans invaded Belgium and largely overran the country. They occasioned widespread suffering by conscripting Belgian labor and confiscating Belgian wealth. The country's very existence as an independent state seemed in danger. Alone of all European belligerents, the Belgians had to rely on their colonial empire as a territorial base as well as a major economic resource —an experience that was to be repeated in World War II. Under such inauspicious circumstances, the Belgians were little inclined to break with their tradition of *dirigisme*.

In 1917 the government passed an ordinance that provided for the compulsory cultivation of cotton and of food crops such as manioc, sweet potatoes, rice, and corn to furnish supplies to both the villages and the mines. The cultivators were remunerated for their produce according to fixed, rather than world-market, prices. For all its good intentions, however, the system was ill adjusted for its stated purpose of creating a prosperous peasantry. The cultivator's personal income remained small, fixed prices reduced the villager's freedom of choice and diminished his economic incentive, and discontent was rife and resistance widespread.

The system also militated against the interests of small merchants, whether their native tongue was Portuguese, Greek, or Swahili. Village traders could have played a major part in developing the country's resources by offering low-cost marketing facilities to producers in the bush. Unlike substantial merchants, they were willing to travel over vast distances, to shoulder high risks, to devote much time to individual transactions, and to buy or sell in "penny packets." Their mode of doing business was adjusted to the needs of producers who harvested crops in small quantities and who were so poor that they would bargain over one or two needles. Petty dealers, moreover, were dependent on their customers' personal goodwill; they could neither compel the peasants to sell their crops nor oblige them to buy the hawkers' wares. Unlike officials, traders could not insist on paying fixed prices; they had to rely on economic incentives by force of circumstance.[37]

But the village trader's economic function was little understood by men like Thys and Delcommune, who looked askance at low-caste hawkers. A system of genuine laissez faire, enabling the villagers to sell their time and labor to their own best advantage, would in fact have benefited both the rulers and the ruled. Such was the opinion of Anglo-Saxon missionaries and of British and German traders with a humanitarian bent, not to speak of the hawkers themselves. Yet laissez faire was entirely alien to an administration as hierarchical and *étatiste* in its tradition as the Belgian establishment in the Congo. Free trade never had a chance. After the end of World War I, the system of compulsory cultivation was further extended, especially for the purpose of enlarging and diversifying African peasant production. The Belgians continued to use compulsion to conscript African villagers for the construction of public works, roads in particular, a form of investment that required a great deal of unskilled labor at a time when mechanical road-making equipment had not yet become available for use in the bush.

At the same time, Belgian governance involved changes for the better. The Belgians did away with the traditional "restraints on trade," the elaborate network of internal tolls, tributes, labor services, and other exactions that had been enforced by former chiefs and warlords. New skills were imported, and new occupations unknown to tribal societies were created. Africans began to work as machinists, police sergeants, telegraphists, hospital assistants, clerks, carpenters, masons, painters, postal officials, and similar functionaries. Black men became the noncommissioned officers of empire. Internecine wars ceased, indigenous armies disappeared, and the slave trade, raids and counterraids, became part of the

205

past. Belgian rule, once regularized and cast into bureaucratic forms, was more sparing of human life than precolonial regimes had been. Ritual cannibalism and witchcraft executions gradually died out, as did the more lurid forms of dealing with suspected witches, such as drowning, hanging, burning at the stake, live burial, or slow impalement.

The success of Belgian policies depended, in the last instance, on the African chiefs whom the colonial administration employed as its local agents. In theory, the Belgians intended to use indigenous institutions for the purpose of governance. The administration accordingly had enacted a decree in 1910 providing that Africans should be governed by traditional chiefs recognized by the district commissioner through a formal "investiture." Execution of this policy, however, left much to be desired. Belgian officials tried to assimilate the chiefs into the colonial hierarchy, but the officials often were too little acquainted with local customs and languages to appoint the right men; the boundaries of provinces and districts were frequently drawn across tribal lines. Sometimes a local impostor or the head of a minor faction in a clan dispute managed to have himself invested as a chief. In other cases, the true tribal authority, shrinking from association with the Belgians, put forward a straw man who formally wielded authority under Belgian supervision while the real power remained in traditional hands. Sometimes the local Belgian administrator, unfamiliar with the local dialect and local ways, conferred power on a "reliable" policeman or court interpreter; commoners or even former slaves occasionally stepped into positions of dignity.

In particular, the Belgians continued the policy of permitting subject peoples to break away from their erstwhile overlords. In some cases, subordinate clans were recognized as independent political units. Hence the process of administrative fragmentation continued. By 1914 there were as many as 3,653 independent *chefferies*; by 1919 their number had risen to 6,059. Fragmentation permitted the Belgians to install a number of pliable men, some of them former

206

soldiers or officials, some of them former slaves. In this way they probably weakened the institution they meant to sustain. According to Louis Franck, writing after World War I:

> In many regions of the colony, the *chefferies* are too small. Many chiefs lack authority. Is this surprising? The means by which the chiefs once made themselves obeyed have disappeared. The chiefs know it and they say so.
>
> One of the heirs to a powerful line . . . said to me, "Bula Matari, if I had the powers which my father possessed, I would know how to make myself obeyed. But will you restore them to me?"[38]

Extensive reform was delayed, and for years the Belgian administration continued to operate with many of the methods and preconceptions that had characterized Free State governance.

Church and State in the Congo

The earliest Christian evangelists in the Congo were the Portuguese. But Portuguese influence, though considerable in the sixteenth century, did not last; hopes of creating a Luso-African form of feudalism, complete with black dukes, black princes, and black counts, collapsed. The first modern missionaries to work in the country came from Great Britain, the United States, France, and Belgium. They pioneered Western education—especially the Protestants, who placed special emphasis on reading the Bible. They also worked to transmit technical skills to their pupils. Missionaries translated books into indigenous languages, compiled dictionaries, and promoted certain indigenous languages to the status of linguae francae, including Lingala, a composite idiom that was widely used in education, in the army, and in the administration.

In numerical terms, the missionaries did not count for much. The means and manpower available to mission societies were limited. Even with the best will in the world they

207

could only educate a tiny percentage of the Congolese population. In 1908 there were supposedly 587 missionaries of all denominations in the country, and the total number of mission pupils was 46,075; 19,380 of these went to Catholic schools, and 26,695 to Protestant schools.[39] The general level of instruction remained modest; only a small proportion of the students acquired even the "three Rs." Missionary progress thus was slow. The white man's lore was alien to the people, and his creed made far greater demands upon the convert than did Islam. Believers were expected to set aside all wives but one, and they could no longer participate in a vast range of village rituals. Moreover, Christianity required an elaborate superstructure of schools and churches. Most of this investment was paid for by European mission supporters, yet African believers were expected to contribute. Their new training and their new obligations fitted them more for a cash economy than for the village life in which they had been brought up.

Initially the vast majority of villagers would have no truck with church or school. Christianity, to a considerable extent, was the creed of slaves, outcasts, and refugees, of men and women without a stake in existing societies. African fathers had no desire to send their children to mission schools where they would pick up eccentric or reprehensible notions and where their labor no longer benefited the kin group. Gradually, however, Africans began to discover the value of the new skills taught by the foreign invaders. Near the turn of the present century many mission societies began to experience a veritable school boom, as young people flocked to the mission stations in large numbers to search out new knowledge. The initial boom collapsed in a renewed surge of resistance, but mission education never again lost its initial impetus; by the early 1920s some 120,000 children were at school, about half of them in Catholic institutions.

The missionary pioneers had not gone to Africa at the risk of their lives for the sake of becoming schoolteachers. They had looked upon themselves as Christ's vanguard,

208

destined to redeem a heathen continent. Living conditions gradually improved. As congregations increased in size, organizational problems grew more complex, and missionaries became organizers and pedagogues rather than preachers. They were forced to leave an ever-growing share of the actual teaching and preaching in the villages to black teachers and catechists. These men formed a new semiliterate or literate elite, part of the new Western-educated stratum of clerks, interpreters, police sergeants, and craftsmen who served the whites in positions of subordinate authority. The catechists were dependent partly upon mission salaries and partly upon the produce of plots worked by themselves or their wives in their spare time.

To the European missionary, education—literary or industrial—began to acquire ever-growing importance as a sovereign tool of evangelization. The differences among the missionary societies in performance and educational philosophy were great. Except for adherents of fundamentalist sects, the Protestants were more inclined to stress learning for all, while the Catholics believed that erudition should be confined to a tiny minority of men with a vocation for the priesthood (the first Congolese priest assumed office in 1917). But whatever their creed, the missionaries had a strong religious ideology to sustain their work. In this respect their approach differed sharply from the narrowly utilitarian outlook of Congo Free State officials. The Leopoldine administration had set up a few technical schools at Boma, Léopoldville, and Stanleyville to train artisans and clerks for service on the railways, in the army, and in the administration. After the *reprise* the state entrusted these institutions to Catholic teaching orders, the Frères des écoles chrétiennes and the Marist brothers.[40]

The choice was a wise one. Missionary resources were scanty. Most contributions came not from millionaires but from middle-class and lower-middle-class supporters overseas—artisans, businessmen, farmers, foremen—men and women for whom missionary donations represented a real

209

sacrifice. Given the paucity of their means, the missionaries acquitted themselves well. They had genuine convictions, an ideological impetus of a depth not common among secular instructors in Free State craft schools. Whatever their educational philosophy, they found that evangelization could not be conducted in a vacuum; the mission stations themselves required craftsmen and farmers to carry on in the bush.

The missionaries began to train artisans, initially for the purpose of changing society. Mission graduates included a small number of brickmakers, bricklayers, masons, gardeners, carpenters, joiners, cooks, and tailors. Protestant missions turned out a few blacksmiths, steamer mechanics, river pilots, steersmen, sailors, printers, bookbinders, and typesetters. The Jesuits placed special emphasis on farming. Their station at Kisantu, for instance, was a great abbey with gardens and plantations; it also had an important industrial establishment with a tannery, a brewery, and cigar and furniture factories. The Baptist Missionary Society set up an industrial training program at Bololo; the American Presbyterians gave similar instruction at Luebo. These and other institutions produced a new kind of African: a skilled worker dependent on wages, fitted primarily to work in the army, in the administration, and in business. The precise economic impact of missionary effort remains hard to measure, but missionaries supplied nearly all the formal Western education that was available to the Congolese. Their training was of some consequence among certain favored ethnic groups such as the Bakongo, who were the first to benefit from missionary instruction, and the Baluba, who had drawn close to the whites for protection against Muslim slaver traders and Chokwe raiders.

In their relations with the administration, the mission societies displayed a considerable degree of ambivalence. Missionaries received many official favors, such as land concessions that could to some extent be exploited commercially. On the other hand, they frequently acted as critics of government; yet few, if any, of them wanted to put an end to

210

colonial rule. They relied upon government protection; yet they wished to work as far from government stations as they could. While their schools turned out skilled clerks and artisans, the missionaries were inclined to denounce the sinful influence of the mine compounds and townships where their graduates were employed.

The Congolese government was equally ambivalent in its approach. In theory, Africans enjoyed full freedom of religious choice under the Belgian flag. A decree issued on 2 May 1910 permitted the *chefferies* to set up schools staffed either by teachers appointed by the *chefs* or by missionaries selected by the *chefs*. Ecclesiastical liberty was assured by international treaty obligations. Even in terms of administrative regulations, liberty of conscience was unrestricted. In actual fact, the administration became increasingly pro-Catholic. The Protestants were mainly "Anglo-Saxon"—Britons and Americans, many of whom looked upon Catholic Belgium with disdain. Most Catholics, on the other hand, were French-speaking Belgians or Frenchmen who were more inclined to sympathize with King Leopold than were the Protestants. There was a faint air of subversion connected with Protestantism. Its believers were determined to create self-sustaining and self-governing African churches, and they put some stress on African participation in church government. British and American Protestants also played an important part in the campaign against the Leopoldine regime. Catholics were more inclined to stress the duties of submission and loyalty to the Free State government. They placed more emphasis on manual work and rural skills than did the Protestants with their literary bent.

The first of the modern missionaries had been Protestants, but Leopold, not surprisingly, favored Catholics on personal as well as national grounds. Most Belgian administrators were inclined to share their monarch's preconceptions. Officials might be anticlerical by personal conviction, but Belgian anticlericalism produced no missionary enthusiasm of its own, no willingness to spread the notions of Holbach and

Voltaire into the Congolese bush. Catholic missionaries, in the anticlericals' eyes, might be superstitious, but at least they were not antinational. There was bitter competitition between Catholics and Protestants to gain control over primary schools in the bush; Catholic and Protestant catechists, rival members of a new ecclesiastical elite, were apt to insult one another or even exchange blows. The administration tended to favor the Catholics in these struggles, and accordingly they gained the upper hand. By 1907 Catholic missionaries outnumbered Protestants by some 400 to 187. In the Congo, the Catholic share of the Christian converts continued to rise.

The Catholic position was further strengthened by a concordat concluded in 1906 between the Congo Free State and the Holy See. Under the terms of this agreement, which was later continued under Belgian colonial auspices, Catholic schools operated under the jurisdiction of the state. The governor-general was to be informed of most of the senior school appointments. Missions were also required to conduct geographical, linguistic, and ethnographic research for the state. Catholic missionaries acquired great power, especially in their own *villages chrétiens* (mission settlements located outside the jurisdiction of local chiefs). The Catholics strove to keep their Protestant competitors out of areas they had already evangelized. They claimed that Catholics alone could be relied upon to support Belgian rule, and they obtained free land grants as well as small but steadily growing financial support from the administration (see Table 23). For better or for worse, the missionary establishment became yet another arm of government in African eyes.

In terms of numbers, the missionary impact was small; by 1908 the Catholics had perhaps 125,000 converts, the Protestants 70,000. But their impact in the religious and educational fields was considerable, except in the eastern Congo, Kivu, and parts of Katanga. Despite bitter disagreements, clergymen and soldiers, district officers and capitalists pur-

212

TABLE 23

Congo Education Budget
(In Thousands of Belgian Francs)

Year	Total Budget	Education Budget	Mission Subsidies		Ratio of Educational Expenses to Total
			For Education	For Other Purposes	
1912	47,105	402	50	600	0.85
1914	51,936	594	31	784	1.45
1939	729,365	22,310	13,200	3,799	3.06

SOURCE: These figures are taken from Marvin P. Markowitz, *Cross and Sword: The Political Role of Christian Missions in the Belgian Congo, 1908-1960* (Stanford, 1973), p. 59.

sued related aims. Gospel and civil code ruled supreme. The white overlords became the predominant reference group for the peoples of the Congo, and the newly literate Africans, perhaps thirty thousand in all, were their indispensable auxiliaries.

SEVEN

CONCLUSION

THE modern states of Africa are, for the most part, colonial artifacts. In this respect, the Belgian colonizers were no different from their British, German, and French competitors. Leopold and his successors and servants created the Congo as surely as the Romanov dynasty shaped Russia and the Bourbons built France. Belgian colonization was part of a wider process whereby Europe imposed its military and administrative institutions, its technology, its science, and its world views on a vast congeries of Iron Age states and statelets, on scattered rural communities with no sense of cohesion. Of all the colonial regimes, Bula Matadi was peculiarly disliked, not only by its black subjects but also by its white contemporaries in Europe. Edwardian Englishmen who read about the red-rubber scandals in their morning newspaper were inclined to curse the Belgians as a reprehensible lot, hardly superior to Portuguese and Turks. The image of "brave little Belgium" heroically resisting a brutal German ravisher derives from World War I.

At first sight, there seems little evidence that Belgian colonialism was sui generis, for the Belgian colonial impulse had its parallels in other continental countries. Leopold's private colonizing effort had much in common with the use of British and German chartered companies as a means of colonizing on the cheap, of building empires without placing any evident burdens on the metropolitan taxpayer and without engaging the administrative resources of the mother country. Private colonization appeared to be inexpensive. For Belgium, colonization was "artificial"; that is, Belgium had no preexisting interests in the vast territories that it annexed. Even the most enthusiastic protagonists of Belgian expansion could not claim that Belgium built an empire to

214

protect an extant commerce or enterprising missionary bodies. Leopold was not pushed into the Congolese adventure by powerful metropolitan lobbies; Belgian capitalists did not become seriously interested in Central Africa until well after the Congo Free State had been established. Yet this situation was not peculiar to Belgium. When Bismarck secured Cameroun, when Crispi seized Eritrea, Germany and Italy held only negligible economic stakes in Africa. In terms of metropolitan capitalism, the colonial entrepreneurs of Belgium, Italy, Germany, and France were all insignificant: colonization created its own lobbies more than the other way around.

Having established their empires, the European powers used a variety of coercive devices to make their colonies pay. France and Germany, like Belgium, occasionally handed out vast concessions in countries like the French Congo or South-West Africa as a means of attracting scarce capital into remote territories where metropolitan investors were reluctant to risk their funds. Belgian concessionary scandals in the Congo Free State were paralleled by French concessionary scandals in the French Congo. Early colonizers of whatever national origin imposed a variety of demands on their new subjects: *corvées* for building roads, food levies, obligatory porterage for official or military purposes, compulsory agricultural schemes, and forced labor to gather wild rubber. The Germans in East Africa helped to provoke a major rising by insisting on the enforced cultivation of certain cash crops. The British in Rhodesia used taxation as an indirect means of forcing villagers to work for wages or to produce food for sale.

The early periods of repression were commonly followed by eras of reform that embodied a peculiar type of capitalist self-criticism, expressed variously in such terms as *imperial trusteeship, moralisation, Eingeborenenfürsorge*, or *política de atracção*. Statesmen like Bernhard Dernburg in Germany, soldiers like José Norton de Matos in Angola, explorer-publicists like de Brazza in France, and administrators like Sir

CONCLUSION

William Milton and Sir Drummond Chaplin in Rhodesia became increasingly convinced, as did their counterparts in Belgium, that African tribesmen were "economic men" capable of responding to economic incentives. According to the reformers, coercion no longer corresponded to the needs of a developing economy that was dependent on willing workers and satisfied customers.

Belgium used both repression and reform. No Belgian soldier was quite as ruthless as General Lothar von Trotha, the German supreme commander in the South-West African rising of 1905-1906. No British administrator was in advance of enlightened Belgian reformers like Fuchs. Yet there were many differences among the Belgians and their competitors. No other European power granted such enormous powers to a private colonizer as those made over by Belgium to Leopold. Rhodes's British South Africa Company, powerful as it was, never enjoyed a trade monopoly in the country under its sway; the company's operations were subjected to imperial scrutiny in a manner that was inconceivable in the Congo Free State. No other colonialism, not even that of Cecil Rhodes, owed as much to the personality of its founder as did that of Leopold II. No other form of African colonialism, in relative terms, required as large an army as did the Leopoldine kind. No other tropical African colony was as rigorous in the extent of its coercive exploitation as the Congo Free State. No other country had the same "active" trade balance as the Congo, where vast exports of rubber were not balanced by corresponding imports. No other colony in tropical Africa accumulated a comparable public debt, and no other colonial country transferred treasury surpluses from the colony to the motherland in order to finance public works.

Belgian colonial power was exceptionally centralized. There was no legislative council on the British model, not even an advisory *Gouvernementsrat* of the German type to give expression to settler, missionary, and African interests or to act as a brake on executive power. No other country

216

achieved anything like the same measure of interpenetration between capital and state as did the Congo. In Northern Rhodesia, the British mining territory to the east, the great corporations were divided into two powerful competing groups. When they pulled together, they could exercise considerable influence on the government, but they never challenged government supremacy. In the Belgian Congo, however, companies and government almost melded into the same coin. In this respect the Congo developed into an early model of the corporate state.

In contrast to its neighbors, Belgium found colonial reform a traumatic experience. The nation had no colonial tradition, and the idea of colonialism was marginal to Belgian society. The Congolese venture began as an exercise—albeit an utterly futile one—in international humanitarianism; the Free State purportedly represented the principles of free trade and missionary improvement. Leopold faced the task of conquering and holding vast areas with his personal funds and a tiny budget that was more adequate for ruling a county than a country. He had to rely initially on army officers, on foreign volunteers, and on small social enclaves within Belgian society. His administration tried to escape its predicament by a regime of brutal coercion.

Leopold's experiment turned out to be a disaster in economic as well as humanitarian terms. Leopold's Congo was backward compared with colonies like Togo and the Gold Coast that managed to build a modest prosperity on the joint enterprise of merchants and indigenous cultivators freely producing cocoa, palm oil, and other tropical crops in response to world-market demands. The Congo stood for a system of mixed state capitalism comparable in kind, though not in size, to the system prevailing in imperial Russia, where the tsars controlled an elaborate complex of state banks, state railways, state enterprises, and state trading monopolies—the world's largest state-controlled economy at the time. In the Congo there was forced labor; there were atrocities. Humanitarian critics in Great Britain, Germany, and in Belgium itself had a good case, and their stories lost nothing in the telling. The Congo was widely described as a gigantic slave plantation ruled by a sovereign so blood-thirsty that its African population had been diminished by one-half or more. The facts, though incriminating, were not that dramatic. The Congo Free State, a country as large as Western Europe, could not be effectively administered with the limited means at Leopold's disposal. There were no censuses, so statistical estimates concerning the effects of administration policy on the native population meant little. Even today, no one knows exactly how many people live in Zaïre.

In 1908, as we have seen, the Belgian state reluctantly assumed control of Leopold's empire. The administration became less military and more civilian in its composition, less brutalizing and more predictably bureaucratic in its operation. Economic coercion did not come to an end, however. Whereas the impact of the Congo Free State had been restricted by its inability to govern the outlying parts of the territory in an effective manner, the new administration was more effective. By about 1920 a more solid form of governance had been established through the Congo. The requirements of "mobilizing" labor and the enforced cultivation of crops still necessitated a coercive state apparatus, but private buccaneering came to an end. The government was able to protect the personal safety and property of its subjects. Mining along modern capitalist lines became the colony's economic mainstay, replacing an archaic *Raubwirtschaft* based on forced labor and the collection of wild rubber and ivory. There were other reforms. Under the new regime the country's population began to expand. But the original impression of widespread exploitation and terror tended to stick despite all reforms.

Polemical criticism and countercriticism seeped into scholarly studies. Critiques of colonialism, Belgian and foreign, were transported into the sphere of international competition. The ultimate effects of Belgian colonization remain a subject of bitter dispute that hinges not so much on the

Belgian experience but on the wider question of the European role in Africa. Contemporary polemics tend to follow a pattern almost as rigid as the moves in a conventional chess gambit. The censors of colonialism stress the negative aspects of the imperial experience. They point out its coercive aspects, the widespread use of forced labor for railway building, porterage, and road construction; they enlarge on the horrors of red rubber; they explain the destructive effects of European colonization on indigenous culture and on indigenous state systems. Some critics agree that European colonization also had certain positive aspects in that it diffused new industrial techniques; nevertheless, they feel convinced that any advantages that may have derived from the colonial experience were acquired at an excessive price. Others go further. They argue that Europe actually "undeveloped" Africa, that relatively peaceful and prosperous societies were debased by foreign conquest and became dependent fragments of industrialized Europe's rural periphery.

The defenders of European colonialism see the imperial experience in very different terms. To them, Europe was a new Rome imposing its laws and civilization on backward barbarians. As George Martelli, a journalist-historian, once wrote, every building in the Congo more than six feet high was put there by the Belgians. The Belgians were not the first conquerors in the Congo, but they were conquerors with a difference. Unlike Chokwe, Lovale, or Swahili-speaking warlords, they brought entirely new methods of production, administration, and government. They introduced steam power for land and sea transport, deep-level mining, and new seeds for agriculture; they paved the way for modern health, veterinary, and educational services. They spread entirely new forms of scientific knowledge; they diffused literacy; and they laid the foundations of a modern state. Their achievements differed both in quality and quantity from those of ancient Luba lords or Lunda monarchs.

Our own view inclines to the second school of thought. In the foregoing account we have been anxious not to eschew

219

the seamy side of empire. But we see no merit in historical interpretations that romanticize the unromantic societies of precolonial Africa. We continue to share the cultural optimism of men like Livingstone, Marx, and Kipling, all of whom—whatever their differences—looked to technological progress and regarded the steam-driven locomotive not merely as a means of transport, but also as an engine of social liberation.

We are skeptical also of the currently fashionable notions of "revisionist" historiography concerning the rule of Western Europe as the world "city" that exploits the rural "periphery" of the Third World through the extraction of super-profits. First of all, we do not see the problems of the so-called Third World as unique. When Leopold set out to build his empire, every European country still had a "rural periphery" at home. The unification of Italy, for instance, subjected southern Italy to the governance of a centralized state whose rulers were as unsympathetic to the peasants of Calabria and Sicily as were the urban anticlerical bourgeoisie of Brussels to the Catholic villagers of Flanders and to the animist tillers of Kivu. The merchants, politicians, and bureaucrats of Milan and Torino failed to comprehend the predicament of the rural south and commonly interpreted it in purely moralistic terms: Sicilian peasants were said to be thriftless and disinclined to work. In fact, centralized northern government, alien laws, heavy taxation, conscription, and a burgeoning bureaucracy may, for a time, have worsened rather than bettered the southerners' condition. Hence widespread social discontent took many forms, including rural banditry. Wiser and more humane governance, respectful of regional particularities and the Catholic religion, would have softened the blow of "modernization" in southern Italy. Yet we do not regard the unification of Italy and the disappearance of the Neapolitan kingdom as a disaster any more than we bewail the demise of African lordships like that established by Msiri in Katanga.

The nature of "exploitation" raises wider issues, which

220

we have discussed in our books *Burden of Empire: An Appraisal of Western Colonialism in Africa South of the Sahara* and *The Economics of Colonialism*. We do not propose to recapitulate our arguments beyond saying that the concept of exploitation is more complex than is assumed by writers on the Left, Old and New. The enforced production of ivory and rubber was exploitation in the true sense, but its profits were minute within the framework of Belgian capitalism as a whole. The enforced cultivation of crops, practiced even more widely after than before the *reprise*, strikes us as equally obnoxious. (In this respect we share the outlook of enlightened contemporary reformers like Bernhard Dernburg in Wilhelminian Germany or the Aborigines Protection Society in Great Britain.) Given the African tillers' natural ability to conduct their affairs in an economically rational manner, without benefit of bureaucratic dictation, we are convinced that the Belgians, in the long run, lost rather than gained by their cupidity. This contention, evident to Victorian giants like Macaulay, is not acceptable, however, to revisionist scholars.

We also differ from revisionists in other respects. For instance, we do not share their view concerning the alleged role of "low" wages in the accumulation of capital. Revisionist historians widely assume (in a curiously un-Marxist manner) that the rate of wages determines capital accumulation. Common sense observation proves that the opposite is true. We equally take issue with currently fashionable arguments concerning "Third World dependency." These notions stem from Rosa Luxemburg, who argued that capitalists can only keep up their rate of profit by constantly expanding their operations into backward areas along the Western periphery and by moving into surviving "islands" of precapitalist production within the industrialized states. Intellectually, Luxemburg's work towers above that of her latter-day epigoni. Unfortunately, her thesis has little applicability to the facts, as we have sought to point out in *Burden of Empire*.

In summary, Belgian colonization in the Congo, like Western colonization in contemporary Africa as a whole, seems to us part of a wider movement of cultural diffusion whose manifold evils were outweighed in the long run by its benefits. Within this wider movement, Belgium occupied a somewhat peculiar place. Belgian colonization had an unusually strong emphasis on practical aims, both negative and positive. When Belgium began to colonize in Africa, it was one of the most advanced industrial countries in northwestern Europe—and one of the most socially backward. If Belgians were wont to use their unskilled labor migrants at home in a harsh fashion, their performance was even worse in the colonies. Domestic reforms, however, gradually seeped from Belgium into the Congo, and the material performance improved decidedly.

Belgium is a country divided between Flemings and Walloons, a country now in search of a national identity. The ideological superstructure of Belgian imperialism was considerably weaker than that of the British or the French. Belgian colonialism thus was characterized by a timidly defensive mood, one appropriate to a small country that was afraid of losing its colonial empire to more powerful European competitors. But for better or for worse, the Belgian experience shaped modern Zaïre. The colonial legacy will be harder to extirpate than the decolonizers ever imagined.

NOTES

CHAPTER ONE. THE MÉTROPOLE

1. See Adrien de Meeüs, *Histoire des Belges* (Paris, 1958), pp. 414-15; Ben Serge Chlepner, *Cent ans d'histoire sociale en Belgique* (Brussels, 1956), pp. 199-234; and Henri Pirenne, *Histoire de Belgique de ses origines à nos jours*, 4 (Brussels, 1931), 155-59.

2. See especially Ferdinand Baudhuin, *Histoire économique de la Belgique, 1914-1939*, 2d ed., 2 vols. (Brussels, 1946; idem, *Belgique, 1900-1960: Explication économique de notre temps* (Louvain, 1961).

3. This has continued to be true to the present. See, for instance, R. Depré, "Career Pattern of Higher Civil Servants in Belgium," *Res Publica* 2 (1973):261-78.

4. In 1912 a full professor earned about 11,190 francs a year; a *secrétaire général*, 14,400; and the *premier président* of the Cour de cassation (the highest court), 16,690.

5. For a brief account, see Thomas Harrison Reed, *The Government and Politics of Belgium* (Yonkers-on-Hudson, N.Y., 1924), pp. 98-113.

6. Ibid., pp. 96-97.

7. By 1911 there were nine provinces, each under a governor nominated by the king. The provinces were divided into 342 cantons—judicial divisions, each under the court of a *juge de paix*—and 2,623 *communes*. Each *commune* with more than five thousand inhabitants was under a burgomaster appointed by the crown.

8. Quoted in Brian Bond, *The Victorian Army and the Staff College, 1854-1914* (London, 1972), p. 61.

9. For the army, see especially: Emile Wanty, *Le Milieu militaire belge de 1831 à 1914* (Brussels, 1957), passim; Charles Terlinden, ed., *Histoire militaire des Belges* (Brussels, 1931), pp. 312-26; and Guy van Gorp, *Le Recrutement et la formation des candidats officiers de carrière à l'armée belge*, nouv. série, no. 56 (Louvain, 1969), esp. pp. 45-46.

10. Cited from R.J.L. Bebing, "Le Commandant Charles Lemaire, pionnier-vedette de l'Etat indépendant du Congo (1863-1926)," in "Nos officiers," unpublished manuscript, Bibliothèque africaine, Brussels.

11. Quoted in Comte Louis de Lichtervelde, *Léopold of the Belgians*, trans. Thomas H. Reed (London, 1928), p. 37.

12. Ibid., pp. 33, 38, 193ff.

13. See H. L. Wesseling, "The Impact of Dutch Colonialism on European Imperialism," First Indonesian-Dutch Historical Confer-

ence, Noordwijkerhout, 19-22 May 1976. See also J. S. Furnival, *Colonial Policy and Practice: A Comparative Study of Burma and Netherlands India* (Cambridge, 1948), passim, and *Statesman's Year-Book* (London, 1895), pp. 776, 788.

14. Quoted in Neal Ascherson, *The King Incorporated: Leopold II in the Age of Trusts* (London, 1963), p. 51. For the king's financial interests, see the magisterial work by Ginette Kurgan-van Hentenryk, *Léopold II et les groupes financiers belges en Chine: La Politique royale et ses prolongements, 1895-1914* (Brussels, 1972). For the king's personal autocracy, see Jean Stengers, "The Congo Free State and the Belgian Congo before 1914," in *Colonialism in Africa, 1870-1960*, vol. 1, *The History and Politics of Colonialism, 1870-1914*, ed. L. H. Gann and Peter Duignan (Cambridge, 1969), 261-92.

15. Quoted in de Lichtervelde, *Léopold*, p. 153.

16. Marcel Luwel, "Gerson von Bleichröder: L'Ami commun de Léopold II et de Bismarck," *Africa-Tervuren* 11 (1965):3-4, 93-110. For the role of the Congo in diplomacy, see Jonathan E. Helmreich, *Belgium and Europe: A Study in Small-Power Diplomacy* (The Hague and New York, 1976), passim.

17. "Histoire parlementaire belge relative à la question du Congo: 1884-1906," Hellepute Papers, no. 498, Archives générales du Royaume (AGR), Brussels.

18. See William A. Hance, *The Geography of Modern Africa* (New York, 1964), pp. 304-41, which includes maps of the high Katanga (p. 331), the transport network (p. 315), and the vegetation zones (p. 309).

19. See the excellent article by Igor Kopytoff, "The Suku of Southwestern Congo," in *Peoples of Africa*, ed. James Gibbs (New York, 1965), pp. 443-77.

20. For a classical study, see Jan Vansina, *Kingdoms of the Savanna* (Madison, Wis., 1966).

21. For a map of the trade, see Roland Oliver and Anthony Atmore, *Africa since 1800* (Cambridge, 1967), p. 45.

CHAPTER TWO. THE FORCE PUBLIQUE

1. "Bericht des amerikanischen Konsul R. Dorsey Mohun" (c. 1895), Kleine Erwerbungen, no. 118, Bundesarchiv Koblenz.

2. See Belgian Congo, Force Publique, *La Force Publique de sa naissance à 1914: Participation des militaires à l'histoire des premières années du Congo* (Brussels, 1952), p. 506; Liane Ranieri, *Les Relations entre l'Etat indépendant du Congo et l'Italie* (Brussels, 1959), pp. 304-16; and A. J. Whyte, *The Evolution of Modern Italy* (New York, 1965), p. 233.

NOTES

3. Thierry de Maere d'Aertrycke, *Les Officiers scandinaves au service de l'Etat indépendant du Congo et du Congo belge* (Brussels, 1959), pp. 1-34.

4. Quoted in Sigbert Axelson, *Culture Confrontation in the Lower Congo* (Falköping, 1970), p. 218. The second largest civilian profession was missionary service. Between 1878 and 1903 about a hundred Scandinavian missionaries served in the Congo; these included about 25 percent of the Swedes in the country.

5. T. E. Lawrence, *The Seven Pillars of Wisdom: A Triumph* (London, 1945), pp. 22-23.

6. Quoted in Ruth Slade, *King Leopold's Congo: Aspects of the Development of Race Relations in the Congo Independent State* (London, 1962), p. 116.

7. Charles-Adolphe-Marie Liebrechts, *Congo: Suite à mes souvenirs d'Afrique. Vingt ans à l'administration centrale de l'Etat indépendant du Congo (1889-1908)* (Brussels, 1920), pp. 98-99.

8. Quoted in H. Depester, *Les Pionniers belges du Congo* (Tamines, 1927), pp. 114-15.

9. See Van Gorp, *Le Recrutement et la formation des candidats officiers*, passim.

10. In 1913 the peacetime establishment of the Belgian army amounted to 3,532 officers and 44,061 men. The Force Publique in the Congo stood at about one-third the strength of the home army. The Belgian colonial army in Africa thus accounted for a high proportion of the country's military effectiveness.

11. Baljit Singh and Ko-Wang Mei, *Theory and Practice of Modern Guerrilla Warfare* (New York, 1971), pp. 20-23.

12. The total strength of the armed forces in the Belgian Congo in 1912 was about 18,000 officers and men. The German colonial forces comprised 6,000 men, and the Portuguese, 13,000. Only the French maintained a larger military establishment than the Belgians: about 13,500 in West Africa and 7,000 in French Equatorial Africa.

13. Vice-governor of Katanga to the minister of colonies, 16 August 1911, Service du personnel d'Afrique (SPA), 36, Archives africaines, Brussels.

14. See, for instance, the entry in Académie Royale des sciences d'outre-mer (ARSOM), *Biographie coloniale belge*, 5 vols. (Brussels, 1948-1958), 5:cols. 875-82.

15. Cited in ibid., col. 878.

16. Belgian Congo, Force Publique, *La Force Publique*, p. 510. Between 1883 and 1901, 12,452 mercenaries were recruited from other parts of Africa; they comprised 5,585 Hausa, 2,745 Sierra Leoneans, 1,775 Zanzibaris, 708 Liberians, 591 Gold Coasters, 412 Abyssinians, 223 Egyptians, 215 Somalis, and 198 Dahomeans.

NOTES

17. "Bericht des amerikanischen Konsul R. Dorsey Mohun."
18. Guy Burrows, *The Curse of Central Africa* (London, 1903), pp. 92-93.
19. Lieutenant Colonel E. Bujac, *L'Etat indépendant du Congo. Esquisse militaire et politique* (Paris, 1905), pp. 33-35.
20. Burrows, *Curse of Central Africa*, pp. 22, 174-75.
21. Ibid., p. 22.
22. See Belgian Congo, Force Publique, *La Force Publique*, p. 63. In 1900 the annual death rate in training camps was 16 percent, as compared with 7.5 percent in field companies. According to E. L. Woodward, *The Age of Reform, 1815-1870* (Oxford, 1949), pp. 256-57, the mortality rate in the British Foot Guards stationed in Britain was 2.04 percent in 1856; among British soldiers stationed at Jamaica during this period, it stood at 7.5 to 8.0 percent, and in Sierra Leone it reached 75 to 80 percent.
23. Bujac, *L'Etat indépendant du Congo*, pp. 36-48.
24. R. P. Marcel Storme, *La Mutinerie militaire au Kasai en 1895* (Brussels, 1970), pp. 51-62.
25. Ibid. In 1891 the cost of the Force Publique amounted to 2,271,628 francs, or 49 percent of the Free State budget. For 1894, the corresponding figures are 3,308,700 francs and 45 percent; for 1898, 6,870,631 francs and 39 percent; for 1912, 8,762,700 francs and 17 percent.
26. Viscount Mountmorres, *The Congo Independent State: A Report on a Voyage of Enquiry* (London, 1906), p. 62.
27. Soldiers signed on for an initial term of seven years and could subsequently reenlist for periods varying from three to seven years.
28. At the turn of the century, the soldiers' basic pay amounted to ten centimes a day. Corporals received an additional allowance of six centimes, sergeants twenty centimes, *sergents major* twenty-five centimes, and *adjudants* thirty centimes. Sir John Harris calculated that the Belgians paid their African soldiers a total of £44,492 a year: Harris, "Conditions in the Congo and Proposed Reforms, 1908," manuscript Afr. R.. 69, Rhodes House Library, Oxford. Had the Belgians remunerated their soldiers at the same rate as the British in Nigeria, they would have spent £383,562. Belgian remuneration also included trade goods worth £37,700.
29. The Force Publique contained a larger proportion of artillery than any other colonial force. In 1908 it possessed nearly 150 artillery pieces, ranging from 5.7-cm. Nordenfeldt guns to 16-cm. pieces. It also had nineteen Maxim machine guns. Standard infantry equipment was the Albini rifle with bayonet.

226

CHAPTER THREE.
THE BEGINNINGS OF CIVIL ADMINISTRATION

1. See the list of religious affiliations of the governors-general in Marvin P. Markowitz, *Cross and Sword: The Political Role of Christian Missions in the Belgian Congo, 1908-1960* (Stanford, 1973), p. 27.

2. *Le Patriote*, 10 August 1908.

3. According to *Le Patriote*, 18 August 1908, the bureau supported two anticlerical journals, a senator, and a deputy in Italy. It also maintained representatives in the United States and Austria-Hungary. The German embassy in Brussels considered the information given by *Le Patriote* essentially reliable. See Embassy to Foreign Ministry, 19 August 1908, 54 11 [Übername des Kongo Staats durch Belgien], Auswärtiges Amt, Brussel Gesandtschaft, Bonn.

4. In 1886 headquarters were shifted to Boma at the northern shore of the Congo estuary. In 1923 Boma was linked to Léopoldville, which was linked to the Atlantic shore by means of the Léopoldville-Matadi railway and had become an important river port serving the Upper Congo.

5. De Winton to Leopold, 10 April 1885, and Leopold to de Winton, 19 May 1885, no. 47, Sir Francis de Winton, Archives du Palais Royal, Brussels.

6. Mountmorres, *Congo Independent State*, p. 49. Mountmorres gives detailed descriptions of the Belgian administrative machinery.

7. These officials comprised the inspectors of state, the minister of justice, and the department heads in charge of forestry, finance, agriculture, transport, post and telegraph, army, marine, registry, medical service, and "politics" or African affairs.

8. By 1891 there were about 290 officials in the Free State. This number rose to 684 in 1897, and to 1,424 in 1904. See Raymond Leslie Buell, *The Native Problem in Africa*, 2 vols. (New York, 1928), 2:419-20.

9. Copies of correspondence dated 14 April 1906, IRCB (722), no. 73 11, A. Baerts-Léopold correspondence, Archives africaines, Brussels.

10. Interview with Captain J. Becker in *Précurseur*, 17-18 April 1892.

11. "Rapport mensuels sur la situation générale d'Uvira," especially January 1904, Archives du Congo belge, no. 3, *Documents relatifs à l'ancien district du Kivu, 1900-1922* (Léopoldville, 1959), doc. 48.

12. Burrows, *Curse of Central Africa*, p. 272.

13. Liebrechts, *Congo: Suite à mes souvenirs*. See also A. Castelain,

NOTES

The Congo State, Its Origins, Rights and Duties: The Charges of Its Accusers (London, 1907).

14. Instructions by Leopold, 3 November 1894, SPA 123, Archives africaines.

15. Letters from Lerman dated 1 August and 10 October 1888, reprinted in Aleksander Lopasič, *Commissaire-Général Dragutin Lerman, 1863-1918: A Contribution to the History of Central Africa* (Tervuren, 1971).

16. Mountmorres, *Congo Independent State*, pp. 92, 99-100.

17. Burrows, *Curse of Central Africa*, pp. 27, 257.

18. Ibid.

19. Félicien Cattier, *Etude sur la situation de l'Etat indépendant du Congo* (Brussels and Paris, 1906), pp. 33-35.

20. Liebrechts, *Congo: Suite à mes souvenirs*, p. 102.

21. Mountmorres, *Congo Independent State*, p. 73.

22. The high mortality rate among officials contributed to administrative instability. During the early days, the death rate in many districts was so high that only half of those who returned to Belgium after their first term of three years had a chance of surviving for more than a few years.

23. Louis Franck, *Le Congo belge*, 2 vols. (Brussels, 1928), 1:340-41.

24. Charles-Adolphe-Marie Liebrechts, *Léopold II: Fondateur d'empire* (Brussels, 1932), p. 209.

25. Stengers, "Congo Free State," pp. 261-92.

26. Report by the Département de l'intérieur, received 21 October 1906, Baerts-Léopold correspondence, IRCB (722), Archives africaines.

27. Vansina, *Kingdoms of the Savanna*, pp. 208-48.

28. Letter from Lerman, 1 September 1892, in Lopasič, *Commissaire-Général Lerman*, pp. 176-84.

29. The region originally formed part of the Stanley Falls district. In 1897 this was divided into six *zones administratives*; of these, the *zones* of Kambara and Tanganyika made up the Kivu area. Kivu's strategic importance on the frontier of German East Africa led to its reorganization in 1900 as an independent district, known as Territoire Ruzizi-Kivu; it was subdivided into two *zones*, with its principal post at Uviva.

30. Instructions dated 17 May 1900 and 1 October 1902, Archives du Congo belge, *Documents relatifs à l'ancien district du Kivu*.

31. Major Moliteur, "Rapport sur les inspections des détachements de la F.P. des Kalembelembe," 26 August 1913, Archives du Congo belge, no. 3, *Documents relatifs à l'ancien district du Kivu*, doc. 44.

32. "Programme tracé par le capitaine-commandant F. V. van

228

Olsen au personnel de Ruzizi-Kivu," 18 January 1909, Archives du Congo belge, no. 3, *Documents relatifs à l'ancien district du Kivu,* doc. 50.

33. Report by Capitaine-Commandant Stamane, n.d., Archives du Congo belge, no. 3, *Documents relatifs à l'ancien district du Kivu,* doc. 115.

34. Report by Lieutenant Spiltoire, 16 April 1907, Archives du Congo belge, no. 3, *Documents relatifs à l'ancien district du Kivu,* doc. 65.

35. Pierre Salmon, *La Dernière insurrection de Mopoie Bangzegino (1916)* (Brussels, 1969), passim.

36. "Histoire du territoire de Costermansville [c. 1921]," Archives du Congo belge, no. 3, *Documents relatifs à l'ancien district du Kivu,* doc. 68.

CHAPTER FOUR. THE ECONOMICS OF COERCION

1. The outstanding book by A. H. Hopkins, *An Economic History of West Africa* (London, 1973), p. 133, shows how world prices for palm oil, palm kernels, and peanuts dropped sharply during the last decades of the century, owing both to competition from other producers in America, Australia, and India and to the wider impact of depression on consumers in Europe.

2. Eduard Pechuel-Loesche, *Kongoland*, part 1, *Amtliche Berichte und Denkschriften über das Belgische Kongo-Unternehmen* (Jena, 1887), p. 288. The author, a well-known traveler, became an employee in the Congo service and later was a professor of geography at the universities of Jena and Erlangen. His two-part study is highly critical of the Congo enterprise, whose economic possibilities Pechuel-Loesche viewed with much pessimism.

3. "Instruktion II. Beilage zum Schreiben vom 14. September 1882," reprinted in ibid., pp. 20-21.

4. Ibid., p. 267.

5. Cited in Henri Rolin, *La Question coloniale: A Propos d'un livre récent* (Liège, 1906), p. 27. Rolin's monograph was written in response to a bitter attack on the Congolese administration compiled by Félicien Cattier, a colleague of Rolin's at the University of Brussels: Cattier, *Etude sur la situation.* Rolin's view of Africans sharply contradicted those of more enlightened administrators, such as Pechuel-Loesche and Alexandre Delcommune. The latter demolished what he called the myth of African idleness in a once-respected study, *L'Avenir du Congo belge menacé: Bilan des dix premières années (1909-1918) d'administration coloniale gouvernementale; le mal—le remède* (Brussels, 1919), esp. pp. 36-46. Rolin's early mis-

conceptions did not prevent him from later writing an excellent book, *Les Lois et l'administration de la Rhodésie* (Brussels, 1913), a critical examination of the British South Africa Company's administration in the two Rhodesias.

6. See *Le XXe siècle*, 17 March 1909; *Frankfurter Zeitung*, 7 August 1908.

7. Edmund Denille Morel, *History of the Congo Reform Movement*, completed by William Roger Louis and Jean Stengers (Oxford, 1968), p. 41.

8. At one of his greatest parties, North reserved 120 bedrooms in a luxury hotel for any guests who might wish to stay for the night. The walls of the ballroom and dining rooms were decorated with white chrysanthemums, ferns, palms, and flowers; the columns were adorned with the letter *N*—for North as well as for nitrate. North himself was dressed as Henry VIII, and his wife, somewhat incongruously, as Madame Pompadour.

9. Information based on Jean Stenger's entry in ARSOM, *Biographie coloniale belge*, 4:cols. 663-66, and George Pendle, *A History of Latin America* (Harmondsworth, 1963), pp. 147-48.

10. Mountmorres, *Congo Independent State*, p. 59.

11. Burrows, *Curse of Central Africa*, pp. 78, 79.

12. Ibid., pp. 167-68.

13. See, for instance, H. R. Fox Bourne, *Civilisation in Congo-Land: A Story of International Wrong-doing* (London, 1903).

14. See Casement to Landsdowne, 11 December 1903, Great Britain, *Parliamentary Papers*, Africa No. 1 (1904), Cd. 1933. There is a detailed discussion of the question by Roger Anstey, "The Congo Rubber Atrocities—A Case Study," *African Historical Studies* 4, no. 1 (1971):59-73. In 1962 Anstey visited an area that had once been affected by the rubber regime and found a still-active oral tradition concerning the atrocities of the past.

15. A. J. Wauters, *Historie politique du Congo belge* (Brussels, 1911), pp. 243-44.

16. Summary of letter by Wahis, 27 March 1905, in Baerts-Leopold correspondence, IRCB (722), no. 73 11, Archives africaines, Brussels.

17. Mountmorres, *Congo Independent State*, pp. 160-61.

18. Ernst Vohsen, "Deutschland und der Kongostaat," *Berliner Tageblatt*, 7 October 1908.

19. Report by Consul Thesiger to Foreign Office, 9 September 1908, Great Britain, *Parliamentary Papers*, Africa No. 1 (1909), *Further correspondence respecting the taxation of natives and other questions in the Congo Free State*, Cd. 4466.

20. Consul W. G. Thesiger to Sir Edward Grey, 17 March 1908, from Boma, ibid., Cd. 4466.

21. Cited by Axelson, *Culture Confrontation in the Lower Congo*, p. 260.

22. Département de l'intérieur, summary of reports, 23 June 1905, IRCB (722), no. 73 l; summary of reports, 7, 20 March 1906, IRCB (722), no. 73 11, Archives africaines.

CHAPTER FIVE. THE *Reprise*

1. Delcommune, *L'Avenir du Congo belge menacé*, p. 207.

2. The CK was itself a body representing several national interests. British capitalists were represented by A. L. Ochs, a South African diamond merchant and financier, and by V. L. Cameron. Maurice Bunau-Varilla, a Parisian newspaper owner, and Seligman Frères were the main French participants. Within the Compagnie du Congo pour le commerce et l'industrie, Léon Lambert, a banker allied to Leopold, and several other Belgian banks supplied the Belgian contribution. Leopold kept an eye on the company through several directors: Baron Constant Goffinet, who was *administrateur* of the Civil List; the Count d'Oultremont, grand marshal of the court; and Thys. See S. E. Katzenellenbogen, *Railways and the Copper Mines of Katanga* (Oxford, 1973), p. 14.

3. John McKendree Springer, *Pioneering in the Congo* (New York, 1916), p. 31.

4. Stanley Shaloff, *Reform in Leopold's Congo* (Richmond, Va., 1970), p. 151.

5. "Texte coordonné des diverses instructions relatives aux rapports des agents de l'Etat avec les indigènes," reprinted in Pierre Mille, *Au Congo belge* (Paris, 1899), pp. 220-31.

6. Félicien Challaye and Pierre Mille, *Les Deux Congos: Devant la Belgique et devant la France* (Paris, c. 1908), p. 55.

7. Buell, *Native Problem*, 2:443. These companies included: the Union Minière, which was financed in the main by the Société générale and Tanganyika Concessions, Ltd.; the Compagnie du chemin de fer du Bas-Congo au Katanga (CCFK), which was dependent on capital from the Société générale and the Banque d'union parisienne; Forminière, part of whose assets derived from the Ryan-Guggenheim group of the United States; and Leopold's Foundation of the Crown. The mining concessions of the private companies at the time of cession comprised more than 230 million hectares.

8. In 1917 the average mortality in labor camps was 102 per 1,000; among laborers recruited by the Bourse du travail du Katanga the mortality rate was 130. By 1920 the figures had declined to 20

NOTES

and 32, respectively. See Léon Guébels, *Relation complète des travaux de la Commission permanente pour la protection des indigènes* (Gembloux, c. 1952), p. 278.

9. Report by *chef de secteur* André, 26 January 1910, Archives du Congo belge, no. 3, *Documents relatifs à l'ancien district du Kivu*, doc. 66.

10. See the *Proceedings* of the Reichskolonialamt commission on war aims, April 1918, Solf Papers, no. 46, Bundesarchiv, Koblenz. Calculated in reichsmarks, total debts in 1916 amounted to: Belgian Congo, 460 million; Nigeria, 186 million; French West Africa, 154 million; German East Africa, 56,000; Cameroun, 46 million.

11. Jean Stengers, *Combien le Congo a-t-il coûté à la Belgique?* (Brussels, 1957); idem, "Congo Free State," p. 274.

12. See, for instance, Victor Roelens to the Fédération pour la défense des intérêts belges à l'étranger, 15 March 1904, in *Fédération pour la défense des intérêts belges à l'étranger* (Brussels, 1908), pp. 28-32. For biography, see Edouard Janssens and Albert Cateaux, eds., *Les Belges au Congo: Notes biographiques* (Anvers, 1913), pp. 919-49.

13. Fritz Masoin, *Histoire de l'Etat indépendant du Congo*, 2 vols. (Namur, 1912-1913), 2:358.

14. For a detailed discussion, see Jean Stengers, *Belgique et Congo: L'Elaboration de la Charte coloniale* (Brussels, 1963), esp. pp. 201-28.

15. Ibid., p. 212.

16. Roger Anstey, *King Leopold's Legacy: The Congo under Belgian Rule, 1908-1960* (London and New York, 1966), pp. 41-42.

CHAPTER SIX. BELGIAN SOVEREIGNTY

1. See Julien Vanhove, *Histoire du Ministère des colonies* (Brussels, 1968), passim.

2. Renkin to governor-general, 22 December 1913, SPA 113, Archives africaines, Brussels.

3. The first governor-general of the Congo, properly speaking, was Camille Janssen, who assumed the title in 1887. The last effective governor-general was Leo Pétillon, who left office in 1958. The last titular governor-general was Henri Cornelis, whose term in office ended with independence in 1960.

4. The districts established in 1912 were: Stanleyville, Bas-Congo, Moyen-Congo, Equateur, Bangala, Uele, Aruwimi, Katanga, and Kasai.

5. See Commandat-General Bertrand, Uele District, to governor-general, 17 November 1910, SPA 112, no. 31, Archives africaines.

6. Buell, *Native Problem*, 2:465.

7. For details of salaries, see ibid., 2:460, 464, 466; see also Van Gorp, *Le Recrutement et la formation des candidats officiers*, p. 63.

8. Minister of colonies to governor-general, 8 July 1910, SPA 112, no. 31, Archives africaines.

9. By 1928 the *personnel supérieur*, including *commissaires de district* and *administrateurs territoriaux*, included 123 graduates. Among them were 7 *docteurs en droit* and *docteurs en philosophie*, 58 graduates of the Université coloniale d'Anvers, 27 *licenciés en sciences commerciales*, and others. See Belgium, Ministère des colonies, *Annuaires officiels* of the Congo; from 1924 onward they mentioned the officials' academic attainments.

10. Passing marks in the *section supérieure* were allotted as follows for each subject: military organization and administration, 25 (out of 100); administrative organization, 25; bookkeeping, 16; law, 14; hygiene, 10. The Belgians relied on examinations much more than did the British. Depending on the results of their final examinations, graduates were admitted to the service in starting ranks as *commis chef*, *commis de 1ᵉ classe*, or *commis de 2ᵉ classe*.

11. "Status des fonctionnaires et agents de la Colonie, arrêté d'exécution," 15 June 1912, SPA 125, no. 170, Archives africaines.

12. Renkin to Leopold, 23 January 1909, Archives du Palais Royal, Brussels.

13. Memorandum and draft by *2ᵉ direction générale*, 16 March 1912, SPA 115, no. 43, Archives africaines.

14. See Buell, *Native Problem*, 2:466.

15. See minister of colonies to governor-general, 29 July 1910, SPA 112, no. 31; governor-general to minister of colonies, 7 January 1913, and minister of colonies to governor-general, 7 June 1913, SPA 113, no. 34, Archives africaines.

16. Undated report by Inspecteur d'état De Meulemeester enclosed in governor-general to minister of colonies, 3 February 1913, SPA 114, no. 38, Archives africaines.

17. Circular dated 15 April 1913, SPA 113, no. 34, Archives africaines.

18. Governor-general to minister of colonies, 5 July 1914, SPA 114, no. 135, Archives africaines.

19. Commandant-Général Moulaert to governor-general, 24 November 1911, SPA 113, no. 13, Archives africaines.

20. See note by Secrétaire Général Arnold for the director general, 17 July 1913, SPA 123; also Renkin to governor-general, 22 December 1913, SPA 113, Archives africaines.

21. Commander Fiebitz, "Militärpolitischer Bericht," 2 April 1910, RM 3, v. 3027, Bundesarchiv Freiburg.

22. According to the official table of departmental precedence, the magistracy and courts came first in the following order: Direction de la justice, Instruction publique et affaires étrangères, Etat major de la Force Publique, Service territorial et secrétariat général, industry and commerce, health, agriculture, public works, marine and navigation, taxes, post and telegraph, clerical services. See governor-general to minister of colonies, 15 February 1911, SPA 112, no. 32, Archives africaines.

23. André van Iseghem, *Le Statut des fonctionnaires et agents de la colonie du Congo* (Brussels, 1921), esp. p. 2.

24. John McKendree Springer, *The Heart of Central Africa: Mineral Wealth and Missionary Opportunity* (New York, 1909), p. 142.

25. Mille, *Au Congo belge*, pp. 114-15.

26. See Axelson, *Culture Confrontation*, pp. 289-92.

27. These include Becker's *Vie en Afrique, ou trois ans dans l'Afrique Centrale*, 2 vols. (Paris, 1887).

28. The first translation of the entire Bible into Kikongo, by K. E. Laman, appeared in 1904. The same author, a Swede, had previously translated an illustrated science textbook (1901) and a book of arithmetic (1900). For a detailed assessment of Belgian secular literature concerning Congolese Africans, see Association des écrivains et artistes coloniaux de Belgique, *Le Noir congolais vu par nos écrivains coloniaux* (Brussels, 1953).

29. Quoted in Bebing, "Le Commandant Charles Lemaire," p. 12.

30. As part of the process, the Université coloniale de Belgique was set up in 1920 at Antwerp. The Université coloniale, together with the Ecole coloniale at Brussels, trained a well-educated type of senior official. Its courses lasted four years. First-year instruction was in general subjects such as history, philosophy, public law, and political economy; the second year included a variety of Bantu languages, anthropology, elements of botany, and African agriculture. The third year was reserved for military service in the engineer corps. Instruction in the fourth year covered the Lingala tongue, African institutions, tropical hygiene, native policy, colonial finance, and related specialized subjects.

31. "La colonisation et l'occupation des terres au Katanga," c. 1921, Helleputte papers, Archives générales du Royaume; Vice-Governor Wangermee to minister of colonies, 20 November 1912, SPA 114, Archives africaines. For an excellent appraisal of the Belgian colonization attempts, see Bruce Fetter, "Martin Rutten," in L. H. Gann and Peter Duignan, eds., *African Proconsuls: European Governors in Africa* (New York, 1978), p. 374-89, especially pp. 376-81, and also Bruce Fetter, *The Creation of Elisabethville, 1910-1914* (Stanford, 1976).

32. According to Buell, *Native Problem*, 2:445-46: "The government holds twenty-five hundred shares of preferred stock in the American Congo Company, 2,266 2/3 shares in the Compagnie du Congo Belge, 17,800 capital shares and 17,000 dividend shares in the Forminière, forty-two hundred shares of various kinds of stock in the Compagnie du Katanga; three hundred thousand dividend shares in the Great Lakes Railway, and 278,400 shares in the Katanga Railway. Moreover, the colony has two-thirds of the capital of the Comité Spécial of the Katanga and it is entitled to fifty per cent in the net profits of the Société Minière du Bécèka and the Banque du Congo Belge. Since the return of the stocks held by the Foundation of Niederfulbach, the Colony holds shares in thirty-five other companies located in various parts of the world. The present value (1925) of the various holdings of the Colony in these companies is estimated to be more than 1,494,000,000 francs."

33. Communication from the Société anonyme belge pour le commerce du Haut-Congo to the minister of colonies, 20 June 1913, quoted in Delcommune, *L'Avenir du Congo belge menacé*, p. 162.

34. See, for instance, the reports cited in Buell, *Native Problem*, 2:544-45.

35. See the *Proceedings* of the Reichskolonialamt commission on war aims, April 1918, Solf Papers, no. 46, Bundesarchiv Koblenz.

36. For a detailed account, see Mvulunga Mulambu, *Cultures obligatoires et colonisation dans l'ex-Congo belge* (Brussels, 1974), Cahier 6-7, série 2, passim. This is the first important historical study on the period by a Zaïrian, and it is based on Belgian archives that are not normally available to the public.

37. For a brilliant analysis of the pattern of Congolese exploitation written from the Marxist standpoint, see the article by Jean-Philippe Peemans, "Capital Accumulation in the Congo under Colonialism: The Role of the State," in *Colonialism in Africa, 1870-1960*, Vol. 4, *The Economics of Colonialism*, ed. Peter Duignan and L. H. Gann (Cambridge, 1975).

38. Louis Franck, "Quelques aspects de notre politique indigène au Congo," in *Etudes de colonisation comparée*, ed. Louis Franck, 1 (Brussels, 1924):94-95.

39. Barbara Anne Yates, "The Missions and Educational Development in Belgian Africa, 1876-1908" (Ph.D. diss., Columbia University, 1967), p. 49.

40. Ed. de Jonghe, *L'Enseignement des indigènes au Congo belge: Rapport présenté à la 21ᵉ session de l'Institut colonial international à Paris, mai 1931* (Brussels, 1931), pp. 8-9.

BIBLIOGRAPHY

NOTES ON ARCHIVES

The following notes are a brief summary of Belgian sources for the period 1884-1914. For a more detailed description, see Peter Duignan and L. H. Gann, *A Bibliographical Guide to Colonialism in Sub-Saharan Africa*, Volume 5 of *Colonialism in Africa, 1870-1960* (Cambridge, 1973):25-27, 42-43, 71, 360-86. See also Jean Stengers, "Opportunities for African Historical Research in Belgian Archives and Collections," mimeographed (School of Oriental and African Studies, Institute of Commonwealth Studies, African History Seminar, London, 22 May 1974).

Archives du Palais Royal, 2 rue Ducale, Brussels

The materials in the Archive du Palais Royal have been described in Emile Vandewoude, *Inventaire des archives relatives au développement extérieur de la Belgique sous le règne de Léopold II* (see the Publications section below). The materials cover primarily the financial affairs of the king and the diplomatic and political entanglements of the Congo, rather than its internal administration. Most of the Free State archives were destroyed at the king's instigation when Belgium took over the colony; the archives of the Département de l'intérieur and most files of the Département des finances were therefore lost to posterity, although some of the foreign-affairs files survived. Most of the local archives of the Congo Free State administration in Boma were likewise incinerated. The surviving materials include a large amount of personal correspondence between the king and a number of public men and private individuals, including Sir Francis de Winton and Jules Renkin. Leopold was a profuse correspondent; hence a good deal of information survives.

Archives africaines, Place Royale, Brussels

The Archives africaines contain the surviving records of the Free State administration and the archives of the now defunct Ministère des colonies. The Free State's surviving archives (mainly those from the departments of finance, foreign affairs, and justice) were transferred to the Ministère des colonies after the state took over the colony in 1908. They have been described in Madeleine van Grieken-Taverniers, *Inventaire des archives des affaires étrangères de l'Etat indépendant du Congo et du Ministère des colonies, 1885-1914* (see Publications). The Ministère des colonies was dissolved following the Congo's independence in 1960, and its archives were transferred to the Ministry of Foreign Affairs under the name of Archives africaines du Ministère des affaires étrangères. At present, much of this material is still housed in the old building of the Ministère des colonies at the Place Royale, next to the Bibliothèque africaine. In 1978, access was limited to material that is at least fifty years old. Some restricted files, however, have been opened to researchers under special circumstances. Personnel records are not available for public scrutiny. Much of the material has been described in detail by Emile Vandewoude, *Inventaire des archives*, and in Madeleine van Grieken-Taverniers, *Inventaire des archives*. We have made use especially of the series Service du personnel d'Afrique (SPA) and Ministère des colonies, correspondance particulière.

Archives du Congo belge, Kinshasa (Léopoldville), Zaïre

Upon leaving the Congo, the Belgians took with them about five kilometers of archives. These materials are presently under the control of the Archives générales du Royaume. Zaïre and Belgium still dispute the question of their ownership and future disposition. At the time of this writing, the Belgian archivist-général felt that purely administrative archives should be returned to Zaïre as soon as Zaïre is capable of servicing them, while Belgium should retain the main fonds concerned with colonial policy. To all intents and purposes, this material is not yet open to research workers. Brief summaries include "Plan de classification à l'usage de l'administration d'Afrique," mimeographed (Léopoldville: Gouvernement général, Secrétariat général, Sect. archives, 1955).

Archives générales du Royaume (AGR), 2-6, rue de Ruysbroeck, Brussels

The Archives générales du Royaume contain numerous fonds deposited by private donors. These include the cabinet papers of Renkin and the private papers of Renkin, van Eetevelde, Droogmans, Helleputte, and others. Access is complicated. The archives observe a fifty-year rule, and researchers must submit an individual written application to the archivist-général for the use of each fond. We found Renkin's cabinet papers to be of no use; they merely cover the Belgian home front in 1914-1918 and provide an interesting comment on the primary preoccupations of a Belgian colonial minister during World War I.

Musée de Tervuren, Section historique

The Musée de Tervuren's rich collection of private papers, which includes those of Cornet, Lemaire, and Fuchs, has been described to some extent in Musée Royal de l'Afrique Centrale, *Inventaire des archives historiques* (see the Publications section). Materials should be ordered well in advance; it is best to do so by telephone from Brussels (no.: 467-43-01). For a description, see Marcel Luwel, "Inventaire des archives historiques du Musée royal" (see Publications).

PUBLICATIONS

Académie Royale des sciences coloniales. *Inventaire des archives des affaires étrangères de l'Etat indépendant du Congo et du Ministère des colonies, 1885-1914.* Brussels, 1955.

Académie Royale des sciences d'outre-mer (ARSOM). *Biographie coloniale belge.* 5 vols. Brussels: Librairie Falk Fils, 1948-1958.

————. *Bulletin des séances.* 1ère sér., 1930-1954; nouv. sér., vol. 1, 1955.

Africa-Tervuren, 1955. *Amis du Musée Royal de l'Afrique Centrale.* Quarterly. (Supersedes Congo-Tervuren, 1872.)

American University (Washington, D.C.), Special Operations Research Office. *Area Handbook for the Republic of the Congo (Léopoldville).* Washington, D.C.: Foreign Areas Studies Division, 1962.

Andersson, Efraim. *Messianic Popular Movements in the Lower Congo.* New York and Uppsala: Almquist and Wiksells Boktryckeri, 1958.

Anstey, Roger. "The Congo Rubber Atrocities—A Case Study." *African Historical Studies* 4, no. 1 (1971).

————. *King Leopold's Legacy: The Congo under Belgian Rule, 1908-1960.* London and New York: Oxford University Press, 1966.

Archives africaines. *Décrets de l'Etat indépendant du Congo nonpubliés au bulletin officiel.* Vol. 2. Brussels: Ministère des affaires étrangères et du commerce extérieur, 1967.

Archives du Congo belge. *Documents pour servir à l'étude du milieu (histoire) du partie.* Léopoldville, 1959.

————. *Plan de classification à l'usage de l'administration d'Afrique.* Léopoldville: Gouvernement général, secrétariat général, section archives, 1955.

Arnot, F. S. *Bihé and Garenganze: or Four Years' Further Work and Travel in Central Africa.* London: J. E. Hawkins, 1893.

————. *Garenganze: or Seven Years' Pioneering Mission Work in Garenganze.* London: J. E. Hawkins, 1889.

————. *Missionary Travels in Central Africa.* Bath: Office of Echoes of Service, 1914.

Ascherson, Neal. *The King Incorporated: Leopold II in the Age of Trusts.* London: George Allen and Unwin, 1963.

Association des écrivains et artistes coloniaux de Belgique. *Le Noir congolais vu par nos écrivains coloniaux.* Brussels: Académie Royale des sciences colonales, 1953.

Axelson, Sigbert. *Culture Confrontation in the Lower Congo.* Falköping: Gummessons Boktryckeri, 1970.

Banning, Emile. *Mémoires politiques et diplomatiques: Comment fut fondé le Congo belge.* Brussels: La Renaissance du livre, 1927.

Baudhuin, Ferdinand. *Belgique, 1900-1960: Explication économique de notre temps.* Louvain: Institut de recherches économiques et sociales, 1961.

———. *Histoire économique de la Belgique, 1914-1939.* 2d. ed. 2 vols. Brussels: Emile Bruylant, 1946.

Belgian Congo, Force Publique. *La Force Publique de sa naissance à 1914: Participation des militaires à l'histoire des premières années du Congo.* Brussels: Institut Royal colonial belge, 1952.

Belgium. Bibliothèque africaine. *Bibliographie africaine.* Brussels, 1969–.

———. *Inventaire des microfilms des documents relatifs à l'histoire de la Belgique et du Congo conservés au "Public Records Office" à Londres, 1866-1903.* Brussels, c. 1959.

———. *Inventaire des microfilms des papiers Morel, séries A, B, E, F, G, H, I, se rapportant à l'histoire du Congo et conservés à la British Library of Political and Economic Science, London School of Economics and Political Science.* Brussels, c. 1961.

———. *Inventaire. Papiers Jules Cornet, géologue (1865-1929).* Tervuren: Musée Royal de l'Afrique Centrale, 1961.

———. *Liste des acquisitions.* [Brussels, 1940–].

Belgium. Ministère des affaires africaines. Bibliothèque. *Catalogue de la bibliothèque.* Compiled by Th. Simar. Brussels: Vromart, 1922–.

Belgium. Ministère des colonies. *Annuaire official.* Brussels, 1910–.

Belgium. Ministère des colonies. Bibliothèque. *Bibliographie courante.* Brussels, 1947-1968.

Belgium. Ministère du Congo belge et du Ruanda-Urundi. *Document note: Stanley au Congo, 1879-1884.* Brussels, 1960.

Belgium. Parlement. Chambre des représentants. *Recueil à l'usage des fonctionnaires et agents du service territorial au Congo belge.* Brussels, 1900, 1905, 1908, 1910.

Berlage, Jean. *Répertoire de la presse du Congo belge (1884-1958) et du Ruanda-Urundi (1920-1958).* Brussels: Commission belge de bibliographie, 1959.

Berlage, Jos. *Bâtisseurs de l'empire.* Brussels: F. Penez-Dehaye, 1939.

Bond, Brian. *The Victorian Army and the Staff College, 1854-1914.* London: Eyre Methuen, 1972.

Bonhuck, François. *Aux origines de l'Etat indépendant du Congo: Documents tirés d'archives américaines.* Louvain: L'Université Lovanium de Léopoldville, 1966.

Braekman, E. M. *Histoire du Protestantisme au Congo.* Brussels: Editions de la librairie des éclaireurs unionistes, 1961.

Buell, Raymond Leslie. *The Native Problem in Africa.* 2 vols. New York: Macmillan Company, 1928.

Bujac, Lieutenant Colonel E. *L'Etat indépendant du Congo. Esquisse militaire et politique.* Paris: Henri Charles la Vouzelle, 1905.

Burrows, Guy. *The Curse of Central Africa.* London: R. A. Everett, 1903.

Bustin, Edouard. *Lunda under Belgian Rule: The Politics of Ethnicity.* Cambridge, Mass.: Harvard University Press, 1975.

————. *A Study Guide for Congo-Kinshasa.* Boston: Boston University, African Studies Center, 1970.

Carton de Wiart, H. *Beernaert et son temps.* Brussels: La Renaissance du livre, 1945.

Castelain, A. *The Congo State, Its Origins, Rights, and Duties: The Charges of Its Accusers.* London: David Nutt, 1907.

Cattier, Félicien. *Etude sur la situation de l'Etat indépendant du Congo.* Brussels: V. F. Larcier; Paris: A Pedone, 1906.

Ceulemans, R.P.F. *La Question arabe et le Congo (1883-1892).* Brussels: Académie Royale des sciences d'outre-mer, 1959.

Challaye, Félicien, and Mille, Pierre. *Les Deux Congos: Devant la Belgique et devant la France.* Paris: Cahiers de la quinzaine, c. 1908.

Charles, P. *Rapport sur le dossier "Campagne anti-congolaise."* Brussels: Institut Royal colonial belge, 1953.

Chlepner, Ben Serge. *Cent ans d'histoire sociale en Belgique.* Brussels: Université libre de Bruxelles, Institut de sociologie Solvay, 1956.

Congo. *Positions socialistes, 1885-1960.* Brussels: Institut Vandervelde, 1961.

Cornet, René. *Katanga avant les belges et l'expédition Bia-Francqui-Cornet.* Brussels: Cuypers, 1946.

———. *Terre katangaise: Cinquantième anniversaire du Comité spécial du Katanga, 1900-1950.* Brussels: Comité spécial du Katanga, 1950.

Cornevin, Robert. *Histoire du Congo, Léopoldville-Kinshasa: Des Origines préhistoriques à la République démocratique du Congo.* 2d ed. Paris: Berger-Levrault, 1966.

D'Agimont, Chevolier. *Charles Liebrechts, serviteur du Roi souverain (1858-1938).* Brussels: Goemaere, 1962.

Daye, Pierre. *L'Empire colonial belge.* Brussels: Editions du soir, 1923.

De Craemer, Willy, and Fox, Renée C. *The Emerging Physician: A Sociological Approach to the Development of a Congolese Medical Profession.* Stanford: Hoover Institution Press, 1968.

De Jonghe, Ed. *L'Enseignement des indigènes au Congo belge: Rapport présenté à la 21ᵉ session de l'Institut colonial international à Paris, mai 1931.* Brussels: Institut colonial international, 1931.

Delcommune, Alexandre. *L'Avenir du Congo belge menacé: Bilan des dix premières années (1909-1918) d'administration coloniale gouvernementale; le mal—le remède.* Brussels: J. Lebèque et Compagnie, 1919.

————. *La Vérité sur la civilisation au Congo par un Belge.* Brussels: Lebègne, 1903.

De Lichtervelde, Louis. *Léopold of the Belgians.* Translated by Thomas H. Reed. London: Stanley Paul and Company, 1928.

Delvaux, Henri. *L'Occupation du Katanga, 1891-1900: Notes et souvenirs du seul serviteur.* Elisabethville: Imbelco, 1950.

De Maere d'Aertrycke, Thierry. *Les Officiers scandinaves au service de l'Etat indépendant du Congo et du Congo belge.* Brussels: Ecole Royale militaire, 1959.

De Meeüs, Adrien. *Histoire des Belges.* Paris: Arthème Fayard, 1958.

Dennet, R. E. *Seven Years among the Fjort: Being an English Trader's Experiences in the Congo District.* London: Sampson, Law, 1887.

Depester, H. *Les Pionniers belges du Congo.* Tamines: Duculot-Roulin, 1927.

Devroey, E., and Vanderlinden, R. *Le Bas-Congo. Artère vitale de notre colonie.* Brussels: Goemare, 1938.

D'Hooge, R. *Histoire du Congo.* Léopoldville: Force Publique, 1959.

Duignan, Peter, and Gann, L. H., general eds. *Colonialism in Africa, 1870-1960.* 5 vols. Cambridge: Cambridge University Press, 1969-1973. Vols. 1-2: *The History and Politics of Colonialism*, edited by Gann and Duignan. Vol. 4: *The Economics of Colonialism*, edited by Duignan and Gann. Vol. 5: *A Bibliographical Guide to Colonialism in Sub-Saharan Africa*, edited by Duignan and Gann.

Elisabethville, 1911-1961. Brussels: Cuypers, 1961.

Encyclopédie du Congo belge. 3 vols. Brussels: Bieleveld, 1950.

Fédération pour la défense des intérêts belges à l'étranger. Brussels: V. Pourbaix, 1908.

Fetter, Bruce. *The Creation of Elisabethville, 1910-1940.* Stanford: Hoover Institution Press, 1976.

Fonds national de la recherche scientifique. *Inventaire des microfilms de papiers privés relatifs à l'histoire du Congo conservés à la "School of Oriental and African Studies" de l'Université de Londres et au "British Museum."* Brussels, 1959.

Fox Bourne, H. R. *Civilisation in Congo-Land: A Story of International Wrong-Doing.* London: P. S. King and Son, 1903.

Franck, Louis. *Le Congo belge.* 2 vols. Brussels: La Renaissance du livre, 1928.

Furnival, J. S. *Colonial Policy and Practice: A Comparative Study of Burma and Netherlands India.* Cambridge: Cambridge University Press, 1948.

Gann, L. H., and Duignan, Peter, eds. *African Proconsuls: European Governors in Africa.* New York: Free Press, 1978.

————. *Burden of Empire: An Appraisal of Western Colonialism in Africa South of the Sahara.* Stanford: Hoover Institution Press, 1967.

Gibbs, James, ed. *Peoples of Africa.* New York: Holt, Rinehart and Winston, 1965.

Great Britain. Foreign Office. *Report of the Trade and Finances of the Congo Independent State.* London: H.M.S.O., 1897.

Grieken-Taverniers, Madeleine van. "L'Histoire de l'Etat indépendant du Congo et les archives du Ministère du Congo belge et du Ruanda-Urundi." *Archives, bibliothèques et musées de Belgique* 30, no. 1 (1959).

————. *Inventaire des archives des affaires étrangères de l'Etat indépendant du Congo et du Ministère des Colonies, 1885-1914.* Académie Royale des sciences coloniales,

Classe des sciences morales et politiques, mémoire in 8 o, n.s., v. 2, fasc. 2. Brussels, 1955.

Guébels, Léon. *Relation complète des travaux de la Commission permanente pour la protection des indigènes, 1911-1951.* Gembloux, c. 1952.

Halewyck de Hensch, Michel. *La Charte coloniale.* . . . 4 vols. Brussels: M. Weissenbruch, 1910-1919.

————. *Organisation politique et administrative de la colonie.* Brussels: Bibliothèque coloniale internationale, 1936.

Hance, William A. *The Geography of Modern Africa.* New York: Columbia University Press, 1964.

Helmreich, Jonathan E. *Belgium and Europe: A Study in Small-Power Diplomacy.* The Hague: Mouton, 1976. New York: Humanities Press, 1976.

Heyse, Théodore. "L'Académie Royale des sciences coloniales et l'ancien Congo." *Archives bibliothèques et Musée du Belgique* 29, no. 1 (1958).

————. *Contributions au progrès des sciences morales, politiques et économiques relatives aux territoires d'Outremer.* 3 vols. Bibliographica Belgica 32. Brussels: Commission belge de bibliographie, 1957-1961.

————. *Les Eaux dans l'expansion coloniale belge. Contribution bibliographique.* Brussels: Falk Fils, 1936.

————. *Index bibliographique colonial Congo belge et Ruanda-Urundi.* 3 vols. Brussels: Falk Fils, 1939-1940.

Hopkins, A. H. *An Economic History of West Africa.* London: Longmans, 1973.

Hostelet, Georges. *L'Oeuvre civilisatrice de la Belgique au Congo, de 1885 à 1945.* Vol. 1: *L'Oeuvre économique et sociale.* Brussels: Institut Royal colonial belge, 1954. Vol. 2: *Les Avantages dont les blancs et les noirs ont bénéficié et bénéficieront de l'oeuvre civilisatrice de la Belgique au Congo.* Brussels: Académie Royale des sciences coloniales, 1954.

Huybrechts, A. *Les Transports fluviaux au Congo 1925-*

1963. Léopoldville: Institut de recherches économiques et sociales, 1965.

Italiaander, Rolf, ed. *Leopolds Kongo. Dokumente und Pamphlete von Mark Twain, Edmund O. Morel, Roger Casement.* Munich: Rütten und Loening Verlag, 1964.

Janssens, Edouard, and Cateaux, Albert, eds. *Les Belges au Congo: Notes biographiques.* Anvers: Van Hille-de Backer, 1913.
Jean Jadot, artisan de l'expansion belge en Chine. Brussels: Académie Royale des sciences d'outre-mer, 1965.
Joye, Pierre, and Lewin, Rosine. *Les Trusts au Congo.* Brussels: Société populaire d'éditions, 1961.

Kassai, Pierre. *La Civilisation africaine. Etude historique et critique de l'oeuvre africaine de l'organisation intérieure et de l'économie politique de l'Etat indépendant du Congo.* Brussels: Mertens, 1888.
Katzenellenbogen, S. E. *Railways and the Copper Mines of Katanga.* Oxford: Clarendon Press, 1973.
Kurgan-van Hentenryk, Ginette. *Léopold II et les groupes financiers belges en Chine: La Politique royale et ses prolongements, 1895-1914.* Brussels: Palais des académies, 1972.

Lemarchand, René. *Rwanda and Burundi.* London: Pall Mall Press, 1970.
———. "Selective Bibliographical Survey for the Study of Politics in the former Belgian Congo." *American Political Science Review* 54 (September 1960).
Léopold II. *Pensées et réflexions recueillies par George M. Dumont.* Brussels: L'Amitié par le lire, 1948.
Leuven. Koloniaal Universitair Centrum. *Onze Kolonie en de Kolonisatie.* Antwerp: N. V. Standaard Boekhandel, 1946.

Liebrechts, Charles-Adolphe-Marie. *Congo: Suite à mes souvenirs d'Afrique. Vingt ans à l'administration centrale de l'Etat indépendant du Congo (1889-1908)*. Brussels: J. Lebège, 1920.

———. *Léopold II: Fondateur d'empire*. Brussels: Office de publicité, 1932.

Lopasiĉ, Aleksander. *Commissaire Générale Dragutin Lerman, 1863-1918: A Contribution to the History of Central Africa*. Tervuren: Musée Royal de l'Afrique Centrale, 1971.

Louis, William Roger. *Ruanda-Urundi, 1884-1919*. Oxford: Clarendon Press, 1963.

Luwel, Marcel. "Gerson von Bleichröder: L'Ami commun de Léopold II et de Bismarck." *Africa-Tervuren* 11 (1965).

———. "Inventaire des archives historiques du Musée Royal du Congo belge à Terburen." Institut Royal colonial belge, *Bulletin des séances* 25, no. 2 (1954).

Markowitz, Marvin P. *Cross and Sword: The Political Role of Christian Missions in the Belgian Congo, 1908-1960*. Stanford: Hoover Institution Press, 1973.

Masoin, Fritz. *Histoire de l'Etat indépendant du Congo*. 2 vols. Namur: Impr. Picard-Balon, 1912-1913.

Meyers, Joseph. *Le Prix d'un empire*. 3d ed. Brussels: Presses académiques européennes, 1964.

Mille, Pierre. *Au Congo belge*. Paris: Armand Collin, 1899.

Miller, Joseph Calder. *Cokwe Expansion, 1850-1900*. Madison: University of Wisconsin, African Studies Program, 1969.

Moloney, James A. *With Captain Stairs to Katanga*. London: Low, Marston and Company, 1893.

Morel, Edmund Denille. *Great Britain and the Congo: The Pillage of the Congo Basin*. New York: Ferhig, 1969.

———. *History of the Congo Reform Movement*. Completed by William Roger Louis and Jean Stengers. Oxford: Clarendon Press, 1968.

Moulaert, G. *Problèmes coloniaux d'hier et d'aujourd'hui: Pages oubliées. Trente-huit années d'activité coloniale.* Brussels: Edition universelle, 1939.

Mountmorres, Viscount. *The Congo Independent State: A Report on a Voyage of Enquiry.* London: Williams and Norgate, 1906.

Mulambu, Mvulunga. *Cultures obligatoires et colonisation dans l'ex-Congo belge.* Brussels: Centre des études africaines, 1974.

Musée du Congo belge. *Bibliographie ethnographique du Congo belge et des régions avoisinantes.* Tervuren: Musée du Congo belge, 1925–.

Musée Royal de l'Afrique Centrale. *Annales.* Série en 8ᵉ sciences historiques. Tervuren: Musée Royal de l'Afrique Centrale, 1964.

―――. *Bibliographie ethnographique de l'Afrique sud-Saharienne.* Tervuren: Musée Royal de l'Afrique Centrale, 1960–.

―――. *Inventaire des archives historiques.* 2 vols. Tervuren: Musée Royal de l'Afrique Centrale, 1961.

Nouvelles recherches sur la genèse et sa nature (1875-1876). Mémoire no. 10:1. Brussels: Académie Royale des sciences d'outre-mer, 1956.

Oliver, Roland, and Atmore, Anthony. *Africa since 1800.* Cambridge: Cambridge University Press, 1967.

Paneels, E. *De diplomatieke aktiviteit van koning Leopold II. Oprichting van de Onafhankelijke Kongostaat.* Brussels: St. Aloysius Handels School, 1970.

Peemans, Jean-Philippe. "Capital Accumulation in the Congo under Colonialism: The Role of the State." In *Colonialism in Africa*, Vol. 4, *The Economics of Colonialism*, edited by Peter Duignan and L. H. Gann, pp. 165-212.

Peschel-Loesche, Eduard. *Kongoland.* Part I: *Amtliche Berichte und Denkschriften über das Belgische Kongo-Unter-*

nehmen. Part 2: *Unterguinea und Kongostaat als Handels-und Wirtschaftsgebiet.* . . . Jena: Herman Costenoble, 1887.

Pirenne, Henri. *Histoire de Belgique de ses origines à nos jours.* Vol. 4. Brussels: La Renaissance du livre, 1931.

Ranieri, Liane. *Les Relations entre l'Etat indépendant du Congo et l'Italie.* Brussels: Académie Royale des sciences coloniales, 1959.

Reed, Thomas Harrison. *The Government and Politics of Belgium.* Yonkers-on-Hudson, N.Y.: World Book Company, 1924.

Revue belge de géographie. Brussels: Société Royale belge de géographie, 1877–.

Roeykens, P. A. *Les Débuts de l'oeuvre africaine de Léopold II (1875-1879).* Brussels: Académie Royale des sciences d'outre-mer, 1958.

Rolin, Henri. *Les Lois et l'administration de la Rhodésie.* Brussels: E. Bruylant, 1913.

————. *La Question coloniale: A Propos d'un livre récent.* Liège: La Meuse, 1906.

Ryckmans, Pierre. *Dominer pour servir.* Rev. ed. Brussels: Edition universelle, 1948.

Schneren, G. van der, ed. *Onze kolonie en die kolonisatie: Voordrachten en lezingen gehouden in het Koloniaal Universitair Centrum.* . . . Antwerp: N. V. Standaard-Boek-handel, 1946.

Shaloff, Stanley. *Reform in Leopold's Congo.* Richmond, Va.: John Knox Press, 1970.

Slade, Ruth M. *English-Speaking Missions in the Congo Independent State (1878-1908).* Brussels: Académie Royale des sciences coloniales, Classe des sciences morales et politiques, mémoires in 8 o, nouv. sér., vol. 16, fasc. 2, 1959.

————. *King Leopold's Congo: Aspects of the Development of Race Relations in the Congo Independent State.* London: Oxford University Press, 1962.

Springer, John McKendree. *The Heart of Central Africa: Mineral Wealth and Missionary Opportunity.* New York: Methodist Book Concern, 1909.

―――――. *Pioneering in the Congo.* New York: Katanga Press, 1916.

Stengers, Jean. *Belgique et Congo: L'Elaboration de la Charte coloniale.* Brussels: La Renaissance du livre, 1963.

―――――. *Combien le Congo-a-t-il coûté à la Belgique?* Brussels: Académie Royale des sciences coloniales, 1957.

―――――. "The Congo Free State and the Belgian Congo before 1914." In *Colonialism in Africa, 1870-1960,* Vol. 1, *The History and Politics of Colonialism, 1870-1914,* edited by L. H. Gann and Peter Duignan, pp. 261-92.

Terlinden, Charles, ed. *Histoire militaire des Belges.* Brussels: La Renaissance du livre, 1931.

Union minière du Haut Katanga, 1906-1956: Évolution des techniques et des activités sociales. Brussels: L. Cuypers, 1957.

Vandewoude, Emile J.L.M. *Les Archives du personnel d'-Afrique de 1877 à 1918.* Institut Royal colonial belge, *Bulletin des séances* 25, no. 2 (1954).

―――――. *Documents pour servir à la connaissance des populations du Congo belge: Aperçu historique (1886-1933) de l'étude des populations autochtones, par les fonctionnaires et agents du service territorial, suivi de l'inventaire des études historiques, ethnographiques et linguistiques conservées aux archives du Congo belge.* Léopoldville: Section documentation des archives du Congo belge, 1958.

―――――. *Inventaire des archives relatives au développement extérieur de la Belgique sous le règne de Léopold II.* Brussels: Archives générales du Royaume, 1965.

Van Gorp, Guy. *Le Recrutement et la formation des candidats officiers de carrière à l'armée belge.* Nouv. sér., no. 56. Louvain: Université catholique de Louvain, 1969.

Van Grieken, Emile. *La Bibliothèque du ministère des af-*

faires africaines: Son rôle, ses collections et ses ouvrages précieux. Brussels: Académie Royale des sciences d'outre-mer, commission d'histoire, fasc. 82, 1962.

Vanhove, Julien. *L'Histoire du Ministère des colonies.* Brussels: Académie Royale des sciences d'outre-mer, 1968.

Van Iseghem, André. *Le Statut des fonctionnaires et agents de la colonie du Congo.* Brussels: Librairie Albert Davit, 1921.

Vansina, Jan. *Introduction à l'ethnographie du Congo.* Kinshasa: Université Iovanium, 1966.

————. *Kingdoms of the Savanna.* Madison: University of Wisconsin Press, 1966.

Van Zuylen, Pierre. *L'Echequier congolais, ou le secret du roi.* Brussels: Cb. Dessart, 1959.

Verbeken, Auguste. *Mairi: Roi du Katanga. L'Homme rouge du Katanga.* Brussels: L. Cuypers, 1958

Vermeulen, François. *Edmond Picard et le réveil des lettres belges.* Brussels: Académie Royale de langue et de littérature française de Belgique, 1935.

Walraet, Marcel. "Inventaires d'archives et publications de textes." Académie Royale des sciences coloniales, *Bulletin des séances* 3, no. 2 (1957).

Wanty, Emile. *Le Milieu militaire belge de 1831 à 1914.* Brussels: Palais des académies, 1957.

Wauters, Alphonse-Jules. *Bibliographie du Congo, 1880-1895: Catalogue méthodique de 3,800 ouvrages, brochures, notices .et cartes relatifs à la géographie et à la colonisation du Congo.* Brussels: Administration du mouvement géographique, 1895.

————. *Histoire politique du Congo belge.* Brussels: P. van Fleteren, 1911.

Wettenschapelyke bijdrage van Belgie tot de ontwikkeling van centraal Afrik. Brussels: Koninklijke Academie voor Overzeese Wetenschapen, 1562-1633.

Whyte, A. J. *The Evolution of Modern Italy.* New York: W. W. Norton and Company, 1965.

Willequet, Jacques. *Le Congo belge et la Weltpolitik, 1894-1914*. Brussels: Presses universitaires de Bruxelles, 1962.

Woodward, E. L. The Age of Reform, 1815-1870. Oxford: Clarendon Press, 1949.

Yates, Barbara Anne. "The Missions and Educational Development in Belgian Africa, 1876-1908." Ph.D. diss., Columbia University, 1967.

Young, Crawford. *Politics in the Congo: Decolonization and Independence*. Princeton: Princeton University Press, 1965.

INDEX

ABIR. *See* Anglo-Belgian Indian
Rubber Company
Aborigines Protective Society,
221
Abyssinians, in Force Publique,
225
Académie Royale des sciences
d'outre-mer (ARSOM), 64
Administrateurs généraux. See
Governors-general
Administration, Belgian, 3, 8,
16-18, 223
Administration, of Belgian
Congo, 158, 159 fig., 160-63,
164-76, 200, 216-17, 232;
directions générales, 164;
Ministry of Colonies, 165
table; administrative personnel,
166-76; representative bodies,
168; technical support for,
174-76; education of administrators, 176, 179-82, 196-97,
233, 234; life-style and social
structure in, 176, 177-80, 186,
188; recruitment for, 177, 185-
86; blacks in, 182-83; salaries
of administrators, 183 table,
186, 187 table, 188; reform
of, 183-84; and changing
ideology of regime, 188-97;
relations with indigenous
chefferies, 206-7
Administration, of Congo Free
State, 85-115, 227; recruitment
for, 85-86; superstructure of,
86-91; *Comité consultatif*, 91;
district officials, 91-108;
budget, 92 table; coercive
nature of, 108; establishment
of civil authority, 108-15; and

indigenous class structure,
112-13; death rate among
administrators, 228
Afrikaansche Handelsvereeniging,
34
Agriculture, Belgian, 3, 7-8
Agriculture, in Congo, 42, 44, 48,
164; technical staff for, 174;
compulsory cultivation, 203-4
AIC. *See* Association interna-
tionale du Congo
Albert, Lake, 54
Albert I, 158
Algeria, Belgian soldiers in, 22
Anglo-Belgian Indian Rubber
Company (ABIR), 125, 127-
29, 137, 143, 148
Anglo-French entente (Entente
Cordiale; 1904), 148
Angola, Congo trade with, 48,
49, 215
Annales d'ethnographie, 192
Antislavery lobby, Belgian, 27,
61, 126
Antwerp, 3, 127, 143, 177, 234;
as world ivory market, 120,
121; governors-general from,
178
Anversoise. *See* Société anver-
soise du commerce au Congo
Argentina: Belgian trade with
and investment in, 24, 25 table;
Argentinians in Congo ad-
ministration, 100 table
Aristocracy, Belgian, 5-6, 20, 64,
105, 178
Army, Belgian, 18-24, 225. *See
also* Force Publique
Arnold, Nicolas, 129
Arntz, Egide-Rodolphe, 85

255

Association des anciens coloni-
aux, 147
Association internationale du
Congo (AIC), 24, 36, 70
Austrians, in Congo administra-
tion, 100 table

Baeyens, Baron Ferdinand, 143-
44
Bakongo people, 210
Bakussu people, 78, 104
Baluba people, 210
Banking, Belgian, 9, 11-12
Banning, Emile, 33, 87, 125
Banque de Bruxelles, 7, 11
Banque d'outre-mer, 32, 70
Banque d'union parisienne, 231
Baptist Missionary Society, 210
Bas Congo-Katanga railway, 199
Bashilele people, 138-39
Batetela people, 53, 55, 76, 78
Becker, Jérome Joseph, 120, 171
Beerhaert, Auguste, 125
Belcoma Cafegas, 70
Belgian Congo: role in inter-
national politics, 147; judiciary,
169-71; legal structure, 173-
74; changing ideology of re-
gime, 188-97; racism among
administrators, 190-91; literary
portrayals of, 191-97; eco-
nomic reform in, 199-207;
continuity with Congo Free
State, 201; foreign trade, 201;
church-state relations, 207-13;
centrality of mining to economy, 218; state ownership of
concessionary companies, 235.
See also Administration, of
Belgian Congo
Belgium, 3-50; colonial possessions of, xii; population, geography, and history, 3-4, 7;
Walloon-Flemish division, 3-5;
social structure and economy,

5-13; education, 6-7, 8-9; vot-
ing rights, 9-14; foreign trade
and investments, 11-12, 24, 25
table; politics and administration, 13-18, 25; army, 18-24;
missionaries from, in Congo,
207; evaluation of colonial
effort, 218-22
Berlin, Congress of (1884-1885),
35, 89, 116
Bernardin de Saint-Pierre, 33
Bertrand, Colonel, 147
Bihé, Congo, 139
Biographie coloniale belge, 64
Bismarck, Otto von, 215
Bleichröder, Gerson von, 34
Blyden, Dr. E. W., 101
Bolobo, Congo, 136, 210
Boma, Congo, 38, 51, 54, 78,
152; as administrative capital,
88, 92-93, 166, 169, 197, 227;
educational institutions in, 153,
209
Bourse du travail du Katanga,
198, 231
Brazza, Pierre Savorgnan de, 215
British South Africa Company,
39, 96, 126, 216
British West Africa, 141, 183
Brown de Tiège, Alexandre-Jean-
Marie de, 127, 129
Brugmann, Georges, 34
Brussels, 64, 143, 169, 178, 234;
University of, 7, 28, 123, 176
Buell, Raymond Leslie, 176, 201
Bulgarians, in Congo adminis-
tration, 100 table
Bulletin de la société belge de
géographie, 28
Bunau-Varilla, Maurice, 231
Bunge, Edouard-Gustave, 129
Burrows, Guy, 77, 98, 135
Busamba people, 154
Business structure, Belgian, 4, 10-

Education: in Belgium, 6-7, 8-9,
23, 28, 61; in Congo, 153,
207-12, 213 table; for colonial
administrators, 176, 180-82,
196-97, 233, 234
Eetvelde, Edmond van, 86
Egyptians, in Force Publique, 225
Elisabethville (Lubumbashi),
169, 197-98; growth and
development of, 145-46, 152,
198-99
Empain, Baron Edouard, 7, 11,
32, 145
Equateur province, 139, 163, 232
Ethnography, 192, 195-96
Etoile belge, 193
Etudes Bakongo, 195-96
Exports, from Congo, 133, 149
table, 197, 201. *See also
individual products by name*

Fédération des anciens militaires, 27
Finland, citizens of, in Congo
administration, 100 table
Flanders, 3, 177
Forced labor. *See* Labor, forced;
Raubwirtschaft
Force Publique, 52-84, 168, 225;
conquest of Congo Free State
by, 53-58; fighting conditions
and tactics, 54-55, 74-75;
national and social origins of
cadres, 58-65; functions and
conditions of service, 65-72,
113; discipline problems, 66-
67, 77-78; organization and
salaries, 67 table, 68 table,
81-82, 226; death rate, 67,
68 table, 226; advancement
and promotion, 67-69, 82;
blacks in, 73-79, 225; military
modernization, 79-84; arma-
ment, 81, 83, 226; in World
War I, 83-84; portrayal of

Congo by members of, 192-93
Foreign investments, Belgian,
11-12, 24, 25 table
Forestry, technical staff for, 174
Forminère. *See* Société internationale forestière et minière
du commerce
Foundation of the Crown, 231
France, 207, 214, 215, 225;
population density, 7; Belgian
commercial and financial
relations with, 25 table; French
in Congo administration, 100
table; training of colonial
administrators in, 179-80
Franck, Louis, 179, 196, 207
Francqui, Emile, 7, 32
Frankfurter Zeitung, 124
Frères des écoles chrétiennes,
209
Fuchs, Félix, 90, 167-68, 184,
201; politics of, 178; enlightened reforms, 216
Fulero people, 113

German East Africa, 58, 83, 111,
155
Germany, 146, 184, 189; colonial
possessions of, xii, 58; population density, 7; Belgian
commercial and financial relations with, 25 table; colonial
army, 79, 225; Germans in
Congo administration, 100
table; German and Belgian
colonial efforts, compared, 214,
215-16
Ghent, 6, 64, 178; University of,
28, 176
Goffinet, Baron Constant, 129,
231
Gold Coast, 73, 141, 173, 225
Governors-general, 88-91, 166-
67, 232; functions, 166-68;

INDEX

Library of Congress Cataloging in Publication Data

Gann, Lewis H   1924-
  The rulers of Belgian Africa, 1884-1914.

  Bibliography: p.
  Includes index.
  1. Zaire—Politics and government—1885-1908.
2. Zaire—Politics and government—1908-1960.
I. Duignan, Peter, joint author.   II. Title.
DT655.G36   320.9′675′102   79-83989
ISBN 0-691-05277-8